English Grammar Simplified

English Grammar Simplified

by

James C. Fernald

HarperPerennial
A Division of HarperCollins*Publishers*

The first paperbound edition of this book was published in 1968 by Funk & Wagnalls Company. It is here reprinted by arrangement.

ISBN: 0-06-463484-1

01 RRD-H 30 29 28 27 26

PREFACE

It is now over half a century since Dr. Fernald's *English Grammar Simplified* was first given to the public. This book has stood the test of time and public use because it is logically designed and skillfully executed to meet the needs of everyone who wishes to understand English grammar and to improve his speech and writing. The book is designed, as Dr. Fernald pointed out, as a complete summary of English grammar. It is not in the class of small grammars that are made brief by leaving out bodily numerous important matters. Brevity has been secured by eliminating discussions and extended explanations, while retaining every important fact. Dr. Fernald's aim was to include everything in correct English usage that is the legitimate object of rational inquiry.

In preparing this grammar, Dr. Fernald made an intensive study of the best authorities of his day, including the most authoritative treatises on grammar, textbooks in grammar used by reputable public schools, and the *New English Dictionary,* with its unrivaled store of quotations from standard English authors. Everything in this work is the product of extensive study and is therefore dependable.

The plan of this book is simple. Based on the premise that English grammar is the correct use of English words in sentences, this work undertakes to explain these matters and nothing more. Words are grammatically classified as parts of speech, and each part of speech is treated separately. Then the sentence is discussed, beginning with the simple sentence and its division into subject and predicate. Under these heads the uses of the parts of speech are shown in their order, first in the subject and then in the predicate. After the simple sentence has been discussed, the compound and complex sentences are explained as combinations of clauses and simple sentences.

The various exercises consist of extracts from the best literature. They were chosen for their simplicity, beauty, and illustrative value. Each quotation is identified by the name of the author and the work in order to relate the study of grammar to living thought and to a range of good reading.

In this work errors of usage have been infrequently noted, for one does not learn correct speech by studying the incorrect. Nevertheless, some of the most prevalent faults are pointed out, and the reason for their being unacceptable is distinctly explained.

In all of the above ways, Dr. Fernald prepared his grammar so well that it is basically sound today despite the changes that English grammar has undergone. Shedding many of its rhetorical flourishes, English has grown simpler, more direct, and more colloquial. It is at present more attuned to prose than poetry; it strives more for the clarity of science than the richness of art. The fact that both spoken and written English have grown more colloquial and permissive is attested by Webster's *Third New International Dictionary* which is latitudinarian to a degree that some authorities think is excessive. As English has grown less prescriptive and more descriptive, a new mode of grammatical analysis and explanation has developed, known as structural linguistics, the aim of which is to describe language in use rather than to codify and prescribe it.

Despite these developments, this revision, like the previous one, leaves Dr. Fernald's method and approach intact. The work remains, as he would have wished, a basic book of facts established through five centuries of English usage; and it remains so precisely because it is so soundly based on fact rather than on theory. The only alterations that have been necessary are changes to make the work correspond to the facts of current English usage. These changes are of four kinds: (1) the elimination of outmoded grammatical classifications and explanations, (2) the

elimination of rhetorical distinctions that are no longer made,
(3) the inclusion of certain ways of explaining usage that are
now used in lieu of older grammatical explanations, and (4) the
elimination from the exercises of some of the illustrative extracts,
which now verge on the archaic, in favor of current illustrations,
the majority of which are in prose because ours is an age of
prose.

Besides these changes, a section on punctuation and a section
on mechanics have been added. With these additions, *English
Grammar Simplified* becomes a complete guide on the subject
of how to speak and write English and how to put written
material in proper form.

This new edition of *English Grammar Simplified,* with its
alterations and additions, remains a traditional, factual summary
of English grammar. In a period of changing patterns and of a
structural approach to language which is at present not fully
established, a traditional grammar is surely the best kind for the
student, the writer, and the general user who is seeking a practical knowledge of English. Instead of cataloguing a variety of
uses, with exceptions and exceptions to exceptions; instead of
a slippery morass of alternatives which may get by, here are the
facts that have been established by many years of usage and that
still stand. Here are also the facts about the departures from
once-standard practice and about the new practices in current
use.

All of this material is firmly stated and clearly illustrated.
Necessary exceptions to rules are given and explained, along
with cautions against common pitfalls. The exercises following
each unit of work give the student the opportunity of practicing
what he has studied and testing his knowledge of it.

The index has been prepared with especial care to make it
efficient for finding information. Its extent shows the inclusiveness of the work. By the use of the index, every important item
in the book can be readily found. Even some duplication has
been allowed to meet the needs of those who approach the same

topic from different points of view. Furthermore, the text itself contains numerous cross references that lead to supplementary, clarifying information.

This work can be used as a textbook for direct instruction. Its inclusiveness, its organization into logical, progressive units of study, and the exercises are well suited to the classroom, where the text may be taken in its entirety or by sections according to the needs of the students. For these reasons it should also be most useful as a supplementary text either for the class as a whole or for individual students who need additional help.

For individual study outside the classroom, there is great value in a book so accurate and clear and so replete with illustrative exercises that it can be studied without the aid of a teacher, either to explain the principles or to check the progress made. An individual can study this book as a whole by progressing from section to section in easy, logical steps. Or he can eliminate areas of weakness in his knowledge of English grammar by concentrating on the appropriate sections.

This book is also designed to meet the constant demand, in the office, the study, or the home, for a handy reference volume in which to recover quickly some item of correct usage or to settle grammatical complexities and disputed points as they may arise. As a reference book of English grammar, it should prove invaluable to students, parents, writers, and professional people —to everyone who has occasion to seek an authoritative answer to some question of English grammar and usage.

C. G.

INTRODUCTION

This book is an explanation of practical English grammar. Practical English grammar is a comparatively easy and manageable subject—one that any intelligent person can master with patience and a reasonable amount of application. It is the art of using our language-apparatus, which is ready-made and almost as simple as it could be made, to express thought clearly and emphatically. A textbook of grammar defines the various parts of language and explains how they should be used in order to secure effective expression. This book undertakes to give these practical instructions in the clearest possible manner and the least possible space.

WHAT IS GRAMMAR?

Grammar is the treatment of connected words as they are used for the expression of thought. Grammar is not needed for disconnected words like *to, mend, is, it, never, late, too*. But grammar applies to words when they are arranged to express thought: *It is never too late to mend*. Grammar teaches us to connect words so as to express thought without confusion or error. It has two main divisions:

I. The Parts of Speech
II. The Sentence

THE PARTS OF SPEECH

A part of speech is a class or group of words associated according to their use in expressing thought. A single word belonging to any one of these classes is often likewise called a part of speech.

There are eight parts of speech under which all the words in the language may be arranged. The eight parts of speech are the following:

1. Noun	5. Adverb
2. Pronoun	6. Preposition
3. Adjective	7. Conjunction
4. Verb	8. Interjection

Grammar explains what the parts of speech are, how each is used in relation to the others, and what each contributes to the expression of thought. By reducing the more than 400,000 words in our language to eight manageable groups, grammar greatly simplifies language. By learning the eight parts of speech and how to use them, we can manage all of the words in our vocabulary; we can string them together to express simple and complex thoughts.

THE SENTENCE

The sentence is a combination of words that expresses a complete thought. A sentence may be short and simple or long and complex. Every sentence contains two parts, a subject and a predicate. Grammar explains the nature and function of these divisions, the parts of speech essential to each, and other parts of speech that may be used in each division to assist in the expression of a thought.

PARSING

When words and sentences are analyzed in this way, we say that they are *parsed*. To parse a word is to tell what part of speech it is, what its properties are, and how it is related to other words. To parse a sentence is to separate it into its elements and to explain the properties and relations of each word it contains.

This book carefully expounds all of these matters. It explains the parts of speech separately, one by one, in Part I. In Part II it explains the sentence, the classes of sentences there are, and the construction, punctuation, and mechanics of the sentence. In doing so, this book covers the entire range of English grammar and explains words and how they are used in sentences to express thought.

CONTENTS

xiii

Part I
THE PARTS OF SPEECH

THE NOUN

A **noun** is the name of an object or idea.

Every word expresses *some* idea. The verb expresses an idea of action, and the conjunction expresses an idea of connection; but the noun alone *names* its idea and stands for it as its symbol in speech. The noun is the name word.

CLASSES OF NOUNS

Nouns are divided into two main classes: *common* and *proper*.

A **common noun** is the name of any *one* of a class or group of objects. A common noun never begins with a capital letter unless it is the first word in a sentence: *man, boy, girl, house, river, tree*.

A **proper noun** is the official name of a single object or sometimes of a single group of objects. A proper noun always begins with a capital letter: *God*, the *Deity*, *Galileo*, *Baltimore*, the *Potomac*, the *Romans*, the *Alps*, *Boston*, *New York*, *Chicago*, *Washington*.

The distinction between proper and common nouns can be clarified by placing a proper noun in the class to which it belongs:

Proper Noun	Common Noun	Proper Noun	Common Noun
Boston	city	Atlantic	ocean
Mississippi	river	George	man or boy
Virginia	state	France	country or nation

SENTENCES: The chief *river* (common noun) of South America is the *Amazon* (proper noun).

Texas (proper noun) is no longer the largest *state* (common noun) in the United States.

3

Only one other class of nouns needs mention here, namely:

Collective Nouns or Collectives.—A collective noun is a noun singular in number but denoting a whole class or group of objects: *class, family, congregation, flock, number, multitude.* These nouns are noted here as forming a separate class because they take either a singular or a plural verb according to the meaning to be expressed, as will be explained later (p. 210).

EXERCISE

Give the common noun corresponding to each of the following proper nouns.

1. Chicago	6. Gibraltar	11. Germany
2. Wisconsin	7. Mediterranean	12. Yale
3. St. Helena	8. Volga	13. Cadillac
4. Hudson	9. Vesuvius	14. Asia
5. Indian	10. *Hamlet*	15. Mexico

INFLECTION AND DECLENSION

In English grammar the use of the terms *inflection* and *declension* is limited. These terms are defined here because they must sometimes be used to explain the forms and relation of words in a sentence.

Inflection is a change in the form of a word to denote gender, person, number, case, comparison, voice, mood, tense: *foxes* from *fox, greater* from *great, did* from *do,* etc. To *inflect* a word is to make some such change. An inflected form of a word is often itself called an *inflection*.

Declension.—The inflection of nouns or pronouns is called *declension*. An orderly arrangement of the forms of a noun or pronoun by gender, person, number, and case is also called the *declension* of that word.

The changes of form in an English noun are so few that it is not worthwhile arranging them in the order of declension. For the few examples of true declension now remaining in the English language, see PERSONAL PRONOUNS, pp. 26–27.

PROPERTIES OF NOUNS

Nouns have certain qualities or characteristics commonly called **properties.** The properties of nouns are four: *gender, person, number,* and *case.* Of these properties, number and the possessive case are of great importance and will receive extended treatment. The other properties, gender, person, and case (except for the possessive case), are of little importance and will therefore be treated briefly.

1. GENDER

Gender, in the English language, is the classification of nouns and certain pronouns as *masculine, feminine,* or *neuter.* Gender belongs *only to nouns and pronouns.* No other words have any distinctions of gender. English gender is *natural;* that is, it corresponds to sex.

Masculine Gender.—All nouns denoting beings of the male sex are masculine in gender.

Feminine Gender.—All nouns denoting beings of the female sex are feminine in gender.

Neuter Gender.—All nouns denoting objects of no sex are neuter in gender.

English stands entirely alone in making gender a rational and intelligible distinction; males are masculine; females feminine; and inanimate things neuter.

RAMSAY *English Language and English Grammar,*
pt. ii, ch. ii, p. 231.

The vast majority of nouns that denote living beings give no indication of gender. Since these nouns are indeterminate in gender, they are sometimes said to be of *common gender: parent, child, friend, nurse, patient, reporter, singer.*

Thus, *animal* is of indeterminate or common gender. We know that it is *not neuter,* since it denotes a living being, and that is all we do know about its gender. The *animal* may be either male or female; hence the noun is said to be of *indeterminate* or *common gender.*

Indications of Gender in Nouns

The few nouns in English that indicate gender do so in one of three ways:

1. By their meaning. These are commonly associated as far as possible in pairs. Thus:

Masculine	Feminine	Masculine	Feminine
bachelor	spinster	king	queen
boy	girl	man	woman
brother	sister	nephew	niece
father	mother	son	daughter
husband	wife	uncle	aunt

2. By prefixing to the noun whose gender is to be indicated a noun or pronoun whose gender is known: *he*-goat, *she*-wolf, *man*-servant, *maid*-servant.

This is a native English usage that is now obsolete. Instead of such prefixes, modern speakers and writers prefer to use a descriptive adjective, *male* or *female:* a *male* zebra, a *female* elephant. *Man-servant* and *maid-servant* are still in use, but they are now written as one word, without the hyphen.

3. By certain endings of foreign origin: *-ess, -ine,* and *-trix.* These suffixes often involve some change in the form of the words to which they are added. They are almost the only instances of true gender-forms in English.

Among the nouns so modified are the following:

Masculine	Feminine	Masculine	Feminine
abbot	abbess	master	mistress
actor	actress	tiger	tigress
duke	duchess	administrator	administratrix
emperor	empress	executor	executrix
host	hostess	testator	testatrix
lion	lioness	hero	heroine

REMARKS.—These forms are not numerous in ordinary use. One might go through a long life without having occasion to use the words *administratrix, executrix,* or *testatrix.* There is a strong tendency to the disuse of all feminine endings in *-ess.* It is now considered offensive to say or write *authoress, poetess,* or, especially, *Negress, Jewess,* and the like. We refer to the woman, like the man, as *author, poet,* and, if necessary, *Negro* or *Jew.* We even speak of a woman as the *chairman* of a meeting, or as a *postmaster* in the United States mail service.

Gender in English nouns is of practical use only in connection with pronouns of the third person (see PERSONAL PRONOUNS, pp. 26–28). The unimportance of gender in nouns is illustrated by the following sentences:

The *good* BOY will study.
The *good* GIRL will study.
The *good* GROUND will be fruitful.

In each of these sentences, the gender of the noun makes no difference in the use of any other word in the sentence.

The lack of forms to indicate the gender of nouns and adjectives is one of the great advantages of the English language. The use and learning of English is much simpler than that of languages which require one to know the gender-forms of adjectives and nouns before he can speak and write properly.

2. PERSON

Person, in grammar, is a relation of words which indicates an object as speaking, spoken to, or spoken of. Person, in grammar, belongs only to nouns, pronouns, and verbs. The form of the English noun is the same in all persons. The person is known only by the position and connection of words and by the thought to be expressed.

There are, in grammar, three persons, as follows:

First Person.—The object or objects speaking.

Second Person.—The object or objects spoken to.

Third Person.—The object or objects spoken of.

EXAMPLES

First Person   I, John, tell the truth.*
Second Person   John, tell the truth.
Third Person   John tells the truth.

To know the person of an English noun, we have simply to inquire whether it indicates who or what is speaking, or spoken to, or spoken of. Pronouns and verbs help to indicate this, as will be explained under PRONOUN, pp. 25–33; VERB, pp. 90–91.

Personification in Nouns

Personification is a figure of speech which attributes personal nature or character to inanimate things. In personification inanimate objects are sometimes introduced as speaking or being spoken to as if they were persons. Thus:

What ailed thee, O thou *sea,* that thou fleddest? thou, *Jordan,* that thou wast driven back?—*Ps.* 114:5.

---

* NOTE.—An English noun is never used in the *first person singular,* except when in apposition with the pronoun *I,* in which case the pronoun *I* is the subject of the verb. If "I" were here omitted, "John" would be in the *second person,* as in the second example. See, also p. 29.

Here the *sea* and the river *Jordan* are spoken to as if they could hear and understand; hence these nouns are in the *second person* by personification.

> (and what have you to say,
> wind wind wind—did you love somebody
> and have you the petal of somewhere in your heart
> pinched from dumb summer?
>
> E. E. CUMMINGS

Here the wind is addressed as if it were a person endowed with a heart and the ability to speak and to pinch something. Note that *wind* is in the second person, but that gender is not indicated.

Nouns denoting inanimate objects, when thus personified, may be treated as of *masculine or feminine gender,* and referred to by *he* or *she, his, her,* etc. (See PERSONIFICATION IN PRONOUNS, pp. 28–29.)

EXERCISE

Tell the gender and person of each noun in the following extracts.

(1)   Now came still evening on; and twilight gray
         Had in her sober livery all things clad;
         Silence accompanied; for beast and bird,
         They to their grassy couch, these to their nests,
         Were slunk, all but the wakeful nightingale.
                        MILTON *Paradise Lost,* bk. iv, l. 598.

(2)   Thou villain base,
         Know'st me not by my clothes?
                        SHAKESPEARE *Cymbeline,* act iv, sc. 2.

(3)   Sweet babe, in thy face
         Soft desires I can trace,
         Secret joys and secret smiles,
         Little pretty infant wiles.
                        BLAKE *A Cradle Song.*

(4)   I, Paul, have written it with my own hand.—*Philemon* 19.

(5) That ye may be mindful of the commandment of us, the apostles.—*2 Peter* 3:2.

(6) Young Oak! when I planted thee deep in the ground,
I hoped that thy days would be longer than mine;
That thy dark-waving branches would flourish around,
And ivy thy trunk with its mantle entwine.

BYRON *To an Oak at Newstead.*

(7) For I, the Lord thy God, will hold thy right hand, saying unto thee, Fear not; I will help thee.—*Isa.* 41:13.

(8) The value of culture is its effect on character. It avails nothing unless it ennobles and strengthens that. Its use is for life. Its aim is not beauty but goodness.—W. SOMERSET MAUGHAM *The Summing Up.*

(9) The *Nellie*, a cruising yawl, swung to her anchor without a flutter of the sails, and was at rest. The flood had made, the wind was nearly calm, and being bound down the river, the only thing for it was to come to and wait for the turn of the tide.—JOSEPH CONRAD *Heart of Darkness.*

(10) Then you must stay here, for hell is the home of the unreal and of the seekers for happiness. It is the only refuge from heaven, which is, as I tell you, the home of the slaves of reality.—G. B. SHAW *Man and Superman,* act iii.

(11) The mass of men lead lives of quiet desperation. What is called resignation is confirmed desperation.—THOREAU *Walden,* ch. 1.

(12) Fortune, we are told, is a blind and fickle foster-mother, who showers her gifts at random upon her nurslings. But we do her a grave injustice if we believe such an accusation.—SAMUEL BUTLER *The Way of All Flesh,* ch. 5.

(13) Let the day glare: O Memory, your tread
Beats to the pulse of suffocating night—
Night peering from his dark but fire-lit head
Burns on the day his tense and secret light.

ALLEN TATE *Ode to Fear.*

(14) My little horse must think it queer
To stop without a farmhouse near
Between the woods and frozen lake
The darkest evening of the year.

ROBERT FROST *Stopping by Woods
on a Snowy Evening.*

(15)   O world! O life! O time!
         On whose last steps I climb,
             Trembling at that where I had stood before:
         When will return the glory of your prime?
         No more—oh, never more.

SHELLEY Lament.

3. NUMBER

In nouns, pronouns, and verbs, **number** is the property which indicates whether one object is meant, or more than one.

In English there are two numbers, the *singular* and the *plural*. The singular number is used to denote one object; the plural, to denote more than one. The plurals of English nouns are formed *regularly* and *irregularly*.

Regular Plurals

RULE.—English nouns regularly form their plurals by adding *s* or *es* to the singular.

This rule is so universal that, when there is nothing to indicate the contrary, the plural of an English noun may be instantly formed by adding *s* or *es* to the singular. (The exceptions to this rule, which are few in number and mostly in words derived from foreign languages, are noted on pp. 13–15.)

Choice of S or ES

Plurals That Add S Only.—When a noun ends in a letter whose sound will readily unite or coalesce with the sound of *s*, s is added to form the plural: *boy, boys; hat, hats; book, books; top, tops; time, times; engine, engines.*

Plurals That Add ES.—When a noun ends in a letter whose sound will not readily unite or coalesce with the sound of *s*, *es* is added, forming a separate syllable, for the sake of euphony, or agreeableness of sound: *fox, foxes; church, churches; bush, bushes.*

Nouns That Form Plurals in ES Classified

The nouns that form their plurals by adding *es* to the singular may be grouped in the following classes:

Nouns Ending in CH (soft *ch* as in *church*), **S, SH, X, or Z.** —In these nouns the *es* forms a separate syllable:

box	boxes	bush	bushes
church	churches	fox	foxes
gas	gases	match	matches

Nouns Ending in F or FE.—Some nouns ending in *f* or *fe* change *f* to *v* in the *plural* and add *es*. The *es* or *ves* does not form a separate syllable:

beef	beeves	loaf	loaves
calf	calves	self	selves
elf	elves	sheaf	sheaves
half	halves	shelf	shelves
knife	knives	thief	thieves
leaf	leaves	wife	wives
life	lives	wolf	wolves

Staff has an old plural, *staves,* but *staffs* is now more common. *Wharf* forms its plural either in *wharves* or *wharfs,* the latter being now somewhat more frequent.

Other nouns in *f* or *fe* form their plurals by adding *s* only: *chief, chiefs; safe, safes; strife, strifes.*

Nouns Ending in O.—Some nouns ending in *o* add *es:*

calico	calicoes	potato	potatoes
cargo	cargoes	tomato	tomatoes
echo	echoes	torpedo	torpedoes
grotto	grottoes	veto	vetoes
hero	heroes	volcano	volcanoes
Negro	Negroes		

Other words ending in *o* form their plurals by simply adding *s:*

albino	albinos	halo	halos
cameo	cameos	piano	pianos
canto	cantos	soprano	sopranos
embryo	embryos	studio	studios
folio	folios		

For this difference in treatment no certain rule can be given. Whenever one is in doubt about the spelling of a word, one should consult a reliable dictionary.

Nouns Ending in Y.—Nouns ending in *y* preceded by a consonant change *y* to *i*, and add *es* to form the plural:

baby	babies	fancy	fancies
berry	berries	folly	follies
body	bodies	lady	ladies
daisy	daisies	lily	lilies

[In this respect *qu* is treated as a consonant combination equivalent to *kw: colloquy, colloquies; soliloquy, soliloquies.*]

Nouns ending in *y*, preceded by a vowel, add *s* only to form the plural, and do not change the *y:*

boy	boys	monkey	monkeys
chimney	chimneys	pulley	pulleys
donkey	donkeys	valley	valleys
key	keys	volley	volleys

Irregular Plurals

Plurals in EN.—These are: *brother, brethren* (also *brothers;* see p. 14); *child, children; ox, oxen.*

Plurals by Vowel Change.—These are:

dormouse	dormice	man	men
foot	feet	mouse	mice
goose	geese	tooth	teeth
louse	lice	woman	women

Foreign Plurals.—Some nouns derived from foreign languages have both a foreign plural and the regular English plural: *antenna, antennæ, antennas; automaton, automata, automatons.*

Some nouns have only the foreign plural. The plural of *alumnus* is *alumni;* the plural of *alumna* is *alumnæ. Basis* has only the foreign plural *bases.*

To insure correctness one should consult a reliable dictionary for the plural forms of foreign terms and also for their meaning.

Nouns Unchanged in the Plural

Some nouns, especially certain names of animals, are the same in both singular and plural: *species, cod, deer, grouse, sheep, salmon, swine, trout.* (For the plural of *fish* see below under DOUBLE PLURALS.)

Double Plurals

Some nouns have both a regular and an irregular plural with a difference in meaning. Thus:

bandit	bandits (individuals)
	banditti (an organized or collective force)
brother	brothers (of the same family)
	brethren (of the same society)
cannon	cannons (separate pieces of artillery)
	cannon (a quantity considered collectively)
die	dies (stamps for coining, etc.)
	dice (small cubes used in games)
fish	fishes (counted one by one)
	fish (considered by quantity, species or the like)
genius	geniuses (men of genius)
	genii (spirits)

heathen	heathens (individual persons)
	heathen (heathen people collectively)
index	indexes (tables of items)
	indices (mathematical signs, etc.)
memorandum	memoranda (items noted down)
	memorandums (separate lists of items)

Plurals Treated as Singulars

Some nouns plural in form are singular in meaning and use: *means, news, mathematics, politics*. We say: The latest *news* IS——; *mathematics* IS a hard study. *Means* is singular when referring to one thing or method, plural when referring to more than one: THIS IS the only *means;* all other *means* HAVE FAILED.

A noun plural in form is treated as singular when it denotes a collection, group, or amount: THAT *hundred dollars* IS here.

EXERCISE

Give the number of each noun in the following extracts; give the plural of every singular noun and the singular of every plural noun. Also give the rule for the formation of all plurals used.

(1)
>See the mountains kiss high heaven,
>And the waves clasp one another.
>>SHELLEY *Love's Philosophy.*

(2)
>I read
>Of that glad year that once had been,
>In those fallen leaves which kept their green,
>The noble letters of the dead:
>And strangely on the silence broke
>The silent-speaking words.
>>TENNYSON *In Memoriam,* pt. xcv.

(3)
>No shade, no shine, no butterflies, no bees,
>No fruits, no flowers, no leaves, no birds,
>November!
>>HOOD *November.*

(4)   No sadder proof can be given by a man of his own little-ness than disbelief in great men.—CARLYLE *Heroes and Hero Worship*, lect. 1.

(5)   Of a truth men are mystically united; a mystic bond of brotherhood makes all men one.—CARLYLE *Essays*, "Goethe's Works."

(6)   The secrets of life are not shown except to sympathy and likeness.—EMERSON *Representative Men,* "Montaigne."

(7)   The stronger curiosity of the women had drawn them quite to the edge of the Green, where they could examine more closely the Quaker-like costume and the odd deport-ment of the female Methodists. Underneath the maple there was a small cart which had been brought from the wheel-wright's to serve as a pulpit, and round this a couple of benches and a few chairs had been placed.
GEORGE ELIOT *Adam Bede,* ch. 2.

(8)   Nothing—only every tool, bus, car, light,
torch, bulb, print, film, instrument or
communication depending for its life
on electrodynamic power would stop
and stand dumb and silent.
CARL SANDBURG *The People, Yes,* no. 20.

(9)   Nick walked barefoot along the path through the meadow below the barn. The path was smooth and the dew was cool on his bare feet.—ERNEST HEMINGWAY *Ten Indians.*

(10)   On Saturday afternoon Billy Buck, the ranch-hand, raked together the last of the old year's haystack and pitched small forkfuls over the wire fence to a few mildly interested cattle. High in the air small clouds like puffs of cannon smoke were driven eastward by the March wind.—JOHN STEINBECK *The Leader of the People.*

(11)   Except in fairy stories the bashful get less.
A beggar's hand has no bottom.
Polite words open iron gates.
Be polite but not too polite.
CARL SANDBURG *The People Yes,* no. 49.

(12)   Loveliest of trees, the cherry now
Is hung with bloom along the bough,

And stands about the woodland ride
Wearing white for Eastertide.
A. E. HOUSMAN *Loveliest of Trees.*

4. CASE

Case in English grammar denotes a relation of a noun or pronoun to other words in a sentence. In English there are three cases which are named as follows:

The **nominative case** denotes the person or thing about which an assertion is made: The *girl* dances.

The **possessive case** denotes ownership, agency, or a relationship: the *boy's* kite; *Russia's* apologists; the *defendant's* attorney.

The **objective case** denotes (1) a person or thing acted upon, or (2) a person or thing related to another word in a sentence by a connective:

(1) He hit *John.*
(2) I walked *to* the *lake.*

In English, case belongs only to *nouns* and *pronouns*. Except for the possessive case, the form of English nouns does not change to indicate case, as the following sentences show:

The *girl* is here. [nominative]

He hit the *girl.* [objective]

Give it *to* the *girl.* [objective]

The *girl's* doll is broken. [possessive]

The terms *nominative case* and *objective case* are therefore simply convenient labels by which to explain the use of nouns in a sentence and the way they are related to other words in the sentence in order to express the intended thought. (See RULES OF CASE IN NOUNS, B (2), p. 20.)

The Nominative and Objective Cases

Whether a noun is in the *nominative* or the *objective* case can be known only by the way the words in a sentence are arranged and related to express the thought intended. (Compare Part II, pp. 199–200.)

The *nominative case* ordinarily *precedes* its verb: *Cromwell* conquered Charles. Here *Cromwell* is in the nominative case because it precedes *conquered* and exerts the action of that verb on *Charles*.

However, nouns in the nominative case may appear anywhere in a sentence: There under the table crouched *Mary*. Here *Mary* is in the nominative case, even though it follows the verb *crouched,* because it is the word about which the assertion (*crouched*) is made and because all of the other words are clearly related to the verb *crouched*. The word order in this sentence has been reversed to place *Mary* in the emphatic position at the end.

The *objective case* usually *follows* the verb: Cromwell conquered *Charles*. Here *Charles* is in the objective case because it follows the verb *conquered* and receives the action.

Grammatically this sentence may be reversed: Charles conquered Cromwell. Now *Charles* is nominative and *Cromwell* is objective. However this is not the sense intended because it is factually untrue.

Nouns in the objective case may appear anywhere in a sentence: Charles, Cromwell conquered at Naseby. Here *Charles* is objective, even though it is the first word in the sentence, because (1) *Cromwell* precedes the verb and is its subject, and because (2) both fact and grammar dictate that *Charles* is the receiver of the action.

The objective is also the case of words used after a preposition: *as, in, at, on, under*. The boy stood *on* the burning *deck*. (See PREPOSITION, pp. 144.)

The Possessive Case

A noun expressing possession, origin, source, or some other close relation, is in the *possessive case:* my *father's* house; the *man's* character; the *nation's* history; a *day's* pay.

Rules of Case in Nouns*

A. The Nominative Case

1. A noun which is the subject of a finite verb (p. 87) or of a sentence is in the nominative case: The *sun* shines. This is called the *subject nominative*.

2. A noun in the predicate, corresponding to the subject and expressing the same meaning as the subject, or explaining or adding to the meaning of the subject, is in the nominative case: Grant was a great *general*. This is called the *predicate nominative*.

3. A noun attached to the subject by way of explanation, emphasis, or the like, is in the nominative case by apposition (see *D*): The chief, an old *man*, arose. This may be called the *nominative by apposition*.

4. A noun used in direct address is in the nominative case: *Charles*, bring me your book. This may be called the *nominative of direct address*.

5. A noun used without direct connection with any verb, to express an independent idea, is in the nominative case: The *hour* having arrived, the meeting was opened. This is called the *nominative absolute*. The absolute, a construction borrowed from Latin, is considered unnatural and loose in English and is therefore not much used. (See THE NOMINATIVE ABSOLUTE under INDEPENDENT ELEMENTS, Part II, p. 222.)

---

* NOTE.—These rules apply also to the pronoun. See PROPERTIES OF PRONOUNS, p. 25.

B. The Objective Case

1. A noun used as the object of a verb, forming what is called the *direct object,* is in the objective case: He repelled the *intruder.*

2. A noun used as the object of a preposition is in the objective case: from *Boston;* in *London;* to *New York.* This may be called the *objective* after a *preposition.*

It is chiefly in this connection that the noting of the objective case is of practical importance. A noun in the objective case can not be the subject of any finite verb in the same sentence. It is very rarely that the objective case after a verb could be so misused, but with prepositions this is very common. Many persons make the verb agree with the nearest noun, and therefore say or write:

The presence of many strangers were observed.

But *strangers* is in the objective case, after the preposition *of,* and can not, therefore, be the subject of the following verb. We must pass over the prepositional phrase, *of many strangers,* as if it were not there, in order to find the true subject of the verb, which is the noun *presence.* But *presence* is in the singular number, and must take a singular verb, so the sentence becomes:

The *presence* of many strangers *was* observed.

The phrase *of many strangers* is a subject modifier and does not affect the agreement of subject (*presence*) and verb (*was*).

3. The subject of the infinitive is in the objective case. (See p. 87.)

4. A noun which is in apposition with the object of a verb or of a preposition, or with the subject of an infinitive, is in the objective case: Miltiades defeated *Darius,* the Persian *emperor.* This may be called the *objective* by *apposition.* (See *D.*)

C. The Possessive Case

1. The possessive of a *singular* noun is formed by adding *'s: boy, boy's; horse, horse's; sailor, sailor's.*

2. The possessive of *plural* nouns ending in *s* or *es* is formed by adding an apostrophe ('): *boys, boys'; horses, horses'; sailors, sailors'.* Names ending in *s* or *es* usually add only the apostrophe: *Dickens'* novels; *Jeffers'* poems.

3. The possessive of *irregular* plurals is formed by adding *'s* to the plural form: the *mice's* cage; the *oxen's* feet; the *children's* hour.

4. Names of firms, societies, and other groups of closely associated words form their possessive by adding *'s* to the end of the whole expression: *Liddel and Scott's* **Lexicon;** The *American Nautical Society's* headquarters; *Dun and Bradstreet's* publications.

5. Possession shared by two or more nouns is shown by adding *'s* to the last noun: *John and Joseph's* notes (one set of notes jointly owned); *Lincoln and Seward's* correspondence (the correspondence between Lincoln and Seward).

6. Individual possession by two or more nouns is shown by adding *'s* to each noun: *John's and Joseph's* notes (the notes of John and the notes of Joseph); *Lincoln's and Seward's* correspondence (the correspondence of Lincoln and the correspondence of Seward).

7. The possessive of a compound word is formed by adding *'s* to the end of the entire word: my *father-in-law's* house.

EXCEPTIONS.—In some few words, the *s* of the *possessive singular* is omitted, and the apostrophe only is added; especially:

(1) When the singular of the noun ends in an *s* or *z* sound, while the following word also begins with an *s* or *z* sound: for *conscience'* sake; for *Jesus'* sake.

(2) When the singular is a word of many syllables, so that the added syllable with *s* would have a disagreeable effect: *Themistocles'* services to the Athenians. *Themistocles's services* would be possible, but harsh and objectionable in sound.

(3) When the singular ending is *s* in a word of one syllable, no exception is commonly made. The possessive is pronounced as if it ended in *es*. Thus we say: *Jones's* woods; *Keats's* poems.

An Equivalent for the Possessive.—The possessive case of any noun is exactly equivalent to the phrase formed by the preposition *of: Tennyson's* poems or the poems *of Tennyson*.

The Possession of Inanimate Objects.—Inanimate objects do not as a rule take the possessive case. Instead, possession is shown by an *of* phrase: the roof *of the house;* the tip *of the cigar* (never the *house's roof,* the *cigar's tip*).

EXCEPTIONS.—Changing usage now permits the inanimate possessive more and more frequently, especially with words that (1) indicate periods of time, (2) refer to an association of people, or (3) are frequently personified:

(1) a day's pay (the pay for a day)
     a week's vacation (a vacation of a week)

(2) the company's policy
     the government's edict

(3) the ship's crew
     the sun's rays

The use of the inanimate possessive seems to be determined more by euphony than by logical prescription. The *desk's top* is an awkward expression, but *at arm's length* is customary and natural.

A Double Possessive.—Sometimes the form in *'s* and the form with *of* are combined, making a double possessive. Thus we say, "That check *of Thompson's,*" where "That *Thompson's* check" would be awkward, and "That check *of Thompson*" would seem rather flat. We prefer the *possessive* at the end of the phrase, even though it combines two forms, and this mode of expression has become an accepted English idiom.

D. Apposition

(*Applying equally to all the cases*)

RULE.—A noun used to limit, explain, expand, or emphasize the meaning of another noun or pronoun denoting the same person or thing is put by apposition in the same case: Cæsar, *the conqueror,* entered Rome in triumph. The White House, *the home of the President,* is being completely refurnished.

A noun which is in apposition with another noun or with a pronoun is called an *appositive*.

EXERCISE

Give the case of every noun in the following extracts. (This may be made a general review of THE NOUN by giving also gender, person, and number of all nouns included.)

(1)   The manly part is to do with might and main what you can do.—EMERSON *The Conduct of Life.*

(2)   There is character in spectacles—the pretentious tortoise-shell, the meek pince-nez of the school teacher, the twisted silver-framed glasses of the old villager. Babbitt's spectacles had huge, circular frameless lenses of the very best glass; the ear-pieces were thin bars of gold.—SINCLAIR LEWIS *Babbitt,* ch. 1.

(3)   Suit the action to the word, the word to the action.
                                   SHAKESPEARE *Hamlet,* act iii, sc. 2.

(4)   Affection is the broadest basis of good in life.—GEORGE ELIOT *Daniel Deronda,* bk. v, ch. 35.

(5)   We do not count a man's years, until he has nothing else to count.—EMERSON *Society and Solitude.*

(6)   The heads of strong old age are beautiful
Beyond all grace of youth. They have strange quiet,
Integrity, health, soundness, to the full
They've dealt with life and been attempered by it.
ROBINSON JEFFERS *Promise of Peace.*

(7)   O, it is excellent
To have a giant's strength, but it is tyrannous
To use it like a giant.
SHAKESPEARE *Measure for Measure,* act ii, sc. 2.

(8)   Alice did not like shaking hands with either of them first,
for fear of hurting the other's feelings; so, as the best way
out of the difficulty, she took hold of both hands at once:
the next moment they were dancing round in a ring.—LEWIS
CARROLL *Through the Looking-Glass,* ch. 4.

(9)   This is the weather the cuckoo likes,
        And so do I;
When showers benumble the chestnut spikes,
        And nestlings fly;
And the little brown nightingale bills his best,
And they sit outside the "Traveller's Rest,"
And maids come forth sprig-muslin drest,
And citizens dream of the South and West,
        And so do I.
THOMAS HARDY *Weather.*

(10)   Feed the grape and bean
            To the vintner and monger;
        I will lie down lean
            With my thirst and hunger.
EDNA ST. VINCENT MILLAY *Feast.*

(11)   On the second morning in the Chicago hotel Wilbourne
waked and found that Charlotte was dressed and gone, hat,
coat and handbag, leaving a note for him in a big sprawling
untrained hand such as you associate at first glance with a
man until you realize an instant later it is profoundly feminine.—WILLIAM FAULKNER *The Wild Palms.*

(12)   She was dressed in a yellow organdie, a costume of a
hundred cool corners, with three tiers of ruffles and a big
bow in back until she shed black and yellow around her
in a sort of phosphorescent lustre.—F. SCOTT FITZGERALD
The Jelly-Bean.

THE PRONOUN

Pronouns are so frequently the keys or turning points of sentences that they can not be too carefully studied or too thoroughly mastered. A **pronoun** is a word used in place of a noun. The pronoun is used in place of a noun in either of two ways:

1. As a substitute for some definite noun.

The noun for which the pronoun stands or to which it refers is called its *antecedent*. (See PRONOUNS AND ANTECEDENTS, pp. 55–61.) Consider the following sentences:

The son told the *son's* mother that the *son* loved the son's *mother*.

The son told *his* mother that *he* loved *her*.

In the second sentence the pronouns *his, he,* and *her* are substituted for the antecedent nouns *son's, son,* and *mother* respectively.

2. As taking the place and having the effect of a noun without being a substitute for a definite, expressed antecedent. (See pp. 55–56.)

PROPERTIES OF PRONOUNS

Pronouns have the same properties as nouns: *gender, person, number,* and *case.* Since the properties of nouns and pronouns are the same, the definitions given under the noun need not be repeated here. Some pronouns represent these properties more perfectly than any noun (see PERSONAL PRONOUNS, pp. 26–27), but other pronouns represent them very imperfectly.

CLASSES OF PRONOUNS

Pronouns may be divided into six classes or groups, as follows:

CLASSES	PRONOUNS
1. Personal Pronouns	*I, thou, he, she,* and *it*
2. Demonstrative Pronouns	*this* and *that*
3. Interrogative Pronouns	*who, which, what*
4. Relative Pronouns	*who, which, what,* and *that (as, but)*
5. Indefinite Pronouns	*another, any, each, either, none,* etc.
6. Adjective Pronouns	*this, that, any, each, which, what,* etc.

1. PERSONAL PRONOUNS

A **personal pronoun** is one that shows by its form whether the *person speaking,* the *person spoken to,* or the *person or thing spoken of* is referred to. For example:

I represents the person speaking: *I* see the lake.

You (*thou*) represents the person or persons spoken to: *You* may leave now.

He (*she, it*) represents the person or thing spoken of: *He* (*she, it*) is a sight to behold!

Declensions of Personal Pronouns

	FIRST PERSON		SECOND PERSON	
	SINGULAR	PLURAL	SINGULAR	PLURAL
Nom.	I	we	you (thou)	you (ye)
Poss.	my, mine	our, ours	your (thy, thine)	your, yours
Obj.	me	us	you (thee)	you

THIRD PERSON

SINGULAR

	Masculine	*Feminine*	*Neuter*
Nom.	he	she	it
Poss.	his	her, hers	its
Obj.	him	her	it

PLURAL

Nom.	they
Poss.	their, theirs
Obj.	them

Gender in Personal Pronouns

In the first and second persons, singular and plural, and in the third person plural, the pronouns are of common or indeterminate gender. (See COMMON GENDER, under NOUN, pp. 5–6.) Gender is directly expressed only by the three pronouns of the third person and singular number, *he, she,* and *it,* with their subordinate case-forms, *his, him, her, hers,* and *its.* (See SPECIAL USES OF PERSONAL PRONOUNS, pp. 31–34.)

A personal pronoun must agree in gender with its antecedent noun. Thus:

The { **man** **woman** **tree** } requires { **his** **her** **its** } proper food.

Since the noun in the top, middle, or bottom line is the subject of the sentence, the pronoun on the same line, and that pronoun only, must be used to refer to that subject as its antecedent.

The pronoun may indicate gender when its antecedent noun does not. Thus:

My friend left this morning, but missed *his* train.

Here we know that the friend is a male *because* the pronoun *his* is masculine. It is the *pronoun alone* that tells us anything about the gender.

Gender Connections of the Possessive.—It is very important to observe that the English possessive pronoun always takes the gender of the *possessor;* never—as in so many other languages —of the person or thing possessed. We say:

The mother loves *her* son.

Although the noun *son* is masculine, the feminine possessive *her* is attached to it because the possessive pronoun takes the gender of the *antecedent, mother,* and *not* the gender of the *object* possessed.

We may reverse the statement and say,

The son loves *his* mother.

Here the masculine possessive *his* is attached to the feminine noun *mother* because the possessive pronoun here also takes the gender of its *antecedent, son,* the possessor, and *not* of the object possessed. The English method of keeping the possessive of the pronoun to the *gender of the antecedent* preserves the unity of the sentence as no other system can do.

Personification in Pronouns

Personification is a figure of speech which refers to inanimate things as if they were persons. (Compare PERSONIFICATION IN NOUNS, pp. 8–9.) Personification by the use of pronouns occurs when a masculine or feminine pronoun is used to refer to a neuter noun as if that noun represented a male or female person.

Thus poets and orators speak of the sun as *he* and of the moon as *she;* and a sailor speaks of his ship, or a railroad man of his engine or train, as *she.* In like manner, the state, the nation, or the church, if personified, is referred to by a feminine pronoun. Poetically we say of the church, for instance, *"her* altars," *"her* ministry"; but in plain prose we say *"its* membership numbers so many thousand." Evidently the rule for all such nouns is that they are of the neuter gender, like all names of inanimate objects.

Person in Personal Pronouns

Personal pronouns and verbs are the only words in English that indicate person by change of form. (Compare VERB, pp. 90–91.) The forms of personal pronouns for the several persons have been sufficiently indicated in the table of DECLENSION OF PERSONAL PRONOUNS (pp. 26–27).

The following items should be carefully noted:

Personal Pronouns Used With or Without Nouns

1. The pronoun of the first person singular, nominative case, is always expressed by a capital *I*, whatever its place in the sentence, or whatever its connection with other words. Other forms of the pronoun of the first person, singular or plural (*mine, me*), and the pronouns of the second and third person (*he, she,* or *it*) are never capitalized except when used at the beginning of a sentence.

2. The pronoun of the *first person* must always be expressed. A singular or plural noun can never be used in the first person without a pronoun of the first person accompanying it. Thus, in the sentence, "*I,* Thomas, am your brother," if we omit the *I,* we have, "Thomas am your brother," which would be an impossible English construction, instantly felt to be ridiculous.

Consider the following sentences:

I, your brother, arrived yesterday.

We, the men of the community, make the laws.

You must deal with *me,* the attorney.

If the *I, we,* and *me* were omitted, the sentences would be in the *third person* instead of the *first:*

Your brother arrived yesterday.

The men of the community make the laws.

You must deal with the attorney.

3. The pronoun of the *second person* may be expressed or omitted, according to circumstances.

Pronoun Expressed	*Pronoun Omitted*
You, my friends, listen to me!	My friends, listen to me!
You, boys, come here!	Boys, come here!

Both forms are equally correct. The use of the pronoun makes the expression more personal, an effect which may be pleasing between friends, but may sometimes be offensive to strangers. In such imperative sentences (see VERB, (3), pp. 84–85), the use or omission of the pronoun of the second person is a matter of taste or feeling, to be settled by circumstances in each case.

There are other expressions where the pronoun of the *second person* can not be omitted. Thus, in the sentences, *"You* men will go," or, "Will *you* men go?" if we omit the pronoun, we change the sentences to the *third* person: Men will go. Will men go?

4. The pronoun of the *third person* is scarcely ever expressed if the noun is given. Such an expression as, "The man *he* told me," is never used by correct writers or speakers. Commonly, the very way we decide that a noun is in the third person is by the absence of an accompanying pronoun:

First Person	We men are mortal.
Second Person	You men are mortal.
Third Person	Men are mortal.

Number in Personal Pronouns

Personal pronouns have complete forms for both the singular and plural, but in the plural of the third person a single set of forms (*they, their* or *theirs, them*) is used as the common plural of *he, she,* and *it.* These forms for the most part explain themselves, but certain special uses should be noted:

Use of You.—The plural forms, *you, your,* and *yours* are now regularly and almost exclusively used in addressing a single individual. The pronoun of the second person singular (*thou, thy* or *thine, thee*) is now wholly out of use in ordinary writing or conversation. The following caution must be carefully noted, however:

CAUTION.—*You,* when singular in use, must always take a plural verb. We use "you *are,*" "you *were,*" in addressing a single person—never "you *is*" or "you *was.*"

Uses of Thou.—The forms *thou, thy* or *thine, thee,* have now only the three following uses:

(1) In Scriptural language or in prayer. (See THE ANCIENT OR SOLEMN STYLE, pp. 130–134.)

(2) In our older literature, as in the plays of Shakespeare, and very rarely in modern poetry or oratory where the ancient style is imitated or where the older forms are used as especially impressive.

(3) In the conventional language of the Society of Friends, who have, however, introduced some changes peculiar to their mode of speech, using the objective as a nominative with the third person of the verb, and saying, for instance, "thee is" instead of "thou art."

Special Uses of Personal Pronouns

1. **The Indeterminate Masculine.**—The third person singular masculine of the personal pronoun, *he,* is often used to refer

indifferently to persons or either sex: If anyone returns the ring, *he* will receive a reward. Here it is understood that *he* may refer indifferently to man or woman, boy or girl. This use obviates the necessity of saying, *"He* or *she* will receive a reward," "A reward will be given to *him* or *her,"* or the like. *He, his,* or *him,* so used, is of the masculine gender, used indeterminately.

The indeterminate plural forms *they* and *theirs* must not be used to refer to a singular noun. It is incorrect to write: If any boy or girl comes late, *they* will lose *their* seat. In such sentences the masculine forms *he* and *his* should be used for both sexes, as explained in the paragraph above. Otherwise, the form of expression should be changed. The example given here could be written: If any *boys* or *girls* come late, *they* will lose *their* seats. The plural is then correct throughout.

2. **The Indeterminate Neuter.**—The neuter of the personal pronoun often has the peculiar effect of simply dismissing gender from consideration. We refer to a child or an animal, for instance, by the pronoun *it* or *its,* not implying that the individual referred to has no sex, but meaning simply that we do not know or do not care about the sex. Thus we say:

> The *child* was crying for *its* mother.
> The hunter shot the *bird,* and broke *its* wing.

Since *child* and *bird* are each indeterminate in gender, we use *its,* with the understanding that the neuter form gives no indication of gender.

3. **Special Uses of We.**—It is customary for a monarch to use *we, our,* and *us* in referring to himself: *We* hereby decree. This is called the *plural of majesty*.

The editor of a paper or magazine uses *we* in referring to himself: *We* referred in our last issue to the recent act of Congress. This is called the *editorial we* and is at times used also by essayists to make their writing seem less personal.

4. The Indefinite You.—It is common to use *you* as applying indefinitely to any or all persons, and not especially to the person or persons addressed: *You* will win friends by being friendly. That is, *any one* will win friends in this way.

5. The Indefinite It.—The pronoun *it* may sometimes refer to a phrase or clause, or even to an entire sentence, or at times to some implied thought: Some say that matter is eternal, but I do not believe *it;* i.e., I do not believe *the statement* "that matter is eternal."

The pronoun *it* may also be used as the apparent subject of a verb, without referring to anything in particular: *It* rains. *It* is too late to go.

It may be used as an introductory word to represent a phrase or clause that is to follow the verb: *It* is likely that he will come. *It* used in this way is sometimes called an *expletive*. *Here* and *there* are also expletives when they introduce a verb that precedes the subject:

It is thought that he stole the money.

Here come the elephants.

There is no one here. (See THE PRONOUN, Part II, pp. 178–179.)

Formerly *it* was used indefinitely as a supplementary object of a verb, as it is still used in poetry and sometimes in popular speech: Come and trip *it* as we go; foot *it* to town.

CAUTION.—The indefinite *it* must be used with care in order to avoid vagueness and obscurity.

Obscure   While I was trying to study, he talked about the homicide, and *it* disturbed me.

Clear   While I was trying to study, he talked about the homicide, and *his talking* disturbed me.

Vague   My uncle is a lawyer. *It* is a profession that I dislike.

Clear   My uncle is a lawyer. *Law* is a profession that I dislike.

EXERCISE A

Select the personal pronouns from the following extracts and decline each one:

(1)   A friend should bear his friend's infirmities,
But Brutus makes mine greater than they are.
           SHAKESPEARE *Julius Cæsar,* act iv, sc. 3.

(2)   I heard him walking across the floor
As he always does, with a heavy tread.
           LONGFELLOW *The Golden Legend,* pt. ii.

(3)   I am not of that feather to shake off
My friend when he must need me.
           SHAKESPEARE *Timon of Athens,* act i, sc. 1.

(4)   Ever-returning spring, trinity sweet to me you bring,
Lilac blooming perennial and drooping star in the west,
And thought of him I love.
        WHITMAN *When Lilacs Last in the Dooryard Bloom'd.*

(5)   We had the "faith doctor," too, in those days—a woman. Her speciality was toothache. She was a farmer's old wife and lived five miles from Hannibal. She would lay her hand on the patient's jaw and say, "Believe!" and the cure was prompt.—MARK TWAIN *Autobiography.*

(6)   Relieved of Babbitt's bumbling and the soft grunts with which his wife expressed the sympathy she was too experienced to feel and much too experienced not to show, their bedroom settled instantly into impersonality.—SINCLAIR LEWIS *Babbitt,* ch. 2.

(7)   You are a friend, then, as I make it out,
Of our man Shakespeare, who alone of us
Will put an ass's head in Fairyland
As he would add a shilling to more shillings,
All most harmonious.
        EDWARD ARLINGTON ROBINSON *Ben Jonson Entertains*
                  a Man from Stratford.

(8)   He appeared to forget to keep his hold,
        But advanced with her as she crossed the grass.
                                ROBERT FROST *The Fear*.

(9)   "I'm sorry that I spelt the word.
                I hate to go above you,
            Because,"—the brown eyes lower fell,—
            "Because, you see, I love you!"
                                WHITTIER *In School Days*.

(10)   My old man had a big lot of money after that race and
        he took to coming into Paris oftener. If they raced at Trem-
        blay he'd have them drop him in town on their way back to
        Maisons and he and I'd sit out in front of the Café de la
        Paix and watch the people go by.—ERNEST HEMINGWAY
        My Old Man.

EXERCISE B

Tell the number and person of each personal pronoun in the
following extracts and decline the pronoun.

(1)   We sat together at one summer's end,
        That beautiful mild woman, your close friend
        And you and I, and talked of poetry.
                                WILLIAM BUTLER YEATS *Adam's Curse*.

(2)   Let us go then, you and I,
        When the evening is spread out against the sky
        Like a patient etherised upon a table.
                                T. S. ELIOT *The Love Song of J. Alfred Prufrock*.

(3)   "You know nothing? Do you see nothing? Do you remember
       "Nothing?"
                    I remember
       Those are pearls that were his eyes.
       "Are you alive, or not? Is there nothing in your head?"
                    T. S. ELIOT *The Waste Land,* II. "A Game of Chess."

(4)   And you, my father, there on the sad height,
        Curse, bless, me now with your fierce tears, I pray.
        DYLAN THOMAS *Do Not Go Gentle into That Good Night*.

(5)   If you are coming down through the narrows of the
                            river Kiang,
        Please let me know beforehand,

> And I will come out to meet you
>   As far as Cho-fu-Sa.
>   EZRA POUND *The River Merchant's Wife: A Letter.*

(6)   The time you won your town the race
>   We chaired you through the market place;
>   Man and boy stood cheering by,
>   And home we brought you shoulder-high.
>   A. E. HOUSMAN *To an Athlete Dying Young.*

(7)   The first thing that strikes one about the discomfort in which our ancestors lived is that it was mainly voluntary. Some of the apparatus of modern comfort is of purely modern invention; people could not put rubber tyres on their carriages before the discovery of South America and the rubber plant.—ALDOUS HUXLEY *Comfort.*

(8)   We Americans are a backward nation in everything except in the making and using of machines. And we are nowhere more backward than we are in our attitude toward our women.—PEARL BUCK *America's Medieval Women.*

(9)   We look for some reward of our endeavors and are disappointed; not success, not happiness, not even peace of conscience, crown our ineffectual efforts to do well. Our frailties are invincible, our virtues barren; the battle goes sore against us to the going down of the sun.—ROBERT LOUIS STEVENSON *Pulvis et Umbra.*

(10)   The politicians tell us, "You must educate the masses because they are going to be masters." The clergy join in the cry for education, for they affirm that the people are drifting away from church and chapel into the broadest infidelity.—T. H. HUXLEY *A Liberal Education and Where to Find It.*

Case in Personal Pronouns

Personal pronouns have for the most part different forms for the several cases, both in the singular and in the plural. The case forms are sufficiently shown in the table of DECLENSIONS OF PERSONAL PRONOUNS, pp. 26–27.

REMARKS

(1) **Use of You and Ye.**—*You* is the accepted form for both the nominative and the objective cases. *Ye*, formerly used for the nominative, is now archaic and rarely used.

(2) **Possessives Used with Nouns.**—The possessive pronouns *my, our, your, his, her, its,* and *their* are used to qualify nouns precisely as adjectives are used:

my book *our* home *your* hat *their* yard

My, our, your, her, and *their* are never used without a noun which they qualify. *His* and *its* may be used either with or without a noun denoting the object possessed.

(3) **Possessives Used Without Nouns.**—Several possessives of the personal pronouns appear in two forms:

my	our	thy	you	her	their
mine	ours	thine	yours	hers	theirs

Of these, the second of each pair (*mine, ours, thine, yours, hers, theirs*) is almost never used with a noun; it is used alone to represent the possessive and the object possessed. Possession can thus be expressed in either of two ways:

This book is *mine*. He lives in *our* house.
This is *my* book. The house is *ours*.

His and *its* may be used without a noun in precisely the same way:

This is my book; that is *his*.
You have your life; the tree has *its*.

A possessive used without a noun is treated exactly like a noun. It may be either the subject or object of a verb, or the object of a preposition:

Yours is here. [Subject of *is*]
Give me *mine*. [Object of *give*]
Put your book with *mine*. [Object of *with*]

(4) **The Possessive After Of.**—A possessive pronoun may be used without its noun to form a double possessive: this heart of *mine;* that knife of *his.* Although the double possessive is an acceptable form, its use is so infrequent that it should be avoided.

Compound Personal Pronouns

Certain compound personal pronouns are formed by adding the word *self* or *selves* to the possessive of the simple personal pronoun. These compound personal pronouns are:

Singular	*Plural*
myself (ourself)	ourselves
thyself (yourself)	yourselves
himself, herself, itself	themselves

These forms are the same both in the nominative and the objective, and have no possessive. They are used:

1. For emphasis: I will go *myself;* I saw the man *himself.*

2. For reference to the subject of the verb: I hurt *myself;* take care of *yourself;* they support *themselves.* Pronouns thus referring back to the original subject are often called *reflexive pronouns.*

3. Occasionally as substitutes for the simple personal pronouns: This invitation is for *yourself.* Regards to *yourself* and family.

EXERCISE

Give the number and case of each personal pronoun in the following extracts.

(1)
>Afterward you did. And then
>what was printed
>about the Estrella gang—you hid it
>from me,
>you and father. What is it—about
>this murder?
>
>MAXWELL ANDERSON *Winterset,* act i, sc. 2.

(2)   Aw, Joe, you're always making me to do crazy things for you, and *I'm* the guy that gets embarrassed. You just sit in this place and make me do all the dirty work.—WILLIAM SAROYAN *The Time of Your Life,* act i.

(3)   You made Chris feel guilty with me. Whether you wanted to or not, you've crippled him in front of me.—ARTHUR MILLER *All My Sons,* act iii.

(4)   When a girl leaves her home at eighteen, she does one of two things. Either she falls into saving hands and becomes better, or she rapidly assumes the cosmopolitan standard of virtue and becomes worse.—THEODORE DREISER *Sister Carrie,* ch. 1.

(5)   The train was just pulling out of Waukesha. For some time she had been conscious of a man behind. She felt him observing her mass of hair. He had been fidgetting, and with natural intuition she felt a certain interest growing in that quarter. THEODORE DREISER *Sister Carrie,* ch. 1.

(6)   Now Kino reached into a secret place somewhere under his blanket. He brought out a paper folded many times. Crease by crease he unfolded it, until at last there came to view eight small misshapen seed pearls, as ugly and gray as little ulcers, flattened and almost valueless.—JOHN STEINBECK *The Pearl,* I.

(7)   The word was passed among the neighbors where they stood close packed in the little yard behind the brush fence. And they repeated among themselves, "Juana wants the doctor." A wonderful thing, a memorable thing, to want a doctor. To get him would be a remarkable thing.—JOHN STEINBECK *The Pearl,* I.

(8)   Only one brave and beautiful boy of ten named Andy from Salinas ever crossed the old Chinaman. Andy was visiting in Monterey and he saw the old man and knew he must shout at him if only to keep his self-respect, but even Andy, brave as he was, felt the little cloud of fear.—JOHN STEINBECK *Cannery Row,* ch. 4.

2. DEMONSTRATIVE PRONOUNS

The word *demonstrative* comes from the Latin *demonstro,* meaning to point out. A **demonstrative pronoun** is one that directly indicates its antecedent, as if with a pointing finger.

The only demonstrative pronouns are *this* (plural *these*) and *that* (plural *those*). *This* points out an object that is near in space, time, or thought: *This* (in my hand) is my book. *That* points out an object that is comparatively remote in space, time, or thought: *That* book (on the shelf across the room) is yours.

> *This* is my property, and I wish to buy *that* land adjoining.
>
> *This* event happened yesterday; *that,* a century ago.

The antecedent of *this* and *that* may be any single noun, as in the examples given above. *This* and *that* may also refer to a phrase, clause, or sentence, or even to an implied thought. Reference of this kind must, however, be immediately clear and apparent; otherwise the thought will be obscure. The reference in the following examples is broad, but clear:

> Is the atomic theory sound? *That* is what science wishes to ascertain.
>
> Tell me *this,* can I depend on your giving the message promptly? (Here *this* refers to a thought which follows.)
>
> He has given me his word of honor. *That* is good enough for me.

The Demonstratives with *Kind* and *Sort*.—The demonstratives are frequently misused with *kind* and *sort*. *Kind* and *sort* are singular in number since each refers to *one class;* their plurals are *kinds* and *sorts,* meaning two or more classes. Therefore the demonstrative pronouns must agree with them in number as follows:

> *this* kind of flower [several flowers of *one kind*]
>
> *these* kinds of flowers [several *kinds*]
>
> *that* sort of people [people of *one sort*]
>
> *those* sorts of people [several *sorts*]

EXERCISE

Point out and explain the demonstrative pronouns in the following examples.

(1)   No more of that, Hal, an thou lovest me.—SHAKESPEARE *Henry IV*, pt. i, act ii, sc. 4.

(2)   God grants liberty only to those who love it, and are always ready to defend it.—WEBSTER *Speech,* June 3, 1834.

(3)   These are excitements to duty; but they are not suggestions of doubt.—WEBSTER *First Bunker Hill Monument Oration.*

(4)   They look into the beauty of thy mind,
    And that, in guess, they measure by thy deeds.
                                    SHAKESPEARE *Sonnet* lxix.

(5)   How can he find himself on a farm? Is that a life? A farmhand?—ARTHUR MILLER *Death of a Salesman,* act i.

(6)   Look at these feathers and furs that she came here to preen herself in! What's this here? A solid-gold dress, I believe! And this one! What is this here? Fox-pieces!—TENNESSEE WILLIAMS *A Streetcar Named Desire,* sc. ii.

(7)   You misjudge me cruelly. It is true that I have some knowledge of drugs and medicines: I can sometimes cure sickness.
    Is that a crime? These dark rumors, my lord, are only the noise of popular gratitude.
                                    ROBINSON JEFFERS *Medea,* act i.

(8)   These are the days when birds come back,
    A very few, a bird or two,
    To take a backward look.

    These are the days when skies put on
    The old, old sophistries of June,—
    A blue and gold mistake.
                                    EMILY DICKINSON *Indian Summer.*

(9)   This quiet Dust was Gentlemen and Ladies,
        And Lads and Girls;
    Was laughter and ability and sighing;
        And frocks and curls.
    This passive place a farmer's nimble mansion,

>Where Bloom and Bees
>Fulfilled their Oriental Circuit,
>Then ceased like these.
>
>   ʼ EMILY DICKINSON *A Cemetery*.

(10)   It would be nice to lie on the hearthrug before the fire, leaning his head upon his hands, and think on those sentences. He shivered as if he had cold slimy water next his skin. That was mean of Wells to shoulder him into the square ditch because he would not swop his little snuffbox for Wells' seasoned hacking chestnut, the conqueror of forty. —JAMES JOYCE *A Portrait of the Artist As a Young Man*, ch. 1.

3. INTERROGATIVE PRONOUNS

An **interrogative pronoun** is a pronoun used to ask a question. These pronouns, often called simply *interrogatives,* are *who, which,* and *what.* They are the same for all genders, persons, and numbers. *Who* alone has distinction of case, and is declined as follows:

>*Masculine, feminine, and neuter*
>SINGULAR AND PLURAL
>*Nominative*   who
>*Possessive*   whose
>*Objective*   whom

Which and *what* have no declension, being wholly without change of form however used. But to avoid awkwardness, *whose* may be used as the possessive of *which.* (See RELATIVE PRONOUNS, pp. 46–47.)

Awkward   He promulgated laws the severity of which was unprecedented.

Improved   He promulgated laws whose severity was unprecedented.

Although the interrogatives have no gender forms of their own, they may be used with reference to subjects of the different genders, as follows:

Who as an interrogative, is used only for persons, either masculine or feminine.

Which, as an interrogative, may be used either for persons, for animals, or for things, i.e., for a masculine, feminine, or neuter noun.

In reference to persons *who* is *universal; which* is *selective.* That is, *who* asks for any one of all persons; *which* asks for any one of a certain number or group of persons:

Who did this? The answer may be any person or persons, present or absent, living now or in any past time.

Which of you did this? The answer is some *one or more of the group of persons addressed.*

Which of the boys did this? The answer points out some one or more *of a certain number or group of boys,* as the boys of the school, of a class, or the like. That is, *which* selects from a limited number, and not, like *who,* from all persons whosoever.

What, as an interrogative, may apply either to persons, to animals, or to things. As applied to persons, *what* is *descriptive.* That is, *what* asks for the character, occupation, or the like:

"*What* is that man?" The answer may be, "He is a teacher (or a preacher, or a soldier, etc.)." That is, the answer tells what the person is or does. If we asked, "*Who* is that man?" the expected answer would tell his name.

What, as applied to things, is universal, asking for any one of all things: *What* did you find? *What* have we here? *What* do you wish?

When a direct question is made indirect, the interrogative pronoun has much the appearance of a relative although it still remains interrogative.

Direct Question	*Indirect Question*
Who did this?	He asked *who* did this.
Which is that?	He asked *which* that was.
What did you find?	They inquired *what* I found.

In indirect questions the pronouns *who, which,* and *what* are classed as interrogatives because the question is still contained in the phrase, although in different form.

For *who, which,* and *what* as relatives, see RELATIVE PRO-NOUNS, p. 45. For *which* and *what* used with an accompanying noun, see ADJECTIVE PRONOUNS, p. 52.

EXERCISE

Point out and explain the interrogative pronouns in the following examples.

(1)   Why, what is pomp, rule, reign, but earth and dust?
And, live we how we can, yet die we must.
SHAKESPEARE Henry VI, pt. iii, act v, sc. 2.

(2)   Which is the villain? . . . Which of these is he?
SHAKESPEARE Much Ado about Nothing, act v, sc. 1.

(3)   What then remains, but well our power to use,
And keep good humor still, whate'er we lose?
POPE Rape of the Lock, can. v, l. 29.

(4)   And who is he that will harm you, if ye be followers of that which is good?—1 *Peter* 3:13.

(5)   —What did he say?
—Did you go in?
—What did he say?
—Tell us. Tell us.
JAMES JOYCE A Portrait of the Artist
As a Young Man, ch. 1.

(6)   Who was the professor at the University of Wisconsin working out a butter-fat milk tester
Good for a million dollars if he had a patent with sales and royalties?
CARL SANDBURG The People, Yes, no. 89.

(7)   Who was that antique Chinese crook who put over his
       revolution and let out a rooster crow: "Burn all the books!
       History must begin with us!"
       What burned so inside of him that he must burn all the
       books?

CARL SANDBURG *The People, Yes,* no. 71.

(8)   No dark tomb-haunter once; her form all full
       As though with magnanimity of light,
       Yet a most gentle woman; who can tell
       Which of her forms has shown her substance right?

WILLIAM BUTLER YEATS *A Bronze Head.*

(9)   A living man is blind and drinks his drop.
           What matter if the ditches are impure?
           What matter if I live it all once more?

WILLIAM BUTLER YEATS *A Dialogue of
Self and Soul.*

(10)   What are those blue remembered hills?
               What spires, what farms are those?

A. E. HOUSMAN *Into My Heart.*

4. RELATIVE PRONOUNS

A **relative pronoun** is a pronoun that relates to an antecedent and at the same time joins to it a limiting or qualifying clause:

This is the house *that* I prefer.

We found a boatman *who* rowed us across.

He is fond of apples, *which* are healthful.

The relative pronouns in common use are *who, which, what,* and *that.* (See *As* AND *But* AS RELATIVE PRONOUNS, p. 48, also COMPOUND RELATIVES, pp. 48–49.)

Declensions of Relative Pronouns

Of the relatives, *who* alone is declined (compare INTERROGATIVE PRONOUNS, p. 42), as follows:

Masculine and feminine
SINGULAR AND PLURAL

Nominative who
Possessive whose
Objective whom

Which, what, and *that* have no declension; they are the same for all genders, numbers, and cases. *As* and *but* are likewise never declined.

EXCEPTION.—To the statement that *which* is not declined there is an apparent exception of usage, but not of form: *Whose,* the possessive of *who,* is used also as the possessive of *which* by many of the best authors.

> 'Tis beauty truly blent, *whose* red and white
> Nature's own sweet and cunning hand laid on.
>   SHAKESPEARE *Twelfth Night,* act i, 5, l. 257.

> Spires *whose* silent finger points to heaven.
>   WORDSWORTH *The Excursion,* bk. vi, l. 19.

Gender and Relative Pronouns.—Relative pronouns have *no proper distinctions of gender,* but there are certain distinctions of usage, as follows:

Who refers only to *persons,* that is, to intelligent living beings. *Who* does not indicate gender; we say with equal propriety: The boy *who* was there, *or* the girl *who* was there.

As a relative, *which* refers only to animals and to inanimate things:

> The whale, *which* was resting quietly, filled me with terror.

> Consult the dictionary, *which* is a storehouse of knowledge.

NOTE.—*Which* was formerly used for persons, even in the most exalted sense, as in the Authorized Version of the Bible:

"Our father, *which* art in heaven." *Matt.* 6:9. Compare the relative with the interrogative *which,* pp. 42–43.

What, as a relative, is strictly neuter in use, referring only to things without life. (Compare the use of *what* as an interrogative, p. 43.)

Personal Uses of Relative Pronouns.—*Who* and *that* may be used for either the first, second, or third person:

> I, John, *who* also am your brother.—*Rev.* 1:9.

> You *who* are present know the facts, and those *who* are absent will be informed.

> I, *that* speak unto thee am he.—*John* 4:26.

By omission of its antecedent, *who* may be used with the force of a double relative equivalent to the following: *he that, they that, the one* or *ones that.* With the exception of some old proverbial sayings, this usage is now confined to poetry.

> *Whom* the gods would destroy they first make mad.

> Who builds a church to God, and not to Fame,
> Will never mark the marble with his name.
>> POPE *Moral Essays,* ep. iii, 1. 285.

Which and *what,* referring only to animals and to inanimate objects, are used only in the third person.

What as a Double Relative.—The relative *what* sometimes combines an antecedent and relative and is the equivalent of *that which:* Take *what* (*that which*) you want. When an antecedent is expressed, *what* should not be used:

> the man *who* (not *what*) met me

> the house *that* or *which* (not *what*) I live in

Forms with Of in Place of the Possessive.—For the relatives *who* and *which,* we may use either the possessive *whose* or the forms *of whom, of which:*

The boy, *whose* mother we just spoke about, has arrived.

The boy, the mother *of whom* we just spoke, has arrived.

We prefer the stanchions *whose* bases must be set in concrete.

We prefer the stanchions, the bases *of which* must be set in concrete.

The forms *of what* and *of that* are also used:

Here is an outline *of what* we must know.

This is the man *that* I spoke *of*.

In the second illustration, note that *of* follows *that* and is placed at the end of the sentence.

As and But as Relative Pronouns.—*As* is sometimes used as a relative pronoun. This relative use of *as* is most frequent after *such:*

Tears *such as* angels weep, burst forth.—MILTON

The aging salesman wrote *such* orders *as* he could.

But may also be used as a relative pronoun, meaning *that not, who not:*

Nobody *but* has his faults.—SHAKESPEARE

No nation *but* has its villains and traitors.

Compound Relative Pronouns

Who, which, and *what* add the suffix *ever,* with distributive effect, to make the pronoun apply to any one of all persons or things without limitation. The compound relatives are:

whoever, whomever   whichever   whatever

The forms *whosoever, whichsoever,* and *whatsoever,* are archaic and should not be used. (For the use of compound

pronouns in sentence construction, see THE COMPLEX SEN-
TENCE, pp. 233–234.)

EXERCISE

Point out and explain the relative pronouns in the following
extracts; name their antecedents.

(1)   The condition which high friendship demands is ability to
do without it.—EMERSON *Essays,* "Of Friendship."

(2)   Who friendship with a knave hath made,
            Is judged a partner in the trade.
                    GAY *The Old Woman and Her Cats.*

(3)   To wisdom he's a fool that will not yield.
                    SHAKESPEARE *Pericles,* act ii, sc. 4.

(4)   And what they dare to dream of, dare to do.
                LOWELL *Ode at Harvard Commemoration,* 1865.

(5)   Whose game was empires, and whose stakes were thrones;
Whose table earth; whose dice were human bones.
                    BYRON *The Age of Bronze,* st. 3.

(6)   What makes life dreary is the want of motive.—GEORGE
ELIOT *Daniel Deronda,* bk. viii, ch. 65.

(7)   I think that God was on your side; for I have not forgotten
how the wind changed, and how our hearts changed when
you came; and by my faith I shall never deny that it was in
your sign that we conquered. But I tell you as a soldier that
God is no man's daily drudge, and no maid's either.—G. B.
SHAW *St. Joan,* sc. 5.

(8)   Mark what I say: the woman who quarrels with her
clothes, and puts on the dress of a man, is like the man who
throws off his fur gown and dresses like John the Baptist:
they are followed, as surely as the night follows the day, by
bands of wild women and men who refuse to wear any
clothes at all.—G. B. SHAW *St. Joan,* sc. 6.

(9)   But so with all, from babes that play
            At hide-and-seek to God afar,
            So all who hide too well away
            Must speak and tell us where they are.
                    ROBERT FROST *Revelation.*

(10)   We who must die demand a miracle.
               How could the Eternal do a temporal act,
               The Infinite become a finite fact?
               Nothing can save us that is possible:
               We who must die demand a miracle.
                        W. H. AUDEN *For the Time Being.*

5. INDEFINITE PRONOUNS

An **indefinite pronoun** is a pronoun that represents an object indefinitely or generally. The chief indefinite pronouns are *another, any, both, each, either, neither, none, one, other, some, such.*

> *Any* of you may go who wish.

> Has *either* of them been here?

> Bring me *some* of those books.

> May *one* smoke in this room?

All, few, many, much, and *several* are by some treated as indefinite pronouns. Many of the best authorities, however, prefer to treat these words as adjectives which are at times used as nouns, and they will be so considered in this book. The fact that *few, many,* and *much* have comparative and superlative forms seems to rank them distinctly as adjectives, since adjectives only are compared.

Compound Indefinite Pronouns

The chief compound indefinite pronouns are *anybody, anything, everybody, everyone, everthing, nobody,* and *somebody.*

> Did you ask *anybody* to come?

> I would not do it for *anything*.

> That book is *somebody* else's.

> In this world *everything* moves.

Most of these words, together with *something* and *somewhat*, are also used as nouns. Whenever the use of one of these words is in doubt, a reliable dictionary should be consulted.

Indefinite Pronominal Phrases.—Certain groups of words, as *any one, every one, no one, some one,* are pronominal or pronoun phrases used like indefinite pronouns.

Possessive with *Else*.—A peculiar English usage is that when the adverb *else* is associated with one of these phrases the whole expression is used in the possessive case like a single word. Thus we say: *anybody else's, any one else's, somebody else's, some one else's.*

Distributive Pronouns.—The indefinite pronouns *each, either,* and *neither* are sometimes termed *distributive pronouns* because they separate some of the objects referred to from others spoken of in the same connection.

Reciprocal Pronouns.—The indefinite pronouns grouped in the phrases, *each other, one another,* are sometimes called *reciprocal pronouns* because the action of each is regarded as affecting the other. Strictly *each other* should be used only of two persons, *one another* of more than two: The husband and wife loved *each other.* All the firemen were helping *one another.* But this distinction is not always observed.

Gender and Person in Indefinite Pronouns.—The indefinite pronouns are the same in form for all genders and persons.

Number in Indefinite Pronouns.—The indefinite pronouns differ in number as follows:

SINGULAR ONLY—*another, each, either, neither*
PLURAL ONLY—*both*
SINGULAR OR PLURAL—*some, such, any*
SINGULAR AND PLURAL FORMS—*one, ones; other, others*

None is both singular and plural, but its use with a plural verb is commoner.

Cases of Indefinite Pronouns.—The indefinite pronouns have the same form in the nominative and in the objective case, whether singular or plural. *Another* and *one* form regular possessives, *another's* and *one's; either's, neither's, other's,* and *others'* are more seldom used.

When the intensive *self* is added to *one,* it forms a compound, *oneself.* Formerly, the possessive phrase *one's self* was used.

EXERCISE

Point out and explain the indefinite pronouns in the following examples.

(1)   All are architects of Fate,
    Working in these walls of Time;
   Some with massive deeds and great,
    Some with ornaments of rime.
        LONGFELLOW *The Builders,* st. 1.

(2)   In other part stood one who, at the forge
   Laboring, two massy clods of iron and brass
   Had melted.
       MILTON *Paradise Lost,* bk. xi, l. 564.

(3) Some books are to be tasted, others to be swallowed, and some few to be chewed and digested.—BACON *Essays,* "Of Studies."

(4) I never knew a man in my life who could not bear another's misfortunes perfectly like a Christian.—POPE (Swift's *Thoughts on Various Subjects.*)

(5)   How happy could I be with either,
    Were t'other dear charmer away!
   But while ye thus tease me together,
    To neither a word will I say.
       GAY *Beggar's Opera,* act ii, sc. 2.

(6) The soul is superior to its knowledge, wiser than any of its works.—EMERSON *Essays,* "The Oversoul."

(7) Oh! it is absurd to have a hard-and-fast rule about what one should read and what one shouldn't. More than half of modern culture depends on what one shouldn't read.—OSCAR WILDE *The Importance of Being Earnest,* act i.

(8)   A water-clerk need not pass an examination in anything under the sun, but he must have the Ability in the abstract and demonstrate it practically.—JOSEPH CONRAD *Lord Jim,* ch. 1.

(9)   The schoolmaster was leaving the village, and everybody seemed sorry.—THOMAS HARDY *Jude the Obscure,* ch. 1.

(10)   He did not mean to return till the evening, when the new school-teacher would have arrived and settled in, and everything would be smooth.—THOMAS HARDY *Jude the Obscure,* ch. 1.

6. ADJECTIVE PRONOUNS

Pronouns used like adjectives to modify nouns and other pronouns are called **adjective pronouns** or **pronominal adjectives.** The pronouns used in this way include the following:

The demonstratives *this, that; these, those*

The interrogatives and relatives *which* and *what*

All the indefinite pronouns except *none*

EXAMPLES: *this* book   *that* man   *some* people
             these books   *those* boys   *another* day

Who and *none* and the various personal pronouns are never used as adjectives. Instead of *none* the adjective *no* is used: *no* man, *no* one, *no* others. All other pronouns may be used as adjectives. When a pronoun is used in this way, as in the expression *this man,* it may be called an *adjective pronoun* or a *pronominal adjective.*

EXERCISE

Point out and explain all the adjective pronouns in the following extracts.

(1)   The true University of these days is a collection of books.
—CARLYLE *Heroes and Hero-Worship.*

(2)   Some friendships are made by nature, some by contract, some by interest, and some by souls.—JEREMY TAYLOR *A Discourse on Friendship.*

(3)   This fellow is wise enough to play the fool;
        And to do that well craves a kind of wit.
                    SHAKESPEARE *Twelfth Night,* act iii, sc. 1.

(4)   I have touched the highest point of all my greatness;
        And from that full meridian of my glory,
        I haste now to my setting.
                    SHAKESPEARE *Henry VIII*, act iii, sc. 2.

(5)   He tried each art, reproved each dull delay,
        Allured to brighter worlds, and led the way.
                    GOLDSMITH *The Deserted Village,* l. 169.

(6)   Finding that my fellow-citizens were not likely to offer me any room in the court house, or any currency or living anywhere else, but I must shift for myself, I turned my face exclusively to the woods, where I was better known.—THOREAU *Walden,* ch. 1.

(7)   As the business was to be entered into without the usual capital, it may not be easy to conjecture where those means, that will still be indispensable to every such undertaking, were to be obtained.—THOREAU *Walden,* ch. 1.

(8)   The second lesson I had was given me by a don, both intelligent and charming, who happened to be staying with me when I was correcting the typescript of another book. —W. SOMERSET MAUGHAM *The Summing Up,* ch. 8.

(9)   In those days people believed with a simple downrightness which I do not observe among educated men and women now. It had never crossed Theobald's mind to doubt the literal accuracy of any syllable in the Bible.—SAMUEL BUTLER *The Way of All Flesh,* ch. 12.

(10)   I see something of God each hour of the twenty-four, and each moment then.
                    WHITMAN *Song of Myself.*

(11)   It little profits that an idle king,
        By this still hearth, among these barren crags,
        Matched with an aged wife, I mete and dole

Unequal laws unto a savage race,
That hoard, and sleep, and feed, and know not me.
TENNYSON *Ulysses*.

PRONOUNS AND ANTECEDENTS

The Antecedent.—*Antecedent* is from the Latin *ante,* before, and *cedo,* go, signifying "that which goes before." The word for which a pronoun stands, or to which it refers back, is called the *antecedent*. The antecedent of a pronoun is ordinarily a noun or pronoun:

Here is the *man* who called you.

Mary said that she would go.

He caught the *ball* and threw it back.

She is the girl who spoke.

Pronouns Without Antecedents

A pronoun taking the place and having the effect of a noun, without being a substitute for any definite noun, has no antecedent.

EXAMPLES

(1) The pronoun of the first person, *I,* never has an antecedent. *I* stands for the speaker, just as a noun might, and therefore requires no antecedent.

(2) The pronoun of the second person, *you,* commonly has no antecedent: Are *you* ready?

(3) *It* often has no antecedent: *It* rains. *It* is time to start. In such sentences *it* is used to introduce a verb that precedes the subject and is called an *expletive*. (See THE INDEFINITE IT, pp. 33–34; THE PRONOUN, Part II, pp. 178–179).

(4) The pronoun *what* never has an antecedent, but carries the antecedent within itself, being equivalent to *that which:* Take *what* (that which) you want (see p. 47).

(5) An interrogative pronoun (see pp. 42–44) has no antecedent. To ask a question we use a pronoun because we do not know what noun to use: *Who* is there? *Which* is yours? *What* do you wish?

(6) A pronoun may be used without an antecedent when it is itself the antecedent of another pronoun: *He* who spoke these words is present. In this sentence the pronoun *he* is the antecedent of the pronoun *who,* while *he* itself has no antecedent. *He* represents a person not previously mentioned but afterward described by the relative clause beginning with *who.* Such forms of expression are common.

In the older style such an antecedent is sometimes omitted: "*Who* (i.e. *He* who) steals my purse, steals trash." Here the omitted antecedent is clearly understood.

A pronoun for which no antecedent can be given is used like a noun. It is used in place of a noun without being a substitute for any particular noun, and it differs from a noun by *representing* without *naming* the object for which it stands.

Pronouns Agreeing with Antecedents

A pronoun must agree with its antecedent. Proper agreement is necessary in order to achieve clarity of expression, especially in a compound or complex sentence where the pronoun and antecedent may be far apart and in different clauses.

RULE.—A pronoun agrees with its antecedent in gender, person, and number (see pp. 27–28).

The uses of pronouns according to this rule are ordinarily perfectly clear, and only special uses need be noted here:

Gender

Antecedents of Different Genders.—A plural pronoun is used to refer to two or more singular antecedents joined by *and:*

The father and mother are caring for *their* child.

The boy and girl are playing in *their* yard.

We parents and you childless people have *our* problems.

Note that each of the above illustrations can take only one pronoun, which is the same for all genders. (See under NUMBER, and DECLENSIONS OF PERSONAL PRONOUNS, pp. 26–27; 31.)

EXCEPTIONS

(1) If a pronoun refers to only one of two or more nouns connected by *and,* the pronoun takes the gender of the noun that is its antecedent:

The bride and groom are living at *her* father's house.

The minister and his wife are visiting *his* parents in San Francisco.

In such sentences the gender of the pronoun is always indicated by the sense.

(2) A singular personal pronoun cannot be logically used to refer to two or more singular nouns or pronouns of different genders which are joined by *or* or *nor*. In this case current practice is to ignore logic and make the pronoun agree with the nearest antecedent:

Some lady or *gentleman* has lost *his* ticket.

Some gentleman or *lady* has lost *her* ticket.

In such constructions the problem of agreement in gender can be avoided by changing the form of the expression: Some lady or gentleman has lost *a* purse. The incorrect use of the plural *their* in such cases is noted on p. 32.

Person

When a pronoun refers to two or more singular antecedents of different persons connected by *and, or,* or *nor,* the pronoun chooses among them, preferring the first person to the second and third, and the second to the third:

> You and I must make up *our* quarrel.

> He and I have arranged *our* affairs.

> You and he have made *your* choice.

> Either you or I have misunderstood *our* contract.

> Neither you nor he understand *your* work.

A pronoun that follows two or more connected nouns or pronouns may refer to only one of them, or to neither of them, as its antecedent. In such cases the pronoun takes the person of the antecedent to which it does refer. However, care must be taken to see that the antecedent and the pronoun reference to it are clearly understood. In the following illustrations, *his* refers to some person previously spoken of or mutually understood, but not expressed:

> Both she and I are living in *his* house.

> Neither you nor I can do *his* work.

Number

1. A noun plural in form, but singular in use is referred to by a singular pronoun. (See PLURALS TREATED AS SINGULARS, p. 15.) An adjective pronoun modifying such a pronoun is also in the singular as shown by the last example below:

> The *news* has done *its* work.

> Every *means* tried has failed of *its* purpose.

> *That* hundred dollars has reached *its* destination.

2. A collective noun (p. 4) singular in form may be referred to by either a singular or plural pronoun. A singular pronoun is used to refer to a collective noun, the members of

which act together as a unit. A plural pronoun is used to refer to a collective noun, the members of which act individually:

> The committee has finished *its* work. [The committee works as *one*.]

> The committee *were* divided in *their* opinions. [The members composing the committee act *individually*.]

3. When a singular noun is modified by two or more adjectives denoting different aspects, uses, or varieties of an object, it may take a pronoun (or a verb) in the plural: Greek and Roman architecture *were* different in *their* type.

4. When two or more singular nouns or pronouns are connected by *and,* they are taken jointly, and a pronoun referring to them jointly is in the plural: The brother *and* sister have left *their* home.

EXCEPTIONS

(1) When two or more singular antecedents connected by *and* denote the same person or thing, a pronoun referring to them is singular: The patriot and hero has finished *his* work.

(2) When two or more singular antecedents connected by *and* are modified by *each, every,* or *no,* they are taken separately, and a pronoun referring to them is in the singular: *Each* town and *each* village sent *its* representatives. *No* ship and *no* boat was without *its* flag.

(3) If singular antecedents connected by *and* are emphatically distinguished by some added word or words, such as *also, as well* (*as*), *even, not, too,* or the like, they are as a rule taken separately, and referred to by a pronoun in the singular:

> Age, *and* grief *also,* wrought *its* effect upon him.

> The clerk, *and* the supervisor *as well,* voiced *his* protest.

> The lieutenant, *and even* the captain, expressed *his* regrets.

(4) When two or more singular antecedents are connected by *or, nor, either—or, neither—nor,* they are taken separately, and a pronoun referring to them is in the singular number: *Either* the man *or* the boy will find *himself* in error. *Neither* the trapper *nor* the Indian would yield *his* ground.

(5) When two or more antecedents of different numbers, connected by *or* or *nor,* are referred to by a pronoun, the pronoun agrees with the antecedent nearest to it: *Neither* the mule *nor* the horses had finished *their* oats.

(6) If, however, nouns of different numbers are connected by *and,* there is no perplexity, for the pronoun is, as a rule, in the plural. And the order of the nouns is unimportant: The horses and the mule were eating *their* oats.

Relatives and Antecedents

The antecedent of a relative pronoun is usually a *noun* or *pronoun* in the major clause on which the relative clause itself depends:

There is the *boy whom* we met yesterday. [The antecedent of *whom* is *boy* in the preceding clause.]

He whom you seek is not here. [The antecedent of *whom* is *he* in the major clause.]

Occasionally a relative pronoun is used to refer to a noun phrase or to an entire clause. However, such usage is broad and vague and should therefore be avoided.

Broad　　The speaker declared *that all men are liars, which* I do not believe.

Improved　The speaker declared *that all men are liars, a statement which* I do not believe.

Broad　　He ordered me *to begin work, which* I promptly did.

Improved He ordered me *to begin work;* a *command which* I promptly obeyed.

Personal Pronouns and Relative Clauses

RULE 1.—If the personal pronoun following a relative pronoun refers to the antecedent of the relative, *it takes the gender and number of that antecedent:* I saw a farmer who was feeding *his* cattle. I found the lady who had lost *her* purse.

RULE 2.—If the personal pronoun following a relative refers to an antecedent different from that of the relative, it takes the gender and number of the antecedent referred to: I saw the lady and also the man who had taken *her* purse.

EXERCISE

Give the antecedent, and explain the form, of every pronoun in the following extracts.

(1)   It is not the business of grammar, as some critics seem preposterously to imagine, to give law to the fashions which regulate our speech. On the contrary, from its conformity to these, and from that alone, grammar derives all its authority and value.—GEORGE CAMPBELL *The Philosophy of Rhetoric.*

(2)   Great god whom I shall carve from this gray stone
            Wherein thou liest, hid to all but me,
        Grant thou that when my art hath made thee known
            And others bow, I shall not worship thee.
                ARTHUR GUITERMAN *The Idol-Maker Prays.*

(3)   Holmes had read carefully a note which the last post had brought him.—A. CONAN DOYLE *The Adventure of the Sussex Vampire.*

(4)   Worst of all, he was coming to realize that, for all his rank of inspector and authority, he, Robineau, cut a poor figure beside this travel-stained and weary pilot, crouching in a corner of the car, his eyes closed and hands all grimed with oil.—ANTOINE DE ST.-EXUPÉRY *Night Flight.*

THE ADJECTIVE

An **adjective** is a word used to describe or limit a noun or pronoun. The adjective is therefore said to *modify* a noun or pronoun:

a *large* house	a *high* hill
I am *hungry*.	He seems *weak*.
I have *two* books.	He found it *good*.

CLASSES OF ADJECTIVES

Adjectives may be divided into two classes:

1. **Descriptive adjectives,** stating some quality of the noun or pronoun to which they are applied: a *beautiful* rose, *useful* tools, a *healthy* child.

Descriptive adjectives may be subdivided into various groups:

(*a*) *Participial adjectives: singing* birds, a *learned* man. (See PARTICIPLES under VERB, p. 92 (1).)

(*b*) *Proper adjectives,* i.e., adjectives derived from proper names: an *American* Indian, a *European* language. It must be carefully noted that in English a proper adjective *must always begin with a capital letter*.

2. **Limiting adjectives,** restricting the meaning of the noun or pronoun within some special limit: *one* person; *double* measure; a *daily* paper.

Limiting adjectives are divided into:

(*a*) *Adjectives of quantity,* including the numeral adjectives: *one, two, three,* etc. (see NUMERALS, pp. 71–73), and various adjectives of repetition, division, measure, or frequency: *half, double, fourfold, daily, weekly.*

(*b*) The articles *a* or *an* and *the* (see THE ARTICLES, p. 73–76).

Adjective Use of Nouns and Pronouns

Nouns Used as Adjectives.—Nouns are often used with the force of adjectives: a *brick* house; a *gold* watch. A noun so used is to be treated as a noun *used* as an *adjective.*

Pronouns Used as Adjectives.—Most pronouns, as *this, that, which, what,* etc., may be used like adjectives. (See ADJECTIVE PRONOUNS, p. 53.)

POSITION OF THE ADJECTIVE

With the Noun

The Adjective Preceding Its Noun.—This is, in English, the established usage. It may be given as a rule that the English adjective regularly precedes its noun: a *good* man; a *fine* harvest; a *lofty* spire. (Compare POSITION OF THE ARTICLE, p. 76.)

The Adjective Following Its Noun.—This may occur in the cases given below:

(1) For emphasis: men *good* and *true; joy unspeakable; reasons innumerable.* Placing the adjective out of its usual order causes the mind to give it especial attention. This usage is very common in poetry and in elevated prose.

(2) Certain adjectives are regularly placed after the nouns they modify: *afraid, alert* (often, not always), *alike, alive, alone, ashamed, askew, asleep, averse, awake, aware, else, enough* (usually), *extant, extinct, fraught, pursuant;* also adjectives in certain special combinations, such as notary *public,* that is, a *public* notary; court *martial;* a *martial* (or military) court, and various others.

(3) Certain nouns, *anything, everything, nothing, something,* are regularly followed, but not preceded, by any modifying adjective: *anything* good; *something* important.

(4) When an adjective is modified by any word or phrase which could not well come between the adjective and its noun, the adjective so modified follows its noun: a person *desirous* to do right; a child, *eager* to learn; a mind *conscious* of rectitude (where we could not say "a *desirous to do right* person," or the like).

(5) An adjective may be used as an epithet after its noun, and is then commonly preceded by the article *the:* Frederick *the Great;* Edward *the Seventh.* But when the name of a monarch is written with Roman numerals, the article is not written: Charles II, George IV. In reading such an expression the article is commonly given, so that *Charles II* is usually read, "Charles the Second."

(6) In some expressions the adjective may either precede or follow its noun according to taste or convenience, without fixed rule. Thus we may say either "the *past* month" or "the month *past.*"

With the Pronoun

An adjective directly modifying a pronoun regularly follows that pronoun: We found him *unconscious.*

Adjectives in Combination

Two or more adjectives connected by conjunctions may modify a single noun or pronoun. In a series of adjectives thus used the conjunction is usually omitted except before the last adjective. The child, *faint, weary,* and *sad,* was sitting by the wayside.

Two adjectives without a conjunction may be joined to one noun or pronoun, when the first adjective modifies the complex idea expressed by the other adjective with its noun: A *poor old man* (that is, an *old man* who is *poor*); a *spirited white horse* (that is, a *white horse* that is *spirited*).

The Predicate Adjective

An adjective may be used in the predicate after a verb to modify the subject. An adjective so used is called a *predicate adjective*. The hour is *late*. The boy is *honest*. (See PARTS OF SPEECH IN THE PREDICATE, Part II, pp. 206–207.)

PROPERTIES OF ADJECTIVES

Simplicity.—English adjectives have neither gender, person, number, nor case. This is a fact of great importance and value. When we know the original form of an adjective, we have only to use that form with any noun or pronoun regardless of its gender, person, number, case, or position. In this respect English differs from most other languages, ancient or modern, thus obtaining the advantage of simplicity without loss of clarity.

Thus we may say:

	Singular	*Plural*	
	man	men	(*masculine*)
	woman	women	(*feminine*)
The good	child	children	(*common*)
	house	houses	(*neuter*)
	tree	trees	(*neuter*)

Adjectives have only one property demanding special consideration. This property is called *comparison*.

COMPARISON OF ADJECTIVES

Comparison is the method by which an adjective (or an adverb, p. 138) expresses a greater or less degree of the same quality. There are three degrees of comparison, as follows:

The Positive Degree.—An adjective in the positive degree expresses simply the quality of an object without reference to any other object: a *tall* man; a *sad* story; a *good* book.

The Comparative Degree.—An adjective in the comparative degree shows that an object has more or less of a quality than some other object or objects with which it is compared: a *taller* man; a *sadder* story; a *better* book; a *smaller* house; a *more valuable* gift; a *less probable* explanation.

The Superlative Degree.—An adjective in the superlative degree expresses the greatest or least amount or intensity of a quality that is found among all the objects compared: the *tallest* man in the company; the *saddest* story I ever heard; the *best* book I ever read; the *most important* item; the *least objectionable* method.

Modes of Comparison
Regular Comparison

Adjectives are regularly compared in two different ways:

1. **Comparison by the Suffixes er and est.**—Words of one syllable and some words of two syllables form their comparative by adding the suffix *er* to the positive: *braver*. They form the superlative by adding the suffix *est* to the positive: *bravest*.

Positive	Comparative	Superlative
sad	sadder	saddest
hot	hotter	hottest
wild	wilder	wildest
heavy	heavier	heaviest
jaunty	jauntier	jauntiest

(*a*) When the positive ends in mute final *e*, the final *e* is dropped before adding *er* or *est:* brave, *braver, bravest;* simple, *simpler, simplest.*

(*b*) When the positive is a monosyllable ending in a single consonant preceded by a single vowel, the final consonant is doubled before *er* or *est:* big, *bigger, biggest;* red, *redder, reddest.*

(*c*) When the positive ends in *le,* the mute *e* before the suffix is dropped: able, *abler, ablest;* noble, *nobler, noblest.*

(*d*) When the positive ends in *y* preceded by a consonant, the *y* is changed to *i* before the suffix: dry, *drier, driest;* lovely, *lovelier, loveliest;* silly, *sillier, silliest. Shy* and *sly* may retain the *y.*

(*e*) When an adjective of two syllables is accented on the last syllable, the comparative and superlative may be formed by adding *er* and *est* exactly as to monosyllables: genteel, *genteeler, genteelest;* polite, *politer, politest;* severe, *severer, severest.* These adjectives may also be compared by *more* and *most,* and this method is often preferred.

(*f*) Various other adjectives of two syllables are also compared by *er* and *est,* according to no very definite rule: bitter, *bitterer, bitterest;* clever, *cleverer, cleverest;* cruel, *crueller, cruellest;* handsome, *handsomer, handsomest;* tender, *tenderer, tenderest.* The correct usage in such words can be learned only by careful study of the dictionary and of the best authors.

CAUTION.—Participles used as adjectives, or adjectives of similar form, do not take *er* and *est;* we do not say *tireder, willinger, learnedest.* Instead, we say, *more tired, more willing, most learned.*

2. **Comparison by Adverbs, More and Most, Less and Least.** —Adjectives of more than one syllable (except as noted in the preceding section) generally form their comparative and superlative degrees by prefixing to the positive the adverbs *more* and *most* or *less* and *least.*

(*a*) *Comparison in the ascending series,* as it is called, by *more* and *most,* is that chiefly used with words of more than one syllable: *more* intelligent; *more* competent; *most* satisfactory; *most* unusual.

This method may be often interchanged with that in *er* and *est*, and we may say either *commoner* or *more common; commonest* or *most common.*

When two or more adjectives are connected by *and*, the adverb *more* or *most* may be prefixed to the whole series even though one or more of the words would ordinarily be compared by *er* or *est:* He was the *most* wise, learned, and eloquent of men.

For emphasis or euphony, especially in poetry, *more* or *most* may be employed where *er* or *est* would ordinarily be used: Never was friend *more* true.

(*b*) *Comparison in the descending series,* indicating a diminishing amount or intensity of a quality, is made only by prefixing the adverbs *less* and *least* to the positive: He was *less* estimable. That method would be *least* objectionable.

Double Comparatives or Superlatives.—Where two forms of the comparative or superlative are found, difference of meaning or use may accompany difference of form:

Far, farthest commonly refer to physical distance.

Further, furthest may be used for distance, but are more often applied to advance or reach of thought: This *further* argument is to be considered.

Later, latest are used directly of time.

Latter, last are used of succession in order.

Elder, eldest denote superiority in age with the implication of being old.

Older, oldest imply the qualities of age.

A Special Superlative in *Most*.—A number of adjectives having the effect of superlatives are formed by adding the suffix *most* to the positive of an adjective, adverb, or even to a noun used adjectively: *foremost, endmost, midmost, topmost*. In such cases usually no comparative degree exists.

Irregular Comparison

We have in English a very small list of irregularly compared adjectives:

Positive	Comparative	Superlative
bad evil ill	worse	worst
far	farther further	farthest furthest
good well	better	best
hind	hinder	hindermost hindmost
(in, *adv.*)	inner	innermost inmost
late	later latter	latest last
little	less lesser	least
many much	more	most
old	elder older	eldest oldest
(out, *adv.*)	outer	outermost outmost
(up, *adv.*)	upper	uppermost upmost

Adjectives Without Comparison

The numerals (pp. 71–73) and the articles (pp. 73–76) do not admit of comparison.

Adjectives denoting material, geographical position, etc., are as a rule not compared.

Adjectives expressing some quality that does not admit of degrees are not compared when used in their strict or full sense: *square, perpendicular, circular, absolute, eternal, illimitable, complete, perfect, unique.*

But such adjectives are often used in a modified or approximate sense, and when so used admit of comparison. If we say, "This is *more perfect* than that," we do not mean that either is perfect without limitation, but that *this* has *more* of the qualities that go to make up perfection than *that;* it is *more nearly* perfect. Such usage has high literary authority.

To form a *more perfect* union.—*Constitution of the United States. Preamble.*

USES OF THE COMPARATIVE AND SUPERLATIVE

The Comparative Excludes.—The comparative holds its object separate from the object or objects compared. When we say, *"This* is better than *that,"* we imply that *this* is separate and distinct from *that* by reason of its superiority.

It is an error to say, "I like *this* better than *anything,"* because *anything* includes *this; this* is part of *anything.* We should say, "I like *this* better than *anything else"* because the word *else* separates *this* from the rest of *anything,* and they can then be compared. Similarly, it is an error to say, *"This* storm is worse than *any* I ever saw," because *this storm* of which you speak is included in *any* and would therefore, illogically, be worse than itself. You must separate it from the class in order to compare it by an adjective in the comparative degree: *"This* storm is worse than *any other* I ever saw." The latter expression is correct because *other* is a separating word.

The Superlative Includes.—The superlative views its object as one of the objects compared; it is in the same class or group.

Thus, when we say, *"This* is the best of *all* the apples," we mean that *this* is one of *all,* and we might say with perfect propriety, "This is the best *among* all the apples." The superlative should be used in actual comparisons only when its object is thus *one of the objects compared.*

In unexpressed comparisons the superlative of *high distinction* is also used: This peach is *most delicious.* Be *most careful* in all your work.

Two or More Than Two.—The comparative refers only to *two* objects or sets of objects, whereas the superlative ordinarily refers to *more than two.* This is not, however, an invariable rule. The superlative with two objects is permissible in informal discourse, or in order to gain emphasis: This is the *best* of the *two.* However, careful writers and speakers prefer the expression: This is the *better* of the *two.*

Than after Comparatives.—The comparative is always followed by *than* before the object of the comparison: better *than* this; greater *than* that.

Of after Superlatives.—The superlative is commonly followed by *of* before its object: the best *of* all. But *among, in, within,* or some other inclusive preposition may be used equally well: He was foremost *among* his contemporaries. This building is the highest *in* the city.

THE NUMERALS

Numerals are numbering adjectives. They are of two classes: *cardinals* and *ordinals.*

The **cardinals,** or **cardinal numeral adjectives,** indicate number absolutely, without reference to position or relation: *ten* apples; *fifty* dollars. They are as follows:

1. one	19. nineteen
2. two	20. twenty
3. three	21. twenty-one, etc.
4. four	30. thirty
5. five	40. forty
6. six	50. fifty
7. seven	60. sixty
8. eight	70. seventy
9. nine	80. eighty
10. ten	90. ninety
11. eleven	100. one hundred
12. twelve	101. one hundred and one, etc.
13. thirteen	1000. one thousand
14. fourteen	1100. one thousand, one hundred
15. fifteen	(or, eleven hundred)
16. sixteen	10,000. ten thousand
17. seventeen	1,000,000. one million
18. eighteen	1,000,000,000. one billion [U. S.]

Numerals, like other adjectives, are freely used as nouns: I will take *five*. More than a *hundred* were present. A cardinal numeral, used as a noun, may or may not take the article, and may be either in the singular or plural according to the meaning to be expressed: *

Were there not *ten* cleansed? but where are the *nine?—Luke* 17:17.

Twelve will, believe me, be quite enough for your purpose. —G. B. Shaw *St. Joan*, sc. vi.

The **ordinals,** or **ordinal numeral adjectives,** indicate, not absolute number, but numbered position in a series: the *fifth* chapter; the *hundredth* meridian. They are, corresponding to the cardinals:

* Note.—A numeral preceding and qualifying a *noun* is used as an adjective and of course takes no plural: *ten thousand* men. A numeral used without a noun is itself treated as a noun, and may take the plural form: *tens of thousands* of men.

first	twelfth	thirtieth
second	thirteenth	fortieth
third	fourteenth	fiftieth
fourth	fifteenth	sixtieth
fifth	sixteenth	seventieth
sixth	seventeenth	eightieth
seventh	eighteenth	ninetieth
eighth	nineteenth	hundredth
ninth	twentieth	thousandth
tenth	twenty-first, etc.	millionth, etc.
eleventh		

To express an ordinal number by a figure, *st, d,* or *th* is added to the figure, according to the sound to be represented: 1*st,* 2*d,* 3*d,* 4*th,* etc. Such a form is not considered an abbreviation but a contraction and does not require a period.

A date written in full is expressed by an ordinal number: the *twenty-fifth* of December. When figures are employed for the date no indication of the ordinal is written: Dec. 25, 1915. This, however, is read, "December *twenty-fifth,*" or, by very precise persons, "December *the twenty-fifth.*"

In reading or naming a fraction, the numerator is expressed by a cardinal and the denominator by an ordinal numeral; thus, ⅛ is read *one-eighth.* Where the denominator is 2, it is read *half;* thus, ½ is read *one-half.* In writing out such forms in words, a hyphen is always used.

THE ARTICLE

An article is a limiting adjective serving to designate or point out a noun. An article may be used with or without other adjectives modifying the same noun: *an* apple; *a* girl; *the* boy.

Articles are never applied to pronouns, except in the rare cases when a pronoun is used as a noun: The *it* is here quite indefinite, the word *it* being used, not as a pronoun, but as a noun, the *name* of a word.

There are two classes of articles: the *indefinite* and the *definite*.

The Indefinite Articles

The indefinite articles are *a* and *an*. The indefinite article *a* is used before words beginning with a consonant *sound,* however spelled: *a* man, *a* woman, *a* unit. *A* is also used before some words beginning with a vowel because the vowel is pronounced like a consonant: *a* unit, *a* university, *a* usurer.

The article *an* is used before words beginning with a vowel sound: *an* apple, *an* orange, *an* eye. Before words like *heir, honor,* and *hour* the article *an* is used because these words are pronounced with an initial vowel sound. Before some other words, like *hotel,* either *a* or *an* may be used, depending on whether the user pronounces the word with an initial vowel or consonant sound.

The same rule for the use of the indefinite article applies when any adjective comes between the article and its noun. If the adjective begins with a consonant sound, the article *a* is used before it: *a* good apple; *a* sore arm; *a* deaf ear. If the adjective begins with a vowel sound, the article *an* is used: *an* empty pocket; *an* eager child; *an* only son; *an* ancient custom; *an* unsung hero.

The indefinite articles *a* and *an* indicate any one of a class of objects without choice or discrimination. It is for this reason that these articles are called *indefinite.*

The Definite Article

This is the simple word *the,* always the same in all situations and under all conditions: *the* king; *the* beggar; *the* wise man; *the* fool. *The* dog is mine. I see *the* dog.

The article *the* is pronounced differently before vowel and consonant sounds. Before a vowel *sound,* the final *e* has its long sound, like *ee* in sw*e*et: th*e* apple; th*e* honest witness. Before a consonant *sound,* the *e* becomes obscure, and is pronounced *uh:* th*e* book; th*e* house; th*e* foolish boy.

The always indicates a definite object, either:

1. An object so well known as not to need description: *The* man is here (the man we have been expecting or seeking). This is *the* book (which has been referred to or inquired for).

2. An object about to be described, the word *the* pointing on to a description to come: *The* story (which I am about to relate) is a sad one.

3. An object emphatically designated, as if the only one worthy of consideration: He made *the* speech (preeminently) of the occasion.

A noun preceded by the article *the* often indicates a whole class or species: *The* dog is a useful animal. *Man* or *woman,* however, is used in the general or generic way without the article: *Man* can adapt himself to any climate. *Man* without the article may be used: (a) To denote all mankind, including women and children: *Man* is mortal. (b) To denote male human beings as a class, contrasted with *woman: Man* is more adventurous, *woman* more domestic.

Adjectives with *The* Used as Nouns.—The definite article *the,* used with an adjective alone, gives to the adjective the effect of a noun which may be either singular or plural in meaning, according to the connection of words in the sentence: *The good* (goodness) is more important than *the beautiful* (beauty). *The good* (good people) are commonly also *the happy* (happy people).

The with Comparatives.—*The* in such phrases as "*The* wiser he is, *the* better," is not the article, but an adverb, signifying *"by how much—by so much."* (See COMPARATIVES WITH THE under THE ADVERB, pp. 187–188.)

Many and Few with the Article.—The English language has certain peculiar idioms in the use of *many* and *few*. The very common expression *many a,* used before a noun, has a plural effect, but is properly used with a singular verb: *Many a* man was afraid that day. This is equivalent to saying, "Many men were afraid," but has a special force by seeming to single out the men individually, one by one. So we say, *many a* day, *many a* time, etc.

The expression, *the many,* signifies the greater number of people, most people. The expression *the few* indicates some limited or exclusive class.

The expressions, *a great many, a few,* etc., like collective nouns, take a plural verb or may be referred to by a plural pronoun: *A great many* are missing. *A few* answered to their names. The phrase *a few* denotes a more considerable number than the simple adjective *few: A few* were found by careful search. *Few* were ever found.

Position of the Article

The article regularly precedes its noun and any other adjective modifying the same noun: *a* man; *an* hour; *the* tree; *a* ripe apple; *the* swift stream.

EXCEPTIONS.—After *how, so,* and *too,* the order is, adjective, article, noun: *how* sad *a* story; *so* merry *a* company; *too* harsh *a* judgment.

When the adjective follows its noun, it may carry the article with it: Alexander *the* Great. (See above, MANY AND FEW WITH THE ARTICLE.)

EXERCISE

Point out all adjectives, including numerals and articles, in the following extracts, and state what noun each adjective modifies. Note the instances where the use of the article gives to the adjective the force of a noun. Note comparatives and superlatives.

(1)　　　　　A moral, sensible, and well-bred man
　　　　　Will not affront me, and no other can.
　　　　　　　　　　　COWPER *Conversation,* l. 193.

(2)　　　Life is not so short but that there is always time enough for courtesy.—EMERSON *Social Aims.*

(3)　　　　　Dead hangs the fruit on that tall tree:
　　　　　The lark in my cold hand is dead.
　　　　　　　　　　RICHARD HUGHES *Burial of the Spirit.*

(4)　　　How sweet and gracious, even in common speech,
　　　　　Is that fine sense which men call courtesy!
　　　　　　　　　　JAMES T. FIELDS *Courtesy.*

(5)　　　　A foot more light, a step more true,
　　　　　Ne'er from the heath-flower dashed the dew.
　　　　　　SIR WALTER SCOTT *Lady of the Lake,* can. i, st. 18.

(6)　　　As a case in point, one may well consider that especial glory of English letters, the much-vaunted plays of the Elizabethan and Jacobean dramatists, which justly rank so high in literature that few can endure the altitude.—JAMES BRANCH CABELL *Beyond Life,* ch. 9.

(7)　　　And brown is the papaw's shade-blossoming cup,
　　　　　In the wood near the sun-loving maize.
　　　　　　　　　　WILLIAM FOSDICK *The Maize.*

(8)　　　　　　　　The silent water
　　　Was like another sky where silent stars
　　　Might sleep for ever, and everywhere was peace.
　　　　　　EDWIN ARLINGTON ROBINSON *Tristram.*

(9)　　　　　　　For pity makes the world
　　　Soft to the weak and noble for the strong.
　　　　　　EDWIN ARNOLD *Light of Asia,* bk. v. l. 401.

(10)　　On one side is a field of drooping oats,
　　　Through which the poppies show their scarlet coats.
　　　　　　　　KEATS *Epistle to My Brother George.*

(11)　　　　　Here bloom red roses, dewy wet,
　　　　　And beds of fragrant mignonette.
　　　　　　　　ELAINE GOODALE *Thistles and Roses.*

(12)   A cloud of dark smoke, as from smoldering ruins, went up
        toward the sun now bright and gay in the blue, enameled
        sky.—STEPHEN CRANE *The Red Badge of Courage,* ch. 17.

(13)   Nations shall not quarrel then
                    To prove which is the stronger.
                CHARLES MACKAY *The Good Time Coming.*

(14)   The reasoning of the strongest is always the best.
                                    LA FONTAINE *Fables.*

(15)   But all was false and hollow; tho his tongue
        Dropped manna, and could make the worse appear
        The better reason.
                        MILTON *Paradise Lost,* bk. ii, 1. 112.

(16)   And the best half should have been returned to him.
                    SHAKESPEARE *Timon of Athens,* act. iii, sc. 2.

(17)   When men were all asleep the snow came flying,
        In large white flakes falling on the city brown,
        Stealthily and perpetually settling and loosely lying,
            Hushing the latest traffic of the drowsy town.
                        ROBERT BRIDGES *London Snow.*

(18)   The crimson blossoms of the coral-tree
                In the warm isles of India's sunny sea.
                            MOORE *Lallah Rookh.*

(19)   None but the brave deserves the fair.
                        DRYDEN *Alexander's Feast,* st. 1.

(20)   Suddenly there was a flash of light, and a quantity of lumi-
        nous greenish smoke came out of the pit in three distinct
        puffs,. which drove up, one after the other, straight into the
        still air.—H. G. WELLS *The War of the Worlds,* ch. 5.

THE VERB

A **verb** is a word that expresses action or state of being. Among verbs expressing action are *walk, run, ride, go, come, look, see, call, shout,* etc. Among verbs expressing emotion and state of being are *be, exist, seem, appear, remain,* etc.

The verb is indispensable; without it no sentence can be made. If one says, "I cold," he has not made a sentence and expressed a thought. A verb is needed to express the thought, which might be: I *am* cold, *or*, I *have* a cold. The verb is the only part of speech that can by itself express a thought, e.g., "Go," in which the subject *you* is understood. Because of their prime importance, verbs must be thoroughly studied and mastered.

EXERCISE

Find all verbs in the following extracts.

(1)   A man will turn over half a library to make one book.
SAMUEL JOHNSON *Boswell's Life of Johnson.*   1775.

(2)   You hear that boy laughing? You think he's all fun;
But the angels laugh, too, at the good he has done.
O. W. HOLMES *The Boys,* st. 9.

(3)   Let us have faith that right makes might, and in that faith let us, to the end, dare to do our duty as we understand it.
—ABRAHAM LINCOLN *Address.* Feb. 21, 1859.

(4)   Oh, fear not in a world like this,
And thou shalt know ere long,—
Know how sublime a thing it is
To suffer and be strong.
LONGFELLOW *The Light of Stars,* st. 9.

(5)   Her modest looks the cottage might adorn,
Sweet as the primrose peeps beneath the thorn.
GOLDSMITH *The Deserted Village,* l. 329.

(6)   They never fail who die
           In a great cause.
                    BYRON *Marino Faliero*, act ii, sc. 2.

(7)   The musicians and I drank up all the wine and talked, till
about midnight, and Rosie seemed to be all right now, lying
on the couch, talking, even laughing a bit, eating her sand-
wiches and drinking some tea I'd brewed her.—JACK
KEROUAC *The Dharma Bums*, 15.

(8)   Then he returned home one afternoon and found her at
the work bench again. It was still the table, still in the center
of the room; she had merely turned back the chintz and
shoved the books and magazines to one end.—WILLIAM
FAULKNER *The Wild Palms*, 2.

(9)   He walked with his cold hands clasped over the tails of
his frockcoat, picking his way among packing boxes and
scuttling children. He kept gnawing his lips and clasping and
unclasping his hands. He walked without hearing the yells of
the children or the annihilating clatter of the L trains over-
head or smelling the rancid sweet huddled smell of packed
tenements.—JOHN DOS PASSOS *Manhattan Transfer*, I.

(10)   He was bitterly irritated. He had spent the afternoon with
his sister-in-law, his brother's wife, on Staten Island. Or,
rather, he had wasted it because of her. Soon after lunch she
had phoned him at the office—he was an editor of a small
trade magazine in lower Manhattan—and immediately, with
terrible cries, she implored him to come out, to come at
once. One of the children was sick.—SAUL BELLOW *The
Victim*, I.

CLASSES OF VERBS

1. Transitive and Intransitive Verbs

Verbs are divided *according to their relation to objects* into
two classes: *transitive* and *intransitive*.

A **transitive verb** is a verb that requires an object to express
a complete meaning. A transitive verb expresses an action that
a subject exerts upon an object:

Read this book. [The transitive verb *read* commands the
subject, *you* understood, to read an *object, book*.]

John *struck* him. [The transitive verb *struck* states what the subject *John* did to the object *him*.]

An **intransitive verb** is a verb that does not require an object to complete a thought: The tree *falls*. At the first opportunity the traitor will *flee*.

REMARKS.—Many verbs are both transitive and intransitive, but with a difference of meaning:

Transitive	The prince *succeeds* the king. [*Succeeds* means comes after and takes the place of.]
Intransitive	He *succeeds* in all his undertaking. [*Succeeds* means accomplishes what is attempted.]
Transitive	The girl *filled* the cup with water. [*Filled* means supplied to fullness.]
Intransitive	The girl's eyes *filled* with tears. [*Filled* means became full.]

Many verbs that are used transitively may also be used intransitively when the purpose is to set forth the act while leaving the object unknown or indefinite: The boy *reads* well. Here the purpose is to show *how* the boy reads, not *what* he reads.

2. Principal and Auxiliary Verbs

According to their use verbs are divided into two classes: *principal verbs* and *auxiliary verbs*.

A **principal verb** is one that expresses by itself some act or state, or, if in combination with some other verb, expresses the leading thought of the combination: I *read*. I will *go*.

An **auxiliary verb** * is a verb of incomplete predication that is used with a principal verb to form a verb phrase indicating tense, voice, or mood: I *will* run. I *can* read. You *may* go.

An auxiliary verb is often called simply an *auxiliary*. The common auxiliaries are *be, can, do, have, may, must, shall, will, ought,* and sometimes *let*.

* NOTE.—For CONJUGATIONS OF AUXILIARY VERBS, see pp. 101–108.

3. Regular and Irregular Verbs

According to their changes of form (inflection) verbs are divided into *regular verbs* and *irregular verbs*.

Regular verbs form the past tense (see p. 96) and past participle (see p. 97) by adding *ed* to the simple form of the verb. When the simple form ends in mute *e*, the *e* is dropped before adding *ed*. Some few regular verbs have alternate forms ending in *t: dream, dreamed, dreamed;* or *dream, dreamt, dreamt.*

Present	Past	Past Participle
learn	learned	learned
love	loved	loved
sleep	slept	slept

Irregular verbs form the past tense and past participle otherwise than by adding *ed: give, gave, given; see, saw, seen.* There are only about 200 irregular verbs, including all the auxiliaries, in the English language. A list of irregular verbs with their principal parts will be found on pages 122–129. These verbs should be carefully committed to memory and referred to in any case of doubt.

PROPERTIES OF VERBS

The properties of verbs are *voice, mood, tense, person,* and *number.*

1. VOICE

Voice is that form of the transitive verb that shows whether the subject acts or is acted upon. The distinction of voice belongs only to verbs that are transitive or used transitively. (See, pp. 80–81 and p. 149.)

The Active Voice.—When the subject of a verb is represented as acting, the verb is said to be in the active voice: The sun *attracts* the earth. The girl *is bouncing* a ball.

The Passive Voice.—When the subject of the verb is represented as acted upon, the verb is said to be in the passive voice: The earth *is attracted* by the sun. The boy *was punished* by his father. For the conjugation of the passive voice, see the PASSIVE VOICE under CONJUGATIONS, pp. 114–117.

EXERCISE

Point out (*a*) all the verbs in the active voice; (*b*) all the verbs in the passive voice, in the following sentences.

(1)   The boy learned the lesson.

(2)   The lesson was learned by the boy.

(3)   The hunter killed the deer.

(4)   No one heard a sound.

(5)   No better thing was ever done.

(6)   The deer was killed by the hunter.

(7)   No sound was heard.

(8)   You never did a better thing.

(9)   I was born an American; I live an American; I shall die an American.—WEBSTER *First Bunker Hill Monument Oration.*

(10)   . . . The feather, whence the pen
Was shaped that traced the lives of these good men,
Dropped from an angel's wing.

                    WORDSWORTH *Sonnet.*

(11)   That time you won your town the race
We chaired you through the market-place;
Man and boy stood cheering by,
And home we brought you shoulder-high.
          A. E. HOUSMAN *To an Athlete Dying Young.*

(12)   Flower in the crannied wall,
I pluck you out of the crannies,
I hold you here, root and all, in my hand,
Little flower—but *if* I could understand
What you are, root and all, and all in all,
     I should know what God and man is.
          TENNYSON *Flower in the Crannied Wall.*

2. MOOD

Mood is a form of the verb that indicates the manner in which the speaker views or conceives the state or action of the verb. The word *mood* signifies a mental state or attitude. The word *mode* (manner) is also used, but *mood* is now more common.

The Three Moods

There are three moods,* namely: the *indicative,* the *subjunctive,* and the *imperative.*

1. The **indicative mood** states or questions a fact: I *live* here. It *is* not cold. *Is* this book yours?

2. The **subjunctive mood** denotes an action or state as possible, supposed or imagined, unreal, conditional, doubtful, contrary to fact, or desired:

> If I *go,* I shall go alone.
>
> If I *were* you, I would not go.
>
> I wish he *were* here.

The conjunctions commonly used with the subjunctive are *if, though, lest, unless, that,* and *till. If* is the most frequent indicator of the subjunctive, but the other conjunctions are not uncommon. The conditional conjunction may be omitted by placing the verb or its auxiliary before the subject. *Had* I *been* there (i.e. *If* I *had been* there), it would not have happened.

3. The **imperative mood** is used to express a command, wish, entreaty, or the like: *Study* your lesson. *Have* pity upon me. *Go* in peace.

Imperative means "commanding," and this mode is so named because it is most often used to express command although it has also the other uses mentioned. The imperative is most often

---

* Formerly the potential and infinitive moods were also distinguished, but these distinctions have disappeared from the language and are therefore not treated here.

used without noun or pronoun, but a pronoun of the second person (singular or plural) is usually understood and may be readily supplied.

> *Love* THOU thy land, with love far brought.—TENNYSON.

> Look at the stars! look, look up at the skies!
> O look at all the fire-folk sitting in the air!
> > G. M. HOPKINS *The Starlight Night.*

> Grow old along with me!—BROWNING.

3. THE INFINITIVE

The **infinitive** form is the first principal part of a verb. It is usually, but not always, preceded by *to*. The infinitive expresses the action or state of a verb as unlimited by connection with a subject: *to go; to be; to love.*

The term *the infinitive of a verb* is generally understood to mean the present infinitive form of the active voice. This form is the base or stem of the verb, with or without *to*. *To,* which is frequently the sign of the infinitive, was originally a preposition and is still so classed even though it has largely lost its prepositional force. The infinitive without *to* is sometimes called the *pure infinitive;* it appears as the stem of the verb used after an auxiliary: I shall *love.* He will *call.* They may *go.*

To of the Infinitive Omitted.—The *to* of the infinitive is commonly omitted after the verbs *bid, dare, feel, hear, let, make, need,* and *see,* and also after all the auxiliaries. After the *passive voice* of the above-named verbs that may be used in the passive form, *to* is retained: He was heard *to* enter. He was seen *to* walk.

Uses of the Infinitive

Since the infinitive has the functions of both a verb and a noun, it is called a *verbal noun.* Like a verb the infinitive can do the following:

(1) Take a subject: We wanted *him* to go.

(2) Take an object: to study a *lesson*.

(3) Take a predicate complement: to go *home*.

(4) Take an adverbial modifier: to fly *swiftly*.

The infinitive resembles a noun in that it can perform the chief functions of a noun.

The Infinitive Phrase.—In a sentence the infinitive with its subject or other adjuncts is best treated as *an infinitive phrase,* and parsed as a single element (having the effect of noun, adjective, or adverb, as the case may be). Such a phrase may then be analyzed, when desired, into its constituent elements. Thus, in the sentence, "I wish you to go at once," the object of the verb *wish* is the infinitive phrase, *you to go at once.*

The Infinitive Used as a Noun.—Used as a noun the infinitive, or infinitive phrase, may be

(1) The subject of a finite verb: *To lie* is shameful. *To tell* a lie is shameful. *To speak* falsely is shameful.

(2) The object of a transitive verb or participle: I desire *to go*. Desiring *to go*. I wish *to get* breakfast. I intend *to start* immediately.

(3) The object of a preposition: He is about *to go.*

(4) A predicate nominative: To see is *to believe*. It is safest *to tell* the truth. It is wise *to act* promptly.

(5) The infinitive is sometimes used like an adjective, modifying a noun: a desire *to learn*.

(6) The infinitive is often used adverbially to denote a purpose, a motive, or (after *so—as, then,* or *too*) to denote a result: Be so kind as *to inform* me. He is too honorable *to do* such a thing.*

* NOTE.—The infinitive active is somewhat rarely used in a passive sense: A house *to let* (to be let). You are *to blame* (to be blamed).

(7) An infinitive phrase may be used as an **independent element** of a sentence: *To confess the truth,* I do not care. (See INDEPENDENT ELEMENTS, Part II, p. 223 (5).)

The Subject of the Infinitive.—The infinitive may be used with or without a subject. When a subject is employed, the rule is as follows:

RULE.—The subject of the infinitive is in the objective case: Do you wish *me* to go?

The Split Infinitive.—Many grammarians hold that an adverb should never come between the *to* of the infinitive and the *verb* form: *to* faithfully *study*. Others give this usage a qualified approval. It is probably best not to split an infinitive unless the construction would otherwise be awkward, as the following example shows:

> To an active mind it may be easier to bear along all the qualifications of an idea, than *to* first imperfectly *conceive* such idea, etc.—HERBERT SPENCER *The Philosophy of Style,* pt. iii, par. 28.

The Finite Verb

Infinitive means "unlimited." By contrast, the forms of the verb in all other moods are called *finite* or limited. Hence we have the following:

DEFINITION.—Any form of the verb except the infinitive or participle is called a *finite* verb.

4. TENSE

Tense is a form taken by a verb to indicate action in relation to time: I *live* here. I *lived* here. I *have lived* here. I *will be living* here.

The Six Tenses

There are three great divisions of time: *past, present,* and *future.* In each of these divisions of time, an act may be viewed as simply occurring, or as completed or perfected.

A tense which expresses completed or perfected action grammarians call *perfect.* Hence the three divisions of time give us *six tenses:*

| Present | Past | Future |
| Present Perfect | Past Perfect | Future Perfect |

1. The **present tense** denotes an act or a condition or state that occurs in present time: I *think.* It *rains.* That *is* true. The present tense is also used (*a*) to assert a general truth or habitual action: Food *is* necessary to live. Babies *cry* often; (*b*) to refer to art and artists of the past, in the sense that they are still extant or endure: Homer *is* a great poet. Joyce *uses* the interior monologue.; and (*c*) to narrate the plot of a fictional work: The opening scene of Shaw's *Saint Joan takes* place at the castle of the local baron.

2. The **present perfect tense** expresses action or state viewed as completed or perfected at the present time: I *have finished* this lesson. This *has been* a cold winter.

Past action expressed by the present perfect must come up to and touch the present. The present perfect can not be used of an act that is wholly and only in the past. Thus, we can not say, "I *have written* last year"; instead we must use the simple past: "I *wrote* last year." Hence, the mistake of the foreigner, who says, "I *have come* to America five years ago." He should not use "I *have come*" for an action that is "five years" removed. There he should use the simple past, "I *came.*"

The present perfect tense is formed by prefixing *have* or *has* to the past participle of the principal verb: I *have heard.* He *has gone.*

3. The **past tense** states that something happened or existed at some time in the past: He *went* to town yesterday. The king *was* very powerful. The *past tense* is formed by inflection, as *loved, gave*. (See p. 96.)

4. The **past perfect tense** expresses past action as completed before some other past action or before some specified past time. The past perfect tense is formed by prefixing *had* to the past participle of any verb: I *had finished* my work before you came.

5. The **future tense** is used to make an assertion about an act or condition anticipated in time to come. The future tense is formed by using *shall* or *will* with the root form of any verb: I *shall go*. He *will succeed*.

6. The **future perfect tense** is used to indicate that an anticipated event will be completed or perfected before some other act or time in the future: I *shall have finished* my lesson at ten o'clock. He *will have left* home before you arrive.

The *future perfect tense* is formed by adding *have* to the *shall* or *will* of the future tense: I *shall have paid* the money before the bank closes.

Filling out the scheme of tenses on p. 88 with the verb *write* we have:

Present	*Past*	*Future*
I write	I wrote	I shall write
Present Perfect	*Past Perfect*	*Future Perfect*
I have written	I had written	I shall have written

EXERCISE

Give the mood and tense of each verb in the following extracts.

(1)   And still they gazed, and still the wonder grew,
    That one small head should carry all he knew.
        GOLDSMITH *The Deserted Village*, l. 215.

(2)   If you once understand an author's character, the comprehension of his writings becomes easy.—LONGFELLOW *Hyperion,* bk. i, ch. v.

(3)   Devise, wit; write, pen; for I am for whole volumes in folio.—SHAKESPEARE *Love's Labour's Lost* act i, sc. 2, l. 190.

(4)   Full many a flower is born to blush unseen,
And waste its sweetness on the desert air.
        GRAY *Elegy in a Country Churchyard,* st. 14.

(5)   Houses are built to live in, not to look on; therefore, let use be preferred before uniformity, except where both may be had.—BACON *Essays,* "Of Building."

(6)   When the Gas-man came to himself, the first words he uttered were, "Where am I? What is the matter?" "Nothing is the matter, Tom,—you have lost the battle, but you are the bravest man alive."—HAZLITT *The Fight.*

(7)   Older than all preached Gospels was this unpreached, inarticulate, but ineradicable, forever-enduring Gospel: Work, and there have well-being.—CARLYLE *Labour; Reward.*

(8)   Do what he will, however, the critic will still remain exposed to frequent misunderstandings, and nowhere so much as in this country.—ARNOLD *Essays in Criticism,* Preface.

(9)   This be the verse you grave for me:
Here he lies where he longed to be,
Home is the sailor, home from the sea,
And the hunter home from the hill.
        STEVENSON *Requiem.*

(10)   Yet each man kills the thing he loves,
    By each let this be heard,
Some do it with a bitter look,
    Some with a flattering word,
The coward does it with a kiss,
    The brave man with a sword!
        WILDE *The Ballad of Reading Gaol.*

5. PERSON

The action or state expressed by a verb may be that of (1) the person or persons speaking (*first person*), (2) the person or persons spoken to (*second person*), or (3) the person or persons spoken of (*third person*). The verb thus has *three persons,* and is said to be of the *first, second,* or *third person,* according to its use.

6. NUMBER

A verb may express the action or state of one person or thing, or that of more than one. Verbs therefore have singular and plural forms to express number. The number of the verb must agree with the number of the noun or pronoun used with it.

	SINGULAR	PLURAL
First Person	I *walk*	we *walk*
Second Person	you *walk*	you *walk*
Third Person	he *walks*	they *walk*

Note that only the *third person singular* changes form to indicate number and person. To this rule the only exception is the verb *to be*. The number and person of verbs, both regular and irregular, are set forth in the table of conjugations (pp. 109–120) where they are best learned.

The Participle

A **participle** is a part of the verb that may be used independently as an adjective while retaining the power of a verb to govern an object or take adverbial modifiers.

Two participles are formed directly from the verb stem:

1. The **present participle,** which always ends in *ing,* and represents the action of the verb as incomplete or in progress at the time denoted by the main verb of the sentence: *Being* in the city, I have called upon you. *Seeing* the multitudes, he went up into a mountain.

2. The **past participle,** denoting action *as complete,* but perhaps still in progress, *with reference to the main verb:* He

was a good man, *honored* wherever *known*. He lives, *honored* wherever *known*. He will live *honored* wherever *known*.

Other participles are formed by the aid of auxiliaries, giving three participles in each voice, as follows:

Active Voice

Present	*Past*	*Perfect*
loving	loved	having loved

Passive Voice

Present	*Past*	*Perfect*
being loved	loved	having been loved

The past participle has the same form in either the active or passive voice. It is called simply the *past* participle: He *loved*. He has been *loved*. The past participle is always given as one of the principle parts of the verb: love, loved, *loved;* see, saw, *seen.* Both the present and past participles are used, with auxiliaries, to form the various tenses and moods of the verb: I am *walking.* He has been *seen.* We wondered if he had been *seen,* etc.

Uses of the Participle

The *participle* has two distinct uses:

1. As an **adjective** *without the adjuncts of the verb: singing* birds; *laden* bees; *known* culprits.

2. As an **adjective** *with the adjuncts of the verb:* The birds, *singing* THEIR SWEET SONGS, flitted among the trees. HEAVILY *laden* bees were flying home.

The Participial Phrase.—A participle with any closely associated word or words forms a *participial phrase.* A participial phrase is used as follows:

(1) As an adjective to modify a noun or pronoun: *Crying bitterly,* the child ran to his mother. *Displayed with many other objects,* the picture attracted little attention.

(2) As an adverb to modify the predicate or any adjective or adverb in the predicate: He succeeded *by persisting in the face of defeat.* The player was shrewd *in making that* move.

The Gerund

A **gerund** is the present participial form of a verb used as a noun. Thus a gerund is frequently called a *verbal noun* because it shares the properties of both a verb and a noun. The gerund may be used with the adjuncts of a verb: *Being* is more than *seeing.* Or the gerund may be used without the adjuncts of a verb, thus forming a *gerund phrase: Thinking noble thoughts* tends to noble actions.

Since the gerund functions as a noun, it may be used as follows:

(1) As the subject of a verb: *Singing* is an art.

(2) As the object of a verb: I study *singing.*

(3) As a predicate nominative or complement: Seeing is *believing.*

(4) As object of a preposition: There is a time for *sowing.*

(5) As an appositive: His favorite sport, *swimming,* is healthful.

EXERCISE

Find all the gerunds and present and past participles in the following selections.

(1)   Thus came the lovely spring with a rush of blossoms and music,
       Flooding the earth with flowers, and the air with melodies vernal.

LONGFELLOW *Tales of a Wayside Inn.*

(2)   I was a stricken deer that left the herd
         Long since.
                              COWPER *The Task,* bk. iii, l. 108.

(3)   Fallen, fallen, fallen, fallen,
             Fallen from his high estate,
                 And welt'ring in his blood;
             Deserted at his utmost need,
             By those his former bounty fed;
             On the bare earth expos'd he lies,
             With not a friend to close his eyes.
                              DRYDEN *Alexander's Feast,* l. 77.

(4)   Thought, once awakened, does not again slumber.
                 CARLYLE *Heroes and Hero Worship,* Sect. I.

(5)   A violet by a mossy stone
             Half hidden from the eye!
             Fair as a star when only one
             Is shining in the sky.
                         WORDSWORTH *She Dwelt Among the*
                                     Untrodden Ways.

(6)   There is another man in the modern world who might be
called the antithesis of Mr. Chamberlain in every point, who
is also a standing monument of the advantage of being
misunderstood. Mr. Bernard Shaw is always represented by
those who disagree with him, and, I fear, also (if such exist)
by those who agree with him, as a capering humorist, a
dazzling acrobat, a quick-change artist.—G. K. CHESTERTON
Heretics, "Mr. Bernard Shaw."

(7)   Having emended their name, the morticians proceed to
exalt and magnify their calling. They do this in a very simple,
but entirely effective way: by insisting on the Service which
they render to Humanity.—ALDOUS HUXLEY *Jesting Pilate.*

(8)   You'd see me with my puffy petulant face,
         Guzzling and gulping in the best hotel,
             Reading the Roll of Honour.
                              SIEGFRIED SASSOON *In the Pink.*

(9)   Man, whose young passion sets the spindrift flying,
      Is soon too lame to march, too cold for loving.
                              JOHN MASEFIELD *On Growing Old.*

(10)   More and more as I grow older and more settled in my
views am I bored by common argument, bored not because
I am ceasing to be interested in the things argued about, but
because I see more and more clearly the futility of the
methods pursued.—H. G. WELLS *First and Last Things*.

CONJUGATION

The **conjugation** of a verb is the schematic arrangement of
its forms for voice, mood, tense, person, and number.

THE PRINCIPAL PARTS

The conjugation of a verb is based on its **principal parts**: the
present indicative, the past indicative, and the past participle.
When these parts are known, all the moods and tenses can be
readily formed from them. Thus the entire conjugation of the
verb *love* or the verb *give* can be formed from the following
principal parts:

	PRESENT	PAST	PAST PARTICIPLE
Regular	love	loved	loved
Irregular	give	gave	given

Synopsis.—*Synopsis* is an abbreviated form of conjugation.
It is the orderly arrangement of the forms of a verb by *mood*
and *tense* in a *single number and person*.

THE STEM AND INFLECTED FORMS

The present infinitive form of the verb, with or without *to*,
is the root-form or **stem** of the verb. Thus we speak of "the
verb *do* or *come*." (See THE INFINITIVE, pp. 85–86.)

The inflected forms of the verb are made as follows:

1. **The Present Indicative.**—In all verbs (except the verb *be*
considered later) the stem (*love, call, give, go,* etc.) is used unchanged in the first person singular, and in the first, second, and
third persons plural of this tense. The third person singular adds

s or *es* to the stem: *loves, calls, gives, goes.* Verbs ending in *o* add *es: does, goes.* Verbs ending in *y* change the *y* to *i* before adding *es:* fly, *flies;* carry, *carries.*

2. **The Present Subjunctive.**—The stem of the verb is used unchanged in all persons and numbers of the *present subjunctive.* That is, the present subjunctive differs from the present indicative only by *not* adding *s* or *es* to the stem of the verb in the third person singular:

> *Pres. Indicative, third pers. sing.*   he **gives**
> *Pres. Subjunctive, third pers. sing.*   (if) he **give**

3. **The Past Indicative.**—The past tense of the indicative mood is made from the stem by adding *ed* to the stem of regular verbs and by other changes in irregular verbs. The past tenses of irregular verbs must be learned one by one, each for itself. (See IRREGULAR VERBS, p. 122.)

When the stem of the verb ends in mute *e,* the mute *e* is dropped before adding *ed:* love, *loved;* change, *changed.* When the stem ends in *y,* the *y* is changed to *i* before adding *ed:* dry, *dried;* carry, *carried.*

4. **The Past Subjunctive.**—This is the same as the past indicative (except in the verb *be,* p. 111).

5. **The Imperative.**—This is the simple stem of the verb used unchanged in a command, a request, an exclamation, etc.: *love; call; give; see* there! *help!*

6. **The Present Participle.**—This is formed by adding *ing* to the stem of the verb: *loving; calling; giving.**

---

* NOTE.—When the stem of the verb ends in mute (silent) *e,* the *e* is dropped before adding *ing,* except in the cases following: (1) The final *e* is retained in *hoeing, shoeing,* and *toeing;* (2) The final *e* is retained in the derivatives of *dye, singe, swinge,* and *tinge,* to distinguish *dyeing* from *dying, singeing* from *singing,* etc., and to keep the *g* soft in *tingeing.* Verbs ending in *ie,* as *die, hie, lie, tie, vie,* commonly change *ie* to *y* before *ing: dying, hying, lying, trying, vying.* Some authorities, however, favor the use of *hieing.*

7. The Past Participle.—This is formed by adding *ed* to the stem in regular verbs, precisely as in the past indicative, and by other changes in irregular verbs (see IRREGULAR VERBS, p. 122): *loved; called; given.* In regular verbs the past tense and the past participle are identical in form.

These are all the English verb-forms made by inflection (except certain forms of the verb *be*, pp. 110–111).

Thus in any English verb (excepting the verb *be*) we have never more than five inflected forms: *love, loves, loved, loving, loved; call, calls, called, calling, called; give, gives, gave, giving, given.*

Since in regular verbs the past tense and past participle (as *loved* or *called*) are identical in form, regular verbs have only *four* different inflected forms: These four or five forms give seven parts of the verb: the present indicative, present subjunctive, past indicative, imperative, present infinitive, present participle, and past participle.

The Stem and Inflected Forms of the Verbs
LOVE, CALL, GIVE

INDICATIVE MOOD

PRESENT TENSE *

Singular Number

First Person	I love	I call	I give
Second Person	(same as plural)	(same as pl.)	(same as pl.)
Third Person	he loves	he calls	he gives

Plural Number

First Person	we love	we call	we give
Second Person	you love	you call	you give
Third Person	they love	they call	they give

* NOTE.—For brevity of statement it is common to say, instead of "the present tense of the indicative mood," simply "the *present indicative*." So "the *past indicative*," "the *present subjunctive*," etc.

Condensed Form

On examining the statement given above, we see that we may omit the designations of person and number, which the pronouns sufficiently indicate. Further, we may omit the second person singular because it is the same as the second person plural, and we may also avoid repeating identical forms as "we *love*," "you *love*," "they *love*," in immediate connection. Condensed in this manner, all these forms for each verb may be presented in a single line, as follows:

INDICATIVE MOOD

PRESENT TENSE

I love, he **loves,** we, you, they **love**

I call, he **calls,** we, you, they **call**

I give, he **gives,** we, you, they **give**

Here "we, you, they *love*" is equivalent to "we *love*, you *love*, they *love*," etc. The person and number are sufficiently indicated by the pronoun. (See PERSONAL PRONOUNS, pp. 26–27.) On account of the simplicity and compactness of this condensed form of statement, it will be used wherever practicable for all moods and tenses throughout the conjugations.

PAST TENSE

I, he, we, you, they **loved; called; gave**

That is all there is of the simple past tense of any verb except the verb *be* (see pp. 110–111). Nothing could be imagined more absolutely simple and easy. In all verbs except the verb *be,* when we have learned the form for the *first person singular* of the *past indicative,* we have learned the forms for *all persons* of both numbers.

SUBJUNCTIVE MOOD

PRESENT TENSE

(If) I, he, we, you, they **love; call; give**

It will be seen that this differs from the present indicative only in the third person singular: The indicative form of the third person singular, *loves, calls, gives,* is now very commonly used after *if,* in place of the subjunctive: If he *calls,* I will see him.

PAST TENSE

(Same as the Past Indicative)

This is virtually to say that the subjunctive mode in any verb (except the verb *be*) has no past tense, the past indicative being used instead. The repetition of this form may therefore ordinarily be omitted.

IMPERATIVE MOOD

love; call; give

INFINITIVES

PRESENT TENSE

(to) **love;** (to) **call;** (to) **give**

PARTICIPLES

PRESENT

loving; calling; giving

PAST

loved; called; given

EXERCISE

Give the principal parts of the following verbs, consulting as needed the list of irregular verbs, pp. 122–129. Give the present and past indicative and the present subjunctive mood of each. Give the present infinitive and the present and past participles of each.

Regular Verbs:

accost	construct	frighten	relieve
address	defend	grieve	strengthen
appear	deliver	hasten	support
approach	detain	lament	sustain
believe	fear	present	travel
carry	forward	receive	

Irregular Verbs:

break	get	make	shake
bring	go	mean	spring
burn	grow	pay	swim
catch	hang	quit	take
come	hit	read	tear
dig	hold	ride	wear
feed	know	see	weep
fight	leave	set	write
fly			

VERB PHRASES

All other parts of the English verb are formed, not by inflection, but by the use of *auxiliary verbs,* often called **auxiliaries.** (See CONJUGATIONS OF AUXILIARY VERBS, pp. 101–112.)

The auxiliary verbs are: *be, can, do, have, may, must, shall, will, ought,* and sometimes *let.* The combinations of auxiliary with principal verbs form **verb phrases:** I *will go.* I *shall have gone.* It *may succeed.* That *might have been done.*

REMARKS.—In treating any one of these verb phrases, *the entire phrase* is called *the verb.* Thus, in "I will go," the verb is not *will* nor *go,* but *will go.* In "that might have been done," the verb is not *might* nor *have* nor *been* nor *done;* but the entire verb phrase *might have been done* is to be treated as the verb.

The same is true if any auxiliary, as often happens, is separated from the rest of the verb phrase by intervening words: I *will* certainly *go*. Here the verb is still *will go*. So if we say, "That *might* possibly in such a case *have been done*," the verb is still *might have been done*. All the words of a verb phrase are to be taken *together* to make the *verb* in any construction.

Conjugations of Auxiliary Verbs

Have

We will first consider *have* as the auxiliary * used in forming what are called the "perfect" tenses.

PRINCIPAL PARTS

Present	*Past*	*Past Participle*
have	**had**	**had**

INDICATIVE MOOD

Present Tense   I **have,** he **has,** we, you, they **have**

Past Tense   I, he, we, you, they **had**

Present Perfect and Past Perfect of all Verbs.—By adding to the present or past indicative of *have* the past participle of any verb, we obtain the *present perfect* or *past perfect* of the indicative mood of that verb. Thus:

INDICATIVE MOOD

Present Perfect Tense   I *have,* he *has,* we, you, they *have* **loved; called; given**

Past Perfect Tense   I, he, we, you, they *had* **loved; called; given**

Here the auxiliary verb is in *italic,* and the participle of the principal verb in full-faced type. By adding either participle to

* Note.—For the full conjugation of *have* as a principal verb, see p. 132.

the appropriate form of the pronoun and auxiliary we obtain the complete form for that mood, tense, person, and number of the principal verb: present perfect tense, second person, plural number, you *have* **loved**.

Had Rather, etc.—*Had* has peculiar use in such phrases as, "I *had* rather"; "You *had* better," etc.

> I *had* rather be a doorkeeper in the house of my God than to dwell in the tents of wickedness.—*Ps.* 84:10.

> > I *had* rather be a dog, and bay the moon,
> > Than such a Roman.
> >   SHAKESPEARE *Julius Caesar,* act iv, sc. 3, l. 27.

Currently the phrase *had rather* is rarely used, but *had better* is common.

CAUTION.—*Have* or *had* can not be used as an auxiliary of *can, may, must, shall, will,* or *ought.* Never say "I *had* ought," or "*I'd* ought." (See OUGHT, p. 108.)

Shall

INDICATIVE MOOD

Present Tense   I, he, we, you, they **shall**

Past Tense   I, he, we, you, they **should**

Shall, although grammatically in the present tense, is used to express future action or state, either as a prediction, a command, or a necessity. *Should* is used as an auxiliary. (See p. 106.) So used, *should* often has the sense of obligation; "you *should* help him" is nearly equivalent to "you *ought* to help him."

Will

Present Tense   I, he, we, you, they **will**

Past Tense   I, he, we, you, they **would**

As an auxiliary,* *will,* although grammatically in the present tense, is used to express future action. *Would* is used as an auxiliary to express wish or preference: I *would* go if possible.

Distinctions Between Shall and Will

Formerly *shall* and *will* as auxiliaries of the future tenses were sharply distinguished one from the other. By now, however, the distinctions have all but disappeared from the language. These distinctions are explained here, with the understanding that they are now seldom observed, simply because they may on occasion be encountered.

Shall in the first person simply denotes future fact: I *shall* be there. In the second and third persons, however, *shall* denotes obligation that is imposed by the speaker; hence, "He (she, you, they) *shall* be there" means that they will be compelled to be there by the speaker. Or the compulsion expressed by *shall* in the second and third persons may be imposed by the nature of things or the circumstances of the case, that is, by necessity: "They that wait on the Lord *shall* renew their faith."

Will in the first person denotes the intention or purpose of the speaker. I *will* go means that I *intend* to go; or, if strongly emphasized, it means that I am resolved to go. "We *will* go" has similar meaning. In the second and third persons *will* expresses *simple future action without compulsion.*

Accordingly there are two parallel sets of futures, (1) the declarative future, expressing simple future action, and (2) the purposive future, expressing intention, obligation, command, or necessity. Thus in the indicative mood:

* NOTE.—*Will* is also used as a principal verb in the sense of *resolve, determine.* In this sense it is conjugated as a regular verb, (present) *will,* (past) *willed,* (past partic.) *willed,* (pres. indic., third pers. singular) he *wills,* etc.

The Declarative Future · *The Purposive Future*

I shall			I will		
he will	love		he shall	love	
we shall	call		we will	call	
you will	give		you shall	give	
they will			they shall		

We have likewise two forms of the future perfect tense, declarative and purposive. This tense adds *have* to the simple future in *shall* or *will,* and puts after this combined form the past participle of any verb. Thus:

FUTURE PERFECT TENSE

Declarative · *Purposive*

I *shall*			I *will*		
he *will*		loved	he *shall*		loved
we *shall*	*have*	called	we *will*	*have*	called
you *will*		given	you *shall*		given
they *will*			they *shall*		

The future and future perfect tenses are found only in the indicative mood.

Future Forms in Interrogative Sentences.—In interrogative sentences, however, *will* is not used with the *first person,* since the speaker knows what he intends or purposes, and does not need to ask. Do not say, *"Will* I mail this letter?" For the first person of a question with simple future meaning, *shall* must be used even though it also carries something of the inquiry: "Is it your will?" As, *"Shall* I mail this letter?" *"Shall* we go to dinner?"

For the second person, with simple future meaning, *shall* is used interrogatively in place of *will. "Shall* you go?" is a simple question as to the future, to which we expect the answer "I *shall"* or "I *shall* not." *"Will* you go?" is a question as to purpose, expecting the answer "I *will"* or "I *will* not."

EXERCISE

1. How many auxiliary verbs are there? Repeat the list of auxiliaries in alphabetical order.

2. Give the conjugation of *have* as an auxiliary verb (only the forms in auxiliary use to be given).

3. Conjugate the auxiliaries *shall* and *will*.

4. Conjugate the indicative mood and the present and present perfect subjunctive of each verb in the exercise on p. 100.

May

INDICATIVE MOOD

Present Tense   I, he, we, you, they **may**

Past Tense   I, he, we, you, they **might**

In the indicative mood *may* denotes possibility: I *may* (*might*) go. In interrogative use *may* expresses a request for permission: *May* I come in? In exclamatory use *may* expresses a wish or entreaty: *May* all good attend you!

Can

INDICATIVE MOOD

Present Tense   I, he, we, you, they **can**

Past Tense   I, he, we, you, they **could**

Can denotes possibility.

CAUTION.—It is not well to use *can* to express permission even though it is often so used: *Can* I go home?

Must

Present Indicative—I, he, we, you they **must**

Must expresses absolute or imperative necessity without change of mood, tense, person, or number.

Tenses with May, Can, Must

Present Tense

I
he   **love**
we   *may, can,* or *must* **call**
you   **give**
they

Present Perfect Tense

I
he   **loved**
we   *may, can,* or *must have* **called**
you   **given**
they

Past Tense

I
he   **love**
we   *might, could, would,* or *should* **call**
you   **give**
they

Past Perfect Tense

I
he   **loved**
we   *might, could, would,* or *should have* **called**
you   **given**
they

Do

(*In Auxiliary Use*)

Do, as an auxiliary,* is used only in the present and past

---

* NOTE.—*Do* as a principal verb meaning *perform* or *accomplish* has the full conjugation of an irregular verb: principal parts, *do, did, done.*

indicative and subjunctive and in the imperative: *Do* you *hear* the music? I *did* not *notice. Do come* in.

Present Indicative	I **do,** he **does,** we, you, they **do**
Past Indicative	I, he, we, you, they **did**
Present Subjunctive	(If) I, he, we, you, they **do**
Past Subjunctive	(Same as Past Indicative.)
Imperative	**do**

ERROR.—The use of the past participle, *done,* as an auxiliary is a vulgarism: He has *done* gone.

As an auxiliary, *do* is used in either of three ways:

1. **Do as the Auxiliary of Emphasis.**—*Do* is used for emphatic affirmation: I *do* believe you. I *did* hear those words.

When used as an emphatic auxiliary, the past form *did* often implies some subsequent change: I *did* intend to go (but have now decided otherwise, or become doubtful).

2. **Do as the Auxiliary of Interrogation.**—*Do* is used at the beginning of a sentence to ask a question: *Do* you know the facts? *Did* you meet anyone at the door?

We never use a principal verb in interrogation: *Came* you yesterday? In present and past interrogative sentences, the forms with *do* and *did* have wholly superseded the direct forms. "*Know* you the facts?" "*Met* you anyone?" would seem so antiquated as to be ridiculous, and would not even be readily understood.

3. **Do as the Auxiliary of Negation.**—*Do* is constantly used in denial, with *not* or some other adverb interposed between the auxiliary and its verb: I *did* NOT *go:* I *do* NOT at present *intend* to go.

Such forms as "I *went not,*" "I *saw not*" are wholly out of use in current speech or literature. Where *not* is used alone with a verb there is commonly another verb understood: I think (it is) *not.* I will *not* (*go, do,* or the like).

Ought and Let

Ought and *let* are semi-auxiliaries. They resemble auxiliaries in the fact that neither of them by itself expresses a complete meaning; they differ from auxiliaries in that neither of them is necessary to the conjugation of any mood or tense of any other verb.

Ought further differs from the auxiliary verbs by taking after it the infinitive with *to:* I *ought* to go. *Ought* is used only as present indicative, expressing moral obligation, logical necessity, or (sometimes) reasonable expectation, thus:

Present Indicative—I, he, we, you, they **ought**

CAUTION.—*Ought* can never take *have, be,* or any other auxiliary; expressions like "You *don't* ought," "I *had* ought" are always erroneous. To express past obligation, use *ought* followed by the *perfect infinitive* of the accompanying verb: I ought *to have gone*.

Let has the full conjugation of an irregular verb. Its use as an apparent auxiliary is most common in the imperative mood when it is followed by an infinitive without *to,* that infinitive having as its subject (in the objective case) a pronoun of the first or third person, *me, us, him, her, it, them,* or any noun in the third person: *Let* me go. *Let* him come in. *Let* them state their case. *Let* the child sleep.

A Peculiar Idiom.—The phrase *let alone* is often used in an idiomatic sense different from the literal sense. "Let the child alone," does not mean that the child is to be solitary. The expression means, "Keep your hands off the child," or "Do not interfere with the child." *Leave alone* is similarly used. "Let it *be*" means let the person or thing *be* undisturbed.

Conjugation of the Verb
HAVE
(AS A PRINCIPAL VERB)

TENSES	INDICATIVE MOOD
Present	I **have,** he **has,** we, you, they **have**
Pres. Perf.	I *have,* he *has,* we, you, they *have* **had**
Past	I, he, we, you, they *had*
Past Perf.	I, he, we, you, they *had* **had**
Future:	
(declarative)	I *shall,* he *will,* we *shall,* you, they *will* **have**
(purposive)	I *will,* he *shall,* we *will,* you, they *shall* **have**
Fut. Perf.	
(declarative)	I *shall,* he *will,* we *shall,* you, they *will have* **had**
(purposive)	I *will,* he *shall,* we *will,* you, they *shall have* **had**

TENSES	SUBJUNCTIVE MOOD
Present	(If) I, he, we, you, they **have**
Pres. Perf.	(If) I, he, we, you, they *have* **had**
Past	(Same as Indicative)
Past Perf.	(Same as Indicative)

With *May, Can,* and *Must*

Present	I, he, we, you, they *may* **have** *
Pres. Perf.	I, he, we, you, they *may have* **had** *
Past	I, he, we, you, they *might* **have** †
Past Perf.	I, he, we, you, they *might have* **had** †

IMPERATIVE MOOD
(you) **have**

INFINITIVES

Present	**have** or *to* **have**
Perfect	*to have* **had**

* NOTE.—*Can* or *must* may be substituted for *may*.
† NOTE.—*Could, would,* or *should* may be substituted for *might*.

PARTICIPLES

Present	*Past*	*Perfect*
having	**had**	*having* **had**

EXERCISE

1. Name the auxiliaries that express wish, possibility, or necessity in (*a*) the present tense and (*b*) the past tense.

2. Conjugate the auxiliaries *may, can,* and *must.* Tell from what verbs *could* and *should* are obtained.

3. Take each verb listed in the exercise on p. 100 and conjugate it with the auxiliaries *may, can,* and *must* in all of the tenses.

4. Explain the three uses of *do* as an auxiliary. With what modes and tenses is it used?

Conjugation of the Verb

BE

PRINCIPAL PARTS

Present	*Past*	*Past Participle*
be	**was**	**been**

TENSES	INDICATIVE MOOD
Present	I **am,** he **is,** we, you, they **are**
Pres. Perf.	I *have* **been,** he *has* **been,** we, you, they *have* **been**
Past	I, he, **was,** we, you, they **were**
Past Perf.	I, he, we, you, they *had* **been**
Future:	
(declarative)	I *shall,* he *will,* we *shall,* you, they *will* **be**
(purposive)	I *will,* he *shall,* we *will,* you, they *shall* **be**

Fut. Perf.

(declarative)   I *shall,* he *will,* we *shall,* you, they *will have*
been

(purposive)   I *will,* he *shall,* we *will,* you, they *shall have*
been

TENSES	SUBJUNCTIVE MOOD
Present	(If) I, he, we, you, they **be**
Pres. Perf.	(If) I, he, we, you, they *have* **been**
Past	(If) I, he, we, you, they **were**
Past Perf.	(If) I, he, we, you, they *had* **been**

With May

Present	I, he, we, you, they *may* **be**
Pres. Perf.	I, he, we, you, they *may have* **been**
Past	I, he, we, you, they *might* **be**
Past Perf.	I, he, we, you, they *might have* **been**

IMPERATIVE MOOD

Present	(you) **be**

INFINITVES

Present	**be** or *to* **be**
Perfect	*to have* **been**

PARTICIPLES

Present	*Past*	*Perfect*
being	**been**	*having* **been**

REMARKS

(1) *Be* is used somewhat rarely as a principal verb, equivalent to "exist": Whatever *is* (exists) is right.

(2) As an auxiliary, a form of the verb *be* is joined:

(*a*) With the present participle of any verb, to denote continued or progressive action: I *am* coming. The tree *is* falling. (See PROGRESSIVE CONJUGATION, pp. 117–118.)

(*b*) With the past participle to express the action of the verb with passive force: The bird *was* killed. The signal *was* given. (See PASSIVE VOICE, pp. 114–115.)

(3) *Be* is also used as a connecting verb (frequently called the *copula,* or "link") connecting the subject with something affirmed of the subject: I *am* the man. Truth *is* mighty.

Conjugation of the Regular Verb

LOVE

PRINCIPAL PARTS

Present	Past	Past Participle
love	loved	loved

Active Voice

TENSES	INDICATIVE MOOD
Present	I **love,** he **loves,** we, you, they **love**
Pres. Perf.	I *have,* he *has,* we, you, they *have* **loved**
Past	I, he, we, you, they **loved**
Past Perf.	I, he, we, you, they *had* **loved**
Future:	
(declarative)	I *shall,* he *will,* we *shall,* you, they *will* **love**
(purposive)	I *will,* he *shall,* we *will,* you, they *shall* **love**
Fut. Perf.	
(declarative)	I *shall,* he *will,* we *shall,* you, they *will have* **loved**
(purposive)	I *will,* he *shall,* we *will,* you, they *shall have* **loved**

TENSES	SUBJUNCTIVE MOOD *
Present	(If) I, he, we, you, they **love**
Pres. Perf.	(If) I, he, we, you, they *have* **loved**

* NOTE.—The past and past perfect tenses of the indicative are used without change in conditional sentences with *if,* etc. The subjunctive has no special forms for these tenses.

With Auxiliaries of Possibility, Wish, etc.

Present	I, he, we, you, they *may* **love** *
Pres. Perf.	I, he, we, you, they *may have* **loved** *
Past	I, he, we, you, they *might* **love** †
Past Perf.	I, he, we, you, they *might have* **loved** †

IMPERATIVE MOOD

Present   **love** (thou or you); *do* (thou or you) **love**

INFINITIVES

Present	(to) **love**
Perfect	(to) *have* **loved**

PARTICIPLES

Present	*Past*	*Perfect*
loving	**loved**	*having* **loved**

Conjugation of the Irregular Verb
GIVE

PRINCIPAL PARTS

Present	*Past*	*Past Participle*
give	**gave**	**given**

Active Voice

TENSES	INDICATIVE MOOD
Present	I **give**, he **gives**, we, you, they **give**
Pres. Perf.	I *have*, he *has*, we, you, they *have* **given** ‡
Past	I, he, we, you, they **gave**

* NOTE.—Instead of *may* we may use *can* or *must*.

† NOTE.—Instead of *might* we may use *could*, *would*, or *should*.

‡ CAUTION.—In conjugating an irregular verb, never use the *past tense* instead of the *past participle* after any form of *have*. Never say, "I have *gave*," but "I have *given*"; never "I had *went*," but "I had *gone*"; not "I have *saw*," "I have *came*," but "I have *seen*," "I have *come*," etc.

Past Perf.	I, he, we, you, they *had* **given**
Future:	
(declarative)	I *shall,* he *will,* we *shall,* you, they *will* **give**
(purposive)	I *will,* he *shall,* we *will,* you, they *shall* **give**
Fut. Perf.	
(declarative)	I *shall,* he *will,* we *shall,* you, they *will* **have given**
(purposive)	I *will,* he *shall,* we *will,* you, they *shall* **have given**

TENSES	SUBJUNCTIVE MOOD
Present	(If) I, he, we, you, they **give**
Pres. Perf.	(If) I, he, we, you, they *have* **given**
	(For the past and past perfect, the indicative forms are used throughout.)

With Auxiliaries of Possibility, Wish, etc.

Present	I, he, we, you, they *may* **give**
Pres. Perf.	I, he, we, you, they *may have* **given**
Past	I, he, we, you, they *might* **give**
Past Perf.	I, he, we, you, they *might have* **given**

IMPERATIVE MOOD

Present	(you) **give**

INFINITIVES

Present	(to) **give**
Perfect	(to) *have* **given**

PARTICIPLES

Present	*Past*	*Perfect*
giving	**given**	*having* **given**

Passive Voice

The passive voice of a verb is formed by adding the past participle (*loved, walked, hoped*) to the inflected forms of the

verb *to be*. (See CONJUGATION OF THE VERB BE, pp. 110–111.)
The participles in the passive voice are formed by adding the
past participle of a verb to the present and perfect participles of
the verb *to be*. The passive voice is here illustrated with the verb
love:

TENSES	INDICATIVE MOOD
Present	I *am,* he *is,* we, you, they *are* **loved**
Pres. Perf.	I *have,* he *has,* we, you, they *have been* **loved**
Past	I, he *was,* we, you, they *were* **loved**
Past Perf.	I, he, we, you, they *had been* **loved**
Future:	
(declarative)	I *shall,* he *will,* we *shall,* you, they *will be* **loved**
(purposive)	I *will,* he *shall,* we *will,* you, they *shall be* **loved**
Fut. Perf.	
(declarative)	I *shall,* he *will,* we *shall,* you, they *will have been* **loved**
(purposive)	I *will,* he *shall,* we *will,* you, they *shall have been* **loved**

TENSES	SUBJUNCTIVE MOOD
Present	(If) I, he, we, you, they *be* **loved**
Pres. Perf.	(If) I, he, we, you, they *have been* **loved**
Past	(If) I, he, we, you, they *were* **loved**
Past Perf.	(If) I, he, we, you, they *had been* **loved**

With Auxiliaries of Possibility, Wish, etc. *

Present	I, he, we, you, they *may be* **loved**
Pres. Perf.	I, he, we, you, they *may have been* **loved**
Past	I, he, we, you, they *might be* **loved**
Past Perf.	I, he, we, you, they *might have been* **loved**

IMPERATIVE MOOD

Present	(you) *be* **loved**

* Note.—Instead of *may*, we may use *can* or *must;* instead of *might*,
we may use *could, would,* or *should.*

INFINITIVES

Present	(to) *be* **loved**
Perfect	(to) *have been* **loved**

PARTICIPLES

Present	*Past*	*Perfect*
being **loved**	**loved**	*having been* **loved**

EXERCISE

Turn to the CONJUGATION OF THE VERB *BE* (pp. 110–111), and from that form the passive voice of each of the following verbs by adding its past participle to the various forms of the verb *be,* except that you *substitute* in each case the past participle of the principal verb for the past participle *been.*

If any of the verbs are irregular, look up their past participles in the LIST OF IRREGULAR VERBS, pp. 122–129.

Verbs to be Conjugated in the Passive Voice *

call	believe	tell	hit
give	receive	place	leave
see	discover	set	push
hear	expect	station	send
think	say	take	report

Change from Active to Passive Voice.—A transitive verb in the active voice may be changed to the passive voice as follows:

Active Voice   The engine *draws* the train.
            (The subject of *draws* is *engine;* its object is *train.*)

Passive Voice   The train *is drawn* by the engine.
            (The subject here is the former object *train.* The

---

* NOTE.—This exercise should be given orally and in writing, changing from one to the other.

former subject *engine* is now object of the preposition *by*.)

EXERCISE

Change the following sentences from the active to the passive form. Consult as needed the LIST OF IRREGULAR VERBS, pp. 122–129.

1. A stranger met him at the door.
2. A friend helped him home.
3. A messenger brought the letter.
4. The teacher explained the lesson.
5. All the children told the same story.

Change the following sentences from the passive to the active form.

1. The work was well done by him.
2. A successful flight was made by the airship.
3. The goods were delivered by the express agent.
4. The bill was promptly signed by the president.
5. The game was saved by a home run.
6. The town was destroyed by a cyclone.

The Progressive Conjugation

It is often desirable to represent an action as continuous at any time mentioned or thought of. For that purpose the *present participle* of the principal verb is associated with any form of the auxiliary *be:* I *am waiting* for an answer.

The progressive conjugation differs from the passive in that (1) it is active in meaning, and (2) it adds the **present** instead of the **past** participle to the various forms of the verb *be*. Thus:

INDICATIVE MOOD

Present Tense I *am*, he *is*, we, you, they *are* **working**

Thus the progressive form of any verb is formed by adding its present participle to any mood, tense or participle of the verb *to be*.

EXERCISE

Turn to the CONJUGATION OF THE VERB *BE* (pp. 110–111) and from that form the *progressive conjugation* of each of the following verbs by adding its present participle to each of the various forms of the verb *be*.

Verbs to be Conjugated in the Progressive Form

call	hope	tell	act
give	believe	do	plan
see	receive	go	place
hear	expect	work	sing
think	say	wish	pause

Negative and Interrogative Forms

In interrogative sentences the subject (noun or pronoun) always follows the first auxiliary. In negation the negative adverb *not* follows the first auxiliary. *Never* is, however, freely used with a principal verb: I *never* said that. In the present and past indicative, *do, does,* or *did* is commonly supplied as an auxiliary in negative or interrogative use (see DO, p. 107).

TENSES   INDICATIVE MOOD
(Negative Form)

Present   I *do,* he *does,* we, you, they *do* NOT **wish**
Past   I, he, we, you, they *did* NOT **intend**
Pres. Perf.   I *have,* he *has,* we, you, they *have* NOT **called**
Future:
(declarative)   I *shall,* he *will,* we *shall,* you, they *will* NOT **call**
(purposive)   I *will,* he *shall,* we *will,* you *shall,* they *shall* NOT **call**

(Interrogative Form)

Present	*Do* I, *does* he, *do* we, you, they **wish**
Past	*Did* I, he, we, you, they **intend**
Pres. Perf.	*Have* I, *has* he, *have* we, you, they **called**
Future:	
(declarative)	*Shall* I, *will* he, *shall* we, *will* you, they **call**
(purposive)	——— *, *shall* he, ——— *, *shall* you, they **call**

With Auxiliaries of Possibility, Wish, etc.

TENSES	(Negative Form)
Present	I, he, we, you, they *may* NOT **come**
Past	I, he, we, you, they *might* NOT **come**

(Interrogative Form)

May I, he, we, you, they **come**

Might I, he, we, you, they **come**

Negative-Interrogative Forms

When the negative and interrogative forms are combined, the subject usually follows the first auxiliary, and the negative follows the subject: *Are* you NOT **reading?** *Will* they NOT **answer?** Sometimes the negative adverb precedes the subject, with the effect of emphasizing it: *Did* NOT I **give** that order?

Contracted Forms.—In conversation various contractions of the negative forms are frequently used: I *haven't.* I *don't.* He *didn't. Isn't* it? etc. *Won't* is used as a contraction of *will not,* in all persons and numbers. These forms are not used in formal literary style or in formal letters or documents.

* NOTE.—The forms of the first person with *will* are never used interrogatively. We know our own purpose, and do not ask other people what it is.

CAUTIONS

(1) *Don't* (for *do not*) can not be used in the third person singular since we can not say, "He *do not.*" Never say, "He *don't*" or *"Don't* he?" but, "He *doesn't*" or *"Doesn't* he?"

(2) *Ain't* (for *am, is* or *are not*) is never proper; "I *ain't*" and "he *ain't*" are especially bad.

(3) Often it is better to contract the auxiliary rather than the negative: *I'm not, he's not, they're not, I've not,* etc. *"I'll not"* (for *"I will not"*) is more elegant than "I *won't,*" but less emphatic.

EXERCISE

In the extracts below do the following: (1) Point out all the finite verbs, infinitives, and participles. (2) Tell which of the verbs are regular and which irregular (see LIST OF IRREGULAR VERBS, pp. 122–129). (3) Tell the mood and tense of each finite verb. (4) Explain the use of each infinitive (with or without *to.*) (5) Give the name of each participle (present, past, etc.).

(1)   From morn
     To noon he fell, from noon to dewy eve,
     A summer's day; and with the setting sun
     Dropt from the zenith like a falling star.
              MILTON *Paradise Lost,* bk. i, l. 742.

(2)   How far that little candle throws his beams!
        So shines a good deed in a naughty world.
              SHAKESPEARE *Merchant of Venice,* act v, sc. 1.

(3)   I am in earnest—I will not equivocate—I will not excuse
        —I will not retreat a single inch; AND I WILL BE HEARD.—
        WILLIAM LLOYD GARRISON *Salutatory of the Liberator,*
        vol. 1, no. 1, Jan. 1, 1831.

(4)   Let us have faith that Right makes Might, and in that faith
        let us to the end dare to do our duty as we understand it.
        —ABRAHAM LINCOLN *Address. New York City.* Feb. 21,
        1859.

(5) A Sensitive Plant in a garden grew,
     And the young winds fed it with silver dew,
     And it opened its fan-like leaves to the light,
     And closed them beneath the kisses of night.
                    SHELLEY *The Sensitive Plant*, pt. i.

(6) In a speech to serenaders just before the battle of Gettysburg four and a half months before, Lincoln had referred to the founding of the republic as taking place "eighty odd years since." Then he had hunted up the exact date, which was eighty-seven years hence, and phrased it "Fourscore and seven years ago" instead of "Eighty-seven years since." —CARL SANDBURG *Abraham Lincoln: The War Years*.

(7) Well, it was a nice snowstorm; a fine sight to see the snow falling so quietly and graciously over so much open country. On his cap and shoulders, on the horses' backs and manes, light, delicate, mysterious it fell; and with it a dry cool fragrance was released into the air.—WILLA CATHER *Neighbour Rosicky*.

(8) I don't suppose I could have been called one of Cal's closest friends in college, but I knew him pretty well. In fact, we lived not far from each other, and I used to see him frequently. I'll admit that I never had any notion he'd climb to his present high position and historical fame, but even in those days you could see from the way he worked, and the way he looked at a thing from all sides before he went off half-cocked, that in whatever department of life he might choose, he would make his mark.—SINCLAIR LEWIS *The Man Who Knew Coolidge*, II.

(9) Two other people had been in the lunch room. Once George had gone out to the kitchen and made a ham-and-egg sandwich "to go" that a man wanted to take with him. Inside the kitchen he saw Al, his derby hat tipped back, sitting on a stool beside the wicket with the muzzle of a sawed-off shotgun resting on the ledge.—ERNEST HEMINGWAY *The Killers*.

(10) Euclid alone has looked on Beauty bare.
      Let all who prate of Beauty hold their peace,
      And lay them prone upon the earth and cease
      To ponder on themselves, the while they stare
      At nothing, intricately drawn nowhere

> In shapes of shifting lineage; let geese
> Gabble and hiss, but heroes seek release
> From dusty bondage into luminous air.
> > EDNA ST. VINCENT MILLAY *Euclid Alone Has*
> > *Looked on Beauty Bare.*

IRREGULAR VERBS

(Including Defective and Redundant Verbs)

Irregular verbs are those that form the past tense and past participle otherwise than by adding *ed: give, take.* (See p. 82.)

NOTE.—The irregular verbs must be learned by heart. For such learning there is no substitute; no "royal road" can evade it. They are easily learned by taking a certain number each day, until the two hundred in the list are learned.

Defective verbs are those that lack some of the principal parts: *can, shall.*

Redundant verbs are those that have more than one form for the past tense or past participle: *shrink, swell.*

The letter R. (*regular*) added to any form indicates that the regular form for that part of the verb is also used. (All verbs marked R. are *redundant.* Thus, the *regular* form *awaked* may be used as the past tense or past participle of *awake,* instead of the irregular forms given.)

Present	Past	Past Participle
abide	abode	abode
arise	arose	arisen
awake	awoke, R.	awoke, R.
be	was	been
bear (*bring forth*)	bore bare	born
bear (*carry*)	bore	borne
beat	beat	beaten beat

Present	Past	Past Participle
become	became	become
befall	befell	befallen
beget	{ begot	begotten
	begat }	begot
begin	{ began)	begun
	begun)	
behold	beheld	beheld
belay	belaid, R.	belaid, R.
bend	bent, R.	bent, R.
bereave	bereft, R.	bereft, R.
beseech	besought	besought
bet	bet, R.	bet, R.
bid (*command*)	{ bid	bid
	{ bade	bidden
bind	bound	{ bound
		{ bounden
bite	bit	{ bitten
		{ bit
bleed	bled	bled
blend	blent, R.	blent, R.
bless	blest, R.	blest, R.
blow	blew	blown
break	broke	{ broke
		{ broken
breed	bred	bred
bring	brought	brought
build	built, R.	built, R.
burn	burnt, R.	burnt, R.
burst	burst	burst
buy	bought	bought
can	could	——
cast	cast	cast
catch	caught	caught
chide	chid	chidden

Present	Past	Past Participle
choose	chose	chosen
cleave (*split*)	cleft	cleft
	clove	cloven
cling	clung	clung
clothe	clad, R.	clad, R.
come	came	come
cost	cost	cost
creep	crept	crept
crow	crew, R.	crowed
cut	cut	cut
dare	durst, R.	dared
deal	dealt	dealt
dig	dug, R.	dug, R.
do	did	done
draw	drew	drawn
dream	dreamt, R.	dreamt, R.
dress	drest, R.	drest, R.
drink	drank	drunk
		drunken
drive	drove	driven
dwell	dwelt, R.	dwelt, R.
eat	ate	eaten
engrave	engraved	engraven, R.
fall	fell	fallen
feed	fed	fed
feel	felt	felt
fight	fought	fought
find	found	found
flee	fled	fled
fling	flung	flung
fly	flew	flown
forbear	forbore	forborne
forbid	forbade	forbidden
		forbid

Present	Past	Past Participle
forget	forgot	{ forgotten { forgot
forsake	forsook	forsaken
freeze	froze	frozen
get	got	{ got { gotten
gild	gilt, R.	gilt, R.
gird	girt, R.	girt, R.
give	gave	given
go	went	gone
grave	graved	graven, R.
grind	ground	ground
grow	grew	grown
hang	hung, R.	hung, R.
have	had	had
hear	heard	heard
heave	hove, R.	hove, R.
hew	hewed	hewn, R.
hide	hid	hidden
hit	hit	hit
hold	held	{ held { holden
hurt	hurt	hurt
keep	kept	kept
kneel	knelt, R.	knelt, R.
knit	knit, R.	knit, R.
know	knew	known
lade	laded	laden, R.
lay	laid	laid
lead	led	led
lean	leant, R.	leant, R.
leap	leapt, R.	leapt, R.
learn	learnt, R.	learnt, R.
leave	left	left

Present	Past	Past Participle
lend	lent	lent
let (*permit*)	let	let
let (*hinder*)	let, R.	let, R.
lie * (*recline*)	lay	lain
light	lit, R.	lit, R.
lose	lost	lost
make	made	made
may	might	——
mean	meant	meant
meet	met	met
mow	mowed	mown, R.
must	——	——
ought	——	——
pass	past, R.	past, R.
pay	paid	paid
pen † (*enclose*)	pent, R.	pent, R.
plead	plead, R.	plead, R.
put	put	put
quit	quit, R.	quit, R.
——	quoth	——
rap ‡ (*seize*)	rapt, R.	rapt, R.
read	read	read
reave	reft, R.	reft, R.
rend	rent, R.	rent, R.
rid	rid	rid
ride	rode	ridden
ring § (*sound*)	{ rang } { rung }	rung
rise	rose	risen
rive	rived	riven, R.

* *Lie* (falsify) is regular (*lied, lied*).
† *Pen* (write) is regular (*penned, penned*).
‡ *Rap* (strike) is regular (*rapped, rapped*).
§ *Ring* (surround) is regular (*ringed, ringed*).

Present	Past	Past Participle
run	ran	run
saw	sawed	sawn, R.
say	said *	said *
see	saw	seen
seek	sought	sought
seethe	sod, R.	sodden, R.
sell	sold	sold
send	sent	sent
set	set	set
shake	shook	shaken
shall	should	——
shape	shaped	shapen, R.
shave	shaved	shaven, R.
shear	shore, R.	shorn, R.
shed	shed	shed
shine	shone, R.	shone, R.
shoe	shod	shod
shoot	shot	shot
show	showed	shown, R.
shred	shred, R.	shred, R.
shrink	shrank / shrunk	shrunk / shrunken
shut	shut	shut
sing	sang	sung
sink	sank / sunk	sunk
sit	sat	sat
slay	slew	slain
slide	slid	slid / slidden
sling	slung	slung
slink	slunk	slunk
slit	slit, R.	slit, R.

* Pronounced *sed*.

Present	Past	Past Participle
smell	smelt, R.	smelt, R.
smite	smote / smit	smitten / smit
sow	sowed	sown, R.
speak	spoke	spoken
speed	sped	sped
spell	spelt, R.	spelt, R.
spend	spent	spent
spill	spilt, R.	spilt, R.
spin	spun / span	spun
spit * (*expectorate*)	spat	spit
split	split	split
spoil	spoilt, R.	spoilt, R.
spread	spread	spread
spring	sprang / sprung	sprung
stand	stood	stood
stave	stove, R.	stove, R.
stay	staid, R.	staid, R.
steal	stole	stolen
stick	stuck	stuck
sting	stung	stung
stink	stunk / stank	stunk
strew	strewed	strewn, R.
stride	strode	stridden
strike	struck	struck / stricken
string	strung	strung
strive	strove	striven
strow	strowed	strown, R.

* *Spit* (transfix) is regular (*spitted, spitted*).

Present	Past	Past Participle
swear	swore / sware	sworn
sweat	sweat, R.	sweat, R.
sweep	swept	swept
swell	swelled	swollen, R.
swim	swam / swum	swum
swing	swung	swung
take	took	taken
teach	taught	taught
tear	tore	torn
tell	told	told
think	thought	thought
thrive	throve, R.	thriven, R.
throw	threw	thrown
thrust	thrust	thrust
tread	trod	trodden / trod
wake	woke, R.	woke, R.
wax	waxed	waxen, R.
wear	wore	worn
weave	wove, R.	woven, R.
wed	wed, R.	wed, R.
weep	wept	wept
wet	wet, R.	wet, R.
whet	whet, R.	whet, R.
will	would	——
win	won	won
wind	wound	wound
wit / wot	wist	——
work	wrought, R.	wrought, R.
wring	wrung	wrung
write	wrote	written

THE ANCIENT OR SOLEMN STYLE

Personal forms have almost disappeared from the English verb. Hence they do not repay study, and they are set forth here for reference only. In the following statement, the forms for all persons of the singular number in the "ancient or solemn" style are given in order to keep the unity of the conjugations. The plural forms involving no change are not given.

Auxiliary Verbs

HAVE

The forms of *have* in auxiliary use will be found in the full conjugation of *have* as a principal verb, below.

TENSES	**SHALL**
Present	I *shall*, thou *shalt*, he *shall*
Past	I *should*, thou *shouldst*, he *should*

WILL

Present	I *will*, thou *wilt*, he *will*
Past	I *would*, thou *wouldst*, he *would*

MAY

Present	I *may*, thou *mayst*, he *may*
Past	I *might*, thou *mightst*, he *might*

CAN

Present	I *can*, thou *canst*, he *can*
Past	I *could*, thou *couldst*, he *could*

MUST

Present	I, thou, he *must* (No change.)

DO *

INDICATIVE MOOD

Present	I *do*, thou *dost*, he *doth*
Past	I *did*, thou *didst*, he *did*

* NOTE.—*Do*, as a principal verb, has the full conjugation of an irregular verb. Only the forms in auxiliary use are above given.

SUBJUNCTIVE MOOD

Present   (If) I, thou, he *do*

IMPERATIVE MOOD

Present   *do* thou

BE

INDICATIVE MOOD

Present   I **am,** thou **art,** he **is**
Pres. Perfect   I *have,* thou *hast,* he *hath* **been**
Past   I **was,** thou **wast,** he **was**
Past Perfect   I *had,* thou *hadst,* he *had* **been**
Future:
(declarative)   I *shall,* thou *wilt,* he *will* **be**
(purposive)   I *will,* thou *shalt,* he *shall* **be**
Fut. Perfect:
(declarative)   I *shall,* thou *wilt,* he *will have* **been**
(purposive)   I *will,* thou *shalt,* he *shall have* **been**

SUBJUNCTIVE MOOD

Present   (If) I, thou, he **be**
Pres. Perfect   (If) I, thou, he *have* **been**
Past   (If) I **were,** thou **wert,** he **were**
Past Perfect   (Same as *Past Perfect Indicative.***)**

With Auxiliaries of Possibility, Wish, etc.
(Second Person only)

Present   thou *mayst, canst,* or *must* **be**
Pres. Perfect   thou *mayst, canst,* or *must have* **been**
Past   thou *mightst, couldst, wouldst,* or *shouldst* **be**
Past Perfect   thou *mightst, couldst, wouldst,* or *shouldst have* **been**

IMPERATIVE MOOD

be thou, or *do* thou **be**

The Semi-Auxiliaries

LET

TENSES	INDICATIVE MOOD
Present	I **let**, thou **lettest**, he **letteth**

SUBJUNCTIVE MOOD

Present   (If) I, thou, he **let**

IMPERATIVE MOOD

let thou, or *do* thou **let**

OUGHT

Present   I **ought**, thou **oughtest**, he **ought**

Principal Verbs

HAVE

INDICATIVE MOOD

Present	I **have**, thou **hast**, he **hath**
Pres. Perfect	I *have*, thou *hast*, he *hath* **had**
Past	I **had**, thou **hadst**, he **had**
Past Perfect	I *had*, thou *hadst*, he *had* **had**
Future:	
(declarative)	I *shall*, thou *wilt*, he *will* **have**
(purposive)	I *will*, thou *shalt*, he *shall* **have**
Fut. Perfect:	
(declarative)	I *shall*, thou *wilt*, he *will have* **had**
(purposive)	I *will*, thou *shalt*, he *shall have* **had**

SUBJUNCTIVE MOOD

Present	(If) I, thou, he **have**
Pres. Perfect	(If) I, thou, he *have* **had**
	(*Past* and *Past Perfect* same as in the *Indicative*.)

With Auxiliaries of Possibility, Wish, etc.

TENSES   (Second Person only given)

Present   thou *mayst, canst,* or *must* **have**
Pres. Perfect   thou *mayst, canst,* or *must have* **had**
Past   thou *mightst, couldst, wouldst,* or *shouldst* **have**
Past Perfect   thou *mightst, couldst, wouldst,* or *shouldst have*
                  had

IMPERATIVE MOOD

Present   **have** thou, or *do* thou **have**

LOVE

ACTIVE VOICE

INDICATIVE MOOD

TENSES

Present   I **love,** thou **lovest,** he **loveth**
Pres. Perfect   I *have,* thou *hast,* he *hath* **loved**
Past   I **loved,** thou **lovedst,** he **loved**
Past Perfect   I *had,* thou *hadst,* he *had* **loved**
Future:
(declarative)   I *shall,* thou *wilt,* he *will* **love**
(purposive)   I *will,* thou *shalt,* he *shall* **love**
Fut. Perfect:
(declarative)   I *shall,* thou *wilt,* he *will have* **loved**
(purposive)   I *will,* thou *shalt,* he *shall have* **loved**

SUBJUNCTIVE MOOD

Present   (If) I, thou, he **love**
Pres. Perfect   (If) I, thou, he *have* **loved**
                  (*Past* and *Past Perfect* same as in the *Indicative.*)

IMPERATIVE MOOD

Present   **love** thou, or *do* thou **love**

PASSIVE VOICE

The *passive voice* simply adds the past participle *loved,* to the various forms of the Ancient Style of the verb *be*. (Compare PASSIVE VOICE, pp. 114–115.)

THE ADVERB

An **adverb** is a word used to modify a verb, an adjective, an adverb, or in some cases a noun or pronoun: The birds sing *sweetly*. The error was *instantly* manifest. He spoke *very* hastily. *Not* a drum was heard.

Adverbs Modifying Nouns or Pronouns.—A few adverbs are used to modify nouns or pronouns:

almost	entirely	merely
also	especially	never
altogether	hardly	not
chiefly	likewise	only
particularly	partly	scarcely
simply	solely	too

EXAMPLE.—*Almost* everything was saved. Here *almost* can not modify the verb, for to say, "Everything was *almost* saved" would imply that *everything* was lost.

> *Not* enjoyment and *not* sorrow
> Is our destined end or way.
> > LONGFELLOW *Psalm of Life.*

> Give crowns and pounds and guineas
> But *not* your heart away.
> > A. E. HOUSMAN *When I Was One and Twenty.*

Who will do this work? *Not* I.

This use of *not* is very frequent, both in approved literature and in common speech.

REMARKS

(1) The adverb is to the verb what the adjective is to the noun, having a limiting or descriptive effect.

135

With noun and adjective: That is a *fast* run.

With verb and adverb: He runs *fast.*

The adverb produces a similar effect upon an adjective or another adverb.

(2) An adverb is equivalent to a prepositional phrase with nouns such as *manner, place, time,* and *degree:*

Adverb	Prepositional Phrase
sharply	in a sharp manner
formerly	at a former time
highly	to a high degree
presently	at the present time

(3) If a prepositional phrase can not be substituted for an adverb, an adjective should be used, and not an adverb: He seemed *angry.* He spoke *angrily.* (He spoke *in an angry manner.*) (See ADJECTIVE OR ADVERB, Part II, pp. 213–214.)

CLASSES OF ADVERBS

According to their meaning, adverbs are divided into six classes: Adverbs of

1. Place: *here, there, where.*
2. Time: *now, then, when.*
3. Manner: *how, well, ill, otherwise.*
4. Cause: *therefore, wherefore, why.*
5. Number: *first,* secondly, thirdly,* etc.
6. Degree: *less, more, too,* etc.

SPECIAL GROUPS

Other divisions may be made which may include some of the adverbs already named. Thus:

Interrogative Adverbs, used in asking questions. These include such words as *how, when, whence, where, whither, why.*

* NOTE.—See FIRST AND FIRSTLY, p. 139.

They may be used either in (*a*) direct questions: *Why* did he sell it? or in (*b*) indirect questions: I do not know *why* he sold it.

Affirmative and Negative Adverbs.—*Yes* is called an affirmative adverb, and *no* and *not* are called negative adverbs.

Relative or Conjunctive Adverbs.—Besides their use in denoting place, manner, time, or the like, these adverbs serve also to join a subordinate clause to a principal clause (See the COMPLEX SENTENCE, Part II, pp. 229–230): I saw him *when* he came. Here *when* is an adverb of time modifying *came;* but it also *relates* to the preceding clause *I saw him,* to which it conjoins its own clause.

Among the chief conjunctive or relative adverbs are the following:

as	thence	wherever
how	when	whither
now	whence	where
since	whenever	why
so		

Some of these adverbs have the full effect of conjunctions and closely resemble them. Some other relative adverbs have the conjunctive effect: *after, before, till, until,* etc.

Adverbs in Ly.—The most common ending of English adverbs is *ly,* a suffix originally meaning *like.* An adverb may be formed from almost any adjective in the language by adding the suffix *ly:* * *badly, quickly, promptly,* etc. (For the few exceptions, see SPECIAL USES, SUGGESTIONS, AND CAUTIONS, pp. 138–139; also, FORMS THAT MAY MISLEAD, p. 139.)

---

* NOTE.—Adjectives ending in *y* change the *y* to *i* before adding *ly: ready, readily,* etc. *Due* and *true* omit final *e* before *ly,* forming *duly* and *truly.* Adjectives in *ll* drop the final *l* before adding *ly: full, fully.*

COMPARISON OF ADVERBS

Adverbs, like adjectives, admit of comparison. However, a smaller number of adverbs can be compared, and these are more commonly compared by *more* and *most,* or *less* and *least: wisely, more* wisely, *most* wisely; *keenly, less* keenly, *least* keenly.

Comparisons by *Er* and *Est*.—A few adverbs are compared by adding *er* and *est,* chiefly those that have the same form as the corresponding adjectives:

early	earlier	earliest
hard	harder	hardest
fast	faster	fastest
long	longer	longest
quick	quicker	quickest
soon	sooner	soonest

Irregular Comparison.—Adverbs compared irregularly are the following:

badly / ill	worse	worst
far	farther / further	farthest / furthest
fore	former	foremost / first
late	later	latest / last
little	less	least
much	more	most
near	nearer	nearest / next
well	better	best

SPECIAL USES, SUGGESTIONS, AND CAUTIONS

Adverbs Identical in Form with Adjectives.—The words *deep, early, hard, long, loud, quick,* and some others are sometimes used as adjectives, and sometimes as adverbs; consequently their comparatives and superlatives may also be used in this double relation. Thus we may say:

Adjective	Adverb
a *deep* well	drink *deep*
an *earlier* hour	come *earlier*
a *louder* noise	read *louder*
a *longer* journey	stay *longer*

From the adjective *hard* is formed the adverb *hardly,* which differs in meaning from the adverb *hard,* having the meaning of *scarcely.* The sentence, "He was *hard* pressed," would be changed in meaning if it read, "He was *hardly* pressed."

Like and Near.—These adverbs (as well as the corresponding adjectives) have often the appearance of prepositions.

Like Never a Conjunction.—Such expressions as, "He looks *like I do,*" are erroneous. (See THE CONJUNCTION, pp. 152–155.)

First and Firstly.—*First* is an adverb as well as an adjective. We may say, the *first* man; or, he spoke *first.* Hence, in enumerations, it is correct to say, *first, secondly,* etc. An adverb, *firstly,* has been formed from *first* and is used by many persons; but *first*—without the *ly*—is in preferred use.

Forms That May Mislead.—Not all words ending in *ly* are adverbs; some adjectives have this termination: *cleanly, goodly, homely, lovely, kindly, manly, timely, untimely.* Because such adjectives usually have no corresponding adverbs, the adverbial meaning can only be expressed by an adverbial phrase: in a *lovely* way. *Kindly,* however, is also an adverb, so that we may say, "He has a *kindly* face" (adj.), or, "He spoke *kindly*" (adv.). *Good* does not form *goodly* as its adverb, but uses instead the adverb *well. Goodly* is an adjective, and not an adverb: a *goodly* number.

ERROR.—Care must be taken never to use an adverb in *ly* as an adjective. Do not say, "The rose smells *sweetly*," but "The rose smells *sweet*." Say "I feel *bad*" (not *badly*). However, "I feel *badly*" is now so widely used that it may soon be accepted without question.

Comparatives with The.—*The* preceding a comparative in such expressions as *"the* more," *"the* less;" *"the* sooner, *the* better," is not the definite article but an adverb, signifying "by that," "by as much," "by so much," or the like. The phrase "the sooner *the* better" thus signifies *"by as much as (it is)* sooner, *by so much* (it will be) better."

Adverbs Following Prepositions.—In various phrases, adverbs seem to be used as objects of prepositions: *at once, on high.* (See PREPOSITIONAL PHRASES, pp. 149–150.)

Prepositional Adverbs.—Many prepositional forms without an object are used in connection with various verbs and are then considered adverbs: to look *down,* to stand *up.*

Adverbs as Independent Elements.—Various adverbs are used, often elliptically, as independent elements: *Away!* (equivalent to "go away"): *Up! Forward!* Here the adverb has the force of an interjection.

Similar are the uses of *why, well, now,* etc., at the beginning of a sentence without any direct connection with other words: *Why,* how did you come here? *Well,* that is a surprise. *Now,* who is there?

Yes and No.—These words, used in answer to questions, are independent elements, each being equivalent to a whole sentence: Will you go? *Yes* (equivalent to "I will go"). Is he here? *No* (equivalent to "He is not here").

Position of Adverbs.—The chief rule is that an adverb should be placed as near as possible to the word it is intended to modify. One must be careful not to place the adverb where it may seem to modify a word not intended, or where it may be doubtful which of two words it modifies. For example:

The French *nearly* lost five thousand men. This sentence implies that the French actually saved the whole five thousand after "nearly" losing them. What the writer meant was, "The French lost *nearly* five thousand men," i.e., they actually *lost* almost that number of men.

The adverb *only* modifies either the word or phrase immediately following or immediately preceding it. Hence great care should be taken to place the word *only* so that its reference may not be false or doubtful. For example:

The light, sandy soil *only* favors the fern.

Here *only* would seem to modify favors, and so understood, the statement would not be true, since "the light, sandy soil" *favors* many other things, as the pine tree, for instance. The meaning is that no other soil than "The light, sandy soil" is suitable for the fern. Hence the sentence should be, *"Only* the light, sandy soil favors the fern."

Uses of Only.—*Only* belongs to three parts of speech, being (1) an *adjective* when it modifies a noun or pronoun; (2) an *adverb,* when it modifies a verb, adjective, or adverb; and (3) a *conjunction,* when it connects phrases or clauses. These uses should be carefully distinguished.

There as an Introductory Word.—See Part II, p. 87.

No and Not.—*No* is not used in direct connection with a verb; we do not say "He will *no* come," but "He will *not* come." But *no* is sometimes used as an alternative after *whether:* Send me an answer *whether* or *no.*

The Double Negative.—In English two negatives in the same construction cancel each other and equal an affirmative. The assertion "There was *no* member who was *not* present," is equivalent to "Every member was present." If the two negatives cannot fitly cancel each other, the double use is an error, and one negative or the other should be changed: "I won't *never* go" should be "I *won't* (will *not*) *ever* go," or, "I will *never* go."

EXERCISE

Point out all the adverbs in the following extracts and explain what words they modify or how they are used.

(1)   The first thing naturally when one enters a scholar's study or library is to look at his books. One gets a notion very speedily of his tastes and the range of his pursuits by a glance round his book-shelves.—O. W. HOLMES *The Poet at the Breakfast Table, viii.*

(2)   Music is well said to be the speech of angels.
                                    CARLYLE *Essays,* "The Opera."

(3)   Dip down upon the northern shore,
                    O sweet new year, delaying long;
                 Thou doest expectant nature wrong.
             Delaying long; delay no more.
                                    TENNYSON *In Memoriam.*

(4)   "The great art of riding," the Knight suddenly began in a loud voice, waving his right arm as he spoke, "is to keep——" Here the sentence ended as suddenly as it had begun, as the Knight fell heavily on the top of his head exactly in the path where Alice was walking.—LEWIS CARROLL *Through the Looking-Glass,* ch. 8.

(5)   Here was the sound of water falling only,
             Which is not sound but silence musical
             Tumbling forever down the gorge's wall.
                                    ROBERT PENN WARREN *The Owl.*

(6)   Fair fall all chances
             The heart can long for—and let all women and men Drink deep while they can their happiness. It goes Fast and never comes again.
                        MAXWELL ANDERSON *Mary of Scotland,* act ii, sc. 3.

(7)   Any group of people necessarily represents an approach to a common denominator, and it is probably true that even

individually they tend to conform somewhat to the general pattern. Many have pointed out—I among them—the danger of engulfing our original thinkers in a tide of mediocrity. —CRAWFORD H. GREENWALT *The Culture of the Businessman.*

(8)   But no, he would not give in. Turning sharply, he walked towards the city's gold phosphorescence. His fists were shut, his mouth set fast. He would not take that direction, to the darkness, to follow her. He walked towards the faintly humming, glowing town, quickly.—D. H. LAWRENCE *Sons and Lovers.*

(9)   His soul had arisen from the grave of boyhood, spurning her graveclothes. Yes! Yes! Yes! He would create proudly out of the freedom and power of his soul, as the great artificer whose name he bore, a living thing, new and soaring and beautiful, impalpable, imperishable.—JAMES JOYCE *A Portrait of the Artist As a Young Man.* ch. iv.

(10)   It was falling, too, upon every part of the lonely churchyard on the hill where Michael Fury lay buried. It lay thickly drifted on the crooked crosses and headstones, on the spears of the little gate, on the barren thorns. His soul swooned slowly as he heard the snow falling faintly through the universe and faintly falling, like the descent of their last end, upon all the living and the dead.—JAMES JOYCE *Dubliners,* "The Dead."

THE PREPOSITION

A **preposition** is a word that shows the relation between some word called its *object* and some other word which is its *antecedent:*

	Antecedent	Preposition	Object
I	went	*to*	New York.

A *preposition* is a relation-word; it belongs to the class of words called connectives. The chief relations denoted by prepositions are those of source, destination, direction, situation, position, cause, instrument, agency, etc.

The *antecedent* of a preposition may be a noun, pronoun, adjective, verb, adverb, or an entire phrase:

There is the steamer *for* Liverpool. [Antecedent *steamer*]

Some *of* the pupils were late. [Antecedent *some*]

That is good *for* nothing. [Antecedent *good*]

Run *to* your base. [Antecedent *run*]

He came exactly *at* the moment. [Antecedent *exactly*]

The *object* of a preposition is ordinarily a noun or pronoun: Start for *school*. Give the book to *him*. Instead of a noun or pronoun, however, a preposition may be followed by:

1. A verb, thus forming the regular infinitive: *to go, to be,* etc.

2. An adjective: from *bad* to *worse*.

3. An adverb: at *once,* from *above*.

4. A phrase: There is happiness in *doing right*.

144

POSITION OF THE PREPOSITION

The word *preposition* is derived from the Latin *pre*, before, and *pono*, place. The *preposition* was originally so called because in Latin it was always *placed before* its object. In English the preposition ordinarily precedes its object, but may at times appropriately, and very forcibly, follow its object, even when the preposition thus ends a clause or sentence, as the following example shows:

> The soil out of which such men as he are made is good to be born *on*, good to live *on*, good to die *for* and to be buried *in*. —LOWELL *Among My Books, Second Series,* "Garfield."

When used with the relative pronoun *that*, the preposition *must* follow its object: This is the book *that* I came *for*. In the English language the object of a preposition is the word that *follows it in thought*, not necessarily in position.

RULE.—A noun or pronoun which is the object of a preposition is always in the objective case.

With nouns this rule is of great importance for sentence construction. (See THE OBJECTIVE CASE, under NOUN, PART I, p. 20.) With pronouns that are declined the rule directly affects the form of the word. We must say: from *me;* to *him;* of *us;* to *them;* with *whom*.

CAUTIONS.—When a pronoun is separated by intervening words from the preposition which governs it, care should be taken that it be in the proper objective form; thus: *Whom* does John Donne say the bell tolls for?

(1) We say correctly, *"Whom* was that made *for?"* or *"For whom* was that made?" Such expressions as *"Who* are you looking *for"* have a certain colloquial use, and some authors would allow them as correct, but they are not in the most approved use.

(2) Do not say "for you and I." After the preposition *for* all

pronouns must be in the objective case: for *you* and *me*. The phrase "you and I" is correctly used in the nominative: *You and I* will wait for him. But if "you and I" is used after a preposition, both pronouns must be objective: He will wait for *you and me*. A good test is to apply the preposition directly to each pronoun and see if it fits. "For *you*" is correct, but "for" *I* is obviously wrong. Hence the expression must be "for *you* and *me*."

PREPOSITIONS LISTED AND DISCRIMINATED

The principal English prepositions are the following:

aboard	by	pending
about	concerning	per
above	considering	regarding
across	down	respecting
after	during	save
against	ere	saving
along	except	since
amid(st)	excepting	through
among(st)	for	throughout
around	from	till
aslant	in	to
at	inside	touching
athwart	into	toward(s)
barring	mid	under
before	midst	underneath
behind	notwithstanding	until
below	of	unto
beneath	off	up
beside(s)	on	upon
between	out	via
betwixt	outside	with
beyond	over	within
but	past	without

It is important to remember that most prepositions have more than one meaning, and some have many. False distinctions have been often made by treating one meaning of a preposition as if it were the only meaning. A few distinctions may here be noted, as follows:

Among—Between.—*Between* is used in speaking of two persons or things; *among* in speaking of more than two: Divide the money *between* the two, or, *among* the three.

By—With.—*By* denotes ordinarily the active agent; *with* denotes the instrument: The snow was cleared away *by* workmen *with* shovels. The metal was corroded *by* the acid. *By*, however, is the preferred preposition after *surround:* The city is surrounded *by* mountains. We say infested *with;* disturbed *by*.

During may mean throughout a certain period, as in the phrase "imprisonment *during* life," but "imprisonment *for* life" is often preferred. Or *during* may denote some time or times within the period named: I awoke repeatedly *during* the night. The amount will be paid *during* (within) the coming week.

From—With.—The idioms *differ from* and *different from* are used to distinguish one thing or person from another: An apple *differs from* a pear. John is *different from* his brother. The idiom *differ with* is used of opinion: I differ *with you* about the worth of that painting.

In—Under.—Shall we say *in,* or *under,* the circumstances? *In* if we mean "surrounded by"; *under,* if we mean "influenced or controlled by." *Under* has the meaning of "subject to"; thus, "*under* my signature" means "subject to and authenticated by, my signature," even though my name may be the last thing on the paper.

Of—Off.—*Of* denotes origin, possession, inclusion, material, etc.: He comes *of* a noble family. The tower *of* London; the palace *of* the King; one *of* the number; made *of* brass. *Off* distinctly denotes removal: Keep *off* the grass.

ERROR.—In some localities *off* is incorrectly used for *of. Of* denotes a source of supply; *off* denotes removal from direct contact. We buy sugar *of* the grocer; we pick apples *off* the tree.

With—Against.—*With* ordinarily denotes association or union, but is also used in phrases indicating conflict, opposition, struggle, etc., as the equivalent of *against:* to fight *with;* dispute *with;* have a feud or quarrel *with.* "To fight *with*" is also used as meaning "to fight in conjunction *with*—on the side of": Hannibal fought *with* his father in Spain. Where any confusion of meaning might thus arise, some explanatory word or words should be added.

With—From.—In phrases denoting separation, *with* has nearly, but not quite, the meaning of *from:* to part *with* a keepsake; to dispense *with* a service.

Phrase-Prepositions.—Certain phrases have all the effect of compound prepositions. Among such phrases are the following:

according to	in spite of	in consequence of
on account of	by means of	with reference to
because of	with regard to	in reference to
with *or* in respect to	in regard to	as to

Participial Prepositions.—Many participles are used with the force of prepositions: I spoke with him *concerning* this. Among such participles are:

barring	excepting	regarding
bating	notwithstanding	respecting
concerning	past	saving
considering	pending	touching
during		

Concerning may be exactly rendered by *about,* but is not coextensive with it. *Considering* is commonly used in a depreciatory sense, implying allowance for or deduction of the things considered: He did well *considering* his age.

Associated Prepositions.—Prepositions are sometimes combined to denote various phases of some relation: The wave slipped *from under the brig*. In this sentence the wave did not slip *from* the brig nor *under* the brig, but *from under*. Such a combination is often called a *complex preposition*.

Prepositions Used as Adverbs.—A preposition is often used without an object with the force of an adverb: to look *on;* to look *up;* to sink *down;* to stand *by*.

Inseparable Prepositions.—A preposition may be so closely connected with a certain verb that the expression has all the force of a compound. There are many such combinations: to laugh *at;* to look *into, on, upon, over, through,* or *up;* to attend *to:* We laughed *at* him. I will attend *to* the matter. When followed by one of these prepositions, an intransitive verb may be used in the passive voice: We *were laughed at* by him. The matter *was attended to* by me.

PREPOSITIONAL PHRASES

A prepositional phrase is composed of a preposition and its object together with any words modifying the object. A prepositional phrase may be used as:

1. A *noun,* the subject of a verb, etc.: *For us to retreat* is impossible.

2. An *adjective,* modifying a noun: The caves *of Kentucky* are wonderful.

3. An *adverb,* modifying a verb, an adjective, or another adverb: The river RISES *in the mountains*. The river is CLEAR *in the mountains*. He acted INCONSISTENTLY *with his professions*.

In analyzing sentences it is best to treat the *prepositional phrase as a whole,* as one element of the sentence. Then the phrase can at pleasure be separated into its component parts, and each treated separately.

A prepositional phrase containing an infinitive may be also called an *infinitive phrase* (pp. 184–185), or if containing a participle, a *participial phrase* (pp. 92–93; 213).

EXERCISE

Find all the prepositions in the following extracts, and tell the object and the antecedent of each.

(1)   From Cairo to Teheran, we flew above trade routes and over cities which are as old as anything in our civilization and which have kept the variety and the contrasts of thousands of years of history.—WENDELL WILLKIE *One World,* ch. 2.

(2)   Where the thousands upon thousands of bad sailors that swarm in every ship hide themselves when they are on land is a mystery.—JEROME K. JEROME *Three Men in a Boat.*

(3)   It is the season now to go
        About the country high and low,
        Among the lilacs hand in hand,
        And two by two in fairyland.
                    ROBERT LOUIS STEVENSON *Underwoods,*
                            "It Is the Season Now to Go."

(4)   No man can thoroughly participate in any culture unless he has been brought up and has lived according to its forms, but he can grant to other cultures the same significance to their participants which he recognizes in his own.—RUTH BENEDICT *Patterns of Culture,* ch. 2.

(5)   Write it on your heart that every day is the best day in the year. No man has learned anything rightly, until he knows that every day is Doomsday.—EMERSON *Society and Solitude,* "Work and Days."

(6)   All of the animals excepting man know that the principal business of life is to enjoy it.—SAMUEL BUTLER THE YOUNGER *Notebooks.*

(7)   The manly part is to do with might and main what you can do.—EMERSON *The Conduct of Life.*

(8)   If you look at it from the days of Chaucer, you will see that what you might call the "internal history" of a country

always affects its use of writing. It makes a difference in the expression, in the vocabulary, even in the handling of grammar.—GERTRUDE STEIN *How Writing Is Written.*

(9)   Though I lived and worked in the Third Reich during the first half of its brief life, watching at first hand Adolf Hitler consolidate his power as dictator of this great but baffling nation and then lead it off to war and conquest, this personal experience would not have led me to attempt to write this book, had there not occurred at the end of World War II an event unique in history.—WILLIAM L. SHIRER *The Rise and Fall of the Third Reich,* "Foreword."

(10)   When in the Course of human events it becomes necessary for one people to dissolve the political bands which have connected them with another, and to assume among the powers of the earth, the separate and equal station to which the Laws of Nature and of Nature's God entitle them, a decent respect of the opinions of mankind requires that they should declare the causes which impel them to separation.—*The Declaration of Independence.*

(11)   . . . that we here highly resolve that these dead shall not have died in vain, that this nation under God shall have a new birth of freedom, and that government of the people, by the people, for the people shall not perish from the earth. —ABRAHAM LINCOLN *Gettysburg Address.*

(12)   We the people of the United States, in Order to form a more perfect Union, establish Justice, insure domestic Tranquility, provide for the common defence, promote the general Welfare, and secure the Blessings of Liberty to ourselves and our Posterity, do ordain and establish this Constitution for the United States of America.—*Preamble* TO *The Constitution of the United States of America.*

THE CONJUNCTION

A **conjunction** is a part of speech that connects words, phrases, clauses, or sentences; or that shows relation between sentences.

LIST OF CONJUNCTIONS

The principal conjunctions are the following:

also	nor	unless
although	notwithstanding	what
and	only	when
as	or	whereas
because	provided	whereat
both	save	whereby
but	seeing	wherefore
either	since	wherein
except	so	whereof
for	still	whereupon
however	than	wherever
if	that	whether
lest	then	while
neither	therefore	without
nevertheless	though	yet

(See also the list of CORRELATIVE CONJUNCTIONS, p. 154.)

CLASSES OF CONJUNCTIONS

There are two principal classes of conjunctions: *coordinate* and *subordinate*.

1. **Coordinate Conjunctions.**—A coordinate conjunction is a conjunction that joins two coordinate elements, that is, elements

of equal order or rank, as two nouns, two verbs, two phrases, or two clauses, neither of which is dependent on the other (see THE COMPOUND SENTENCE, Part II, pp. 226–228).

Coordinate conjunctions may be subdivided into *copulative* and *disjunctive* conjunctions.

A *copulative conjunction* is one that denotes addition: *also, and, moreover*.

A *disjunctive conjunction* is one that denotes separation: *but, either, else, however, nevertheless, or, nor, notwithstanding, save, yet*.

2. Subordinate Conjunctions.—A subordinate conjunction is one that joins a subordinate element to the principal element of the sentence: John said *that* he would go. The divisions of subordinate conjunctions are those denoting the following relations:

(1) Time: *since, until, as long as, as soon as*, etc.

(2) Reason, cause or concession: *as, because, for, since*, etc.

(3) Contingency or supposition: *if, though, unless, provided*, etc.

(4) Purpose or result: *lest, that, in order that, so that*.

(5) Comparison: *than*, following adjectives or adverbs in the comparative degree, and also following *else, other, otherwise*, and *rather*. See p. 71; Part II, p. 230.

The independent clauses of compound sentences are joined by coordinate conjunctions (see p. 152); the subordinate clauses of complex sentences are joined to principal clauses by subordinate conjunctions (see PART II, pp. 229–230).

CAUTION 1.—It must be remembered that *lest* means "that not," and we must avoid supplying an unnecessary *not*, which would reverse the meaning. To say, "A young man must take heed *lest* he be *not* ensnared in temptation," would imply that it is desirable that he should be "ensnared." Omit the *not*.

CAUTION 2.—*Like* should not be used as a conjunction; it should not be followed by a subject and verb. *Like* is a preposition; it should be followed by a noun or pronoun in the objective case.

> Act *like him* [not *like he does*].
>
> He looks *like me* [not *like I do*].
>
> He struts *as if he were a general* [not *like he was a general*].
>
> He sings *like Caruso* [not *like Caruso did*].

A headline in a leading New York paper read, "City's New Flag Will Be *Like* Hudson Used." But the reporter who wrote the article had correctly said, "New York will have a new flag which will be *the same as* the banner," etc.

CORRELATIVE CONJUNCTIONS

Correlative conjunctions are those used in pairs. Correlatives are often used in clauses that succeed each other in the same sentence, neither of which makes complete sense without the other.

Correlative conjunctions are:

although—yet	if—then	so—as
as—as	neither—nor	though—yet
as—so	not only—but also	whereas—therefore
both—and	now—now	whether—or
either—or	now—then	

> *Either* he *or* I must do the work.
>
> *Neither* he *nor* I can do the work.
>
> Milton was *not only* a poet, *but also* a man of affairs.
>
> *Both* William *and* Henry will be present.
>
> He does not care *whether* he goes *or* stays.

Or or Nor After Not.—The conjunction *neither* must take *nor* as its correlative: *Neither* France *nor* Italy will yield. The adverbial *not* may take *or* or *nor,* depending on the sense. The correlatives *not . . . or* imply merely not one and not the other: He will *not* come *or* send an agent. But *not . . . nor* is more emphatically negative, suggesting the sense of not one and not *even* the other. He will *not* come *nor* send an agent.

EXERCISE

Find all the conjunctions in the following extracts, and tell what words, phrases, or clauses, they connect.

(1) If there was ever a just war since the world began, it is this in which America is now engaged.—THOMAS PAINE *The Crisis.*

(2) They spoke to the fugitive in my heart as if it were leaves to leaf;
They tapped at my eyelids and touched my lips with an invitation to grief.
But it was no reason I had to go because they had to go.
ROBERT FROST *A Leaf-Treader.*

(3) Character is higher than intellect. . . . A great soul will be strong to live, as well as to think.—EMERSON *The American Scholar.*

(4) No race can prosper till it learns that there is as much dignity in tilling a field as in writing a poem.—BOOKER T. WASHINGTON *Up from Slavery.*

(5) Either the well was very deep, or she fell very slowly, for she had plenty of time as she went down to look about her, and to wonder what was going to happen next.—LEWIS CARROLL *Alice's Adventures in Wonderland,* ch. 1.

(6) The severity of the frost was so extraordinary that a kind of petrifaction sometimes ensued; and it was commonly supposed that the great increase of rocks in some parts of Derbyshire was due to no eruption, for there was none, but to the solidification of unfortunate wayfarers who had been turned literally to stone where they stood.—VIRGINIA WOOLF *Orlando,* ch. 1.

(7)   He who has nothing to assert has no style and can have
none: he who has something to assert will go as far in power
of style as its momentousness and his conviction will carry
him.—G. B. Shaw *Man and Superman*. Epistle Dedicatory.

(8)   I tell you this because I remember you when you were small,
And because I remember all your infant boasts and lies,
And the way you smiled, and how you ran and climbed,
        as no one else quite did, and how you fell and were
        bruised,
And because there is no other person, anywhere on earth,
        who remembers these things as clearly as I do now.
                Kenneth Fearing *Any Man's Advice to His Son*.

(9)   When Doris danced under the oak tree
        The sun himself might wish to see,
        Might bend beneath those lovers, leaves,
        While her her virgin step she weaves
        And envious cast his famous hue
        To make her daft, yet win her too.
                Richard Eberhart *When Doris Danced*.

(10)   If intellect is in some way an expression of sexual appe-
tite, then man is not simply driven, but may gain power over
impulse by directing it.—Jacques Barzun *Intellect and Sex*.

(11)   If things are allowed to drift, it is obvious that the bicker-
ing between Russia and the Western democracies will con-
tinue until Russia has a considerable store of atomic bombs,
and that when that time comes there will be an atomic war.
—Bertrand Russell *The Future of Mankind*.

(12)   What chiefly distinguishes the daily press of the United
States from the press of all other countries pretending to
culture is not its lack of truthfulness or even its lack of
dignity and honor, but its incurable fear of ideas, its constant
effort to evade the discussion of fundamentals by translating
all issues into a few elementary fears, its incessant reduction
of all reflection to mere emotion.—H. L. Mencken *American Culture*.

THE INTERJECTION

An **interjection** is a word used, independently of all grammatical relation, to express strong feeling or to awaken attention or interest: *Ah! Hallo! Ho! Alas!* (See INDEPENDENT ELEMENTS, Part II, pp. 223–224.)

Various parts of speech may be used as exclamations to express surprise or sudden emotion or intense feeling of any kind. They have the force of interjections and are called exclamatory nouns or adjectives, etc.: *What! Never! Good! Heavens! Mercy!*

O and Oh.—The distinction between *O* and *oh* is not now closely observed. The former is the sign of address or wishing and should always be written as a single capital letter: "O pride of Greece! Ulysses stay!" The latter, *oh,* expresses sorrow, pain, surprise, hope, or longing and may begin with a capital or a small letter, according to its position:

> Oh, think not I am faithful to a vow!
> EDNA ST. VINCENT MILLAY

EXERCISE

Find all the interjections in the following extracts.

(1)   Alas! Can I never have peace in the shining instant?— CONRAD AIKEN *At A Concert of Music.*

(2)   If it prove a mind of uncommon activity and power, a Locke, a Lavoisier, a Hutton, a Bentham, a Fourier, it imposes its classification on other men, and lo! a new system. —EMERSON *Self-Reliance.*

(3)   Ah! what a sound will rise, how wild and dreary,
When the death-angel touches those swift keys!
LONGFELLOW *The Arsenal at Springfield.*

(4)   If a man was tossed out of a window when an infant, and so made a cripple for life, or scared out of wits by Indians, it is regretted chiefly because he was thus incapacitated for —business! I think that there is nothing, not even crime, more opposed to poetry, to philosophy, ay, to life itself, than this incessant business.—THOREAU *Life Without Principle.*

(5)   O brown halo in the sky near the moon, drooping upon the
         sea!
      O troubled reflection in the sea!
      O throat! O throbbing throat!
      And I singing uselessly, uselessly all the night.
           WHITMAN *Out of the Cradle Endlessly Rocking.*

(6)   Alas! we have been long led away by ancient prejudices and made large sacrifices to superstition.—PAINE *Thoughts on the Present State of American Affairs.*

(7)   O Captain! my Captain! rise up and hear the bells;
      Rise up—for you the flag is flung—for you the bugle trills,
      For you bouquets and ribbon'd wreaths—for you the shores
         a-crowding,
      For you they call, the swaying mass, their eager faces
             turning;
             Hear Captain! dear father!
             This arm beneath your head!
               It is some dream that on the deck,
                 You've fallen cold and dead.
                   WHITMAN *O Captain! My Captain!*

(8)   To live, to err, to fall, to triumph, to recreate life out of life! A wild angel had appeared to him, the angel of mortal youth and beauty, an envoy from the fair courts of life, to throw open before him in an instant of ecstasy the gates of all the ways of error and glory. On and on and on and on! —JAMES JOYCE *A Portrait of the Artist As a Young Man,* ch. iv.

(9)   Oh, come! Confidence for confidence. First tell me what you used to say to the ladies.—G. B. SHAW *Man and Superman,* act iii.

(10)   Hark! the numbers soft and clear,
             Gently steal upon the ear.
                   POPE *Ode on St. Cecilia's Day.*

Part II
THE SENTENCE

THE SENTENCE

A **sentence** is a combination of words so connected as to express a complete thought: Man is mortal. Is man mortal? How mortal man is!

It is by expressing a complete thought that the sentence differs from its subordinate parts, the phrase and the clause. The *phrase* merely indicates a thought which it does not completely express: Man *being* mortal. (See PHRASES, p. 167.) The *clause* expresses only part of a thought: *Because* man is mortal. (See CLAUSES, p. 166.) Since neither the phrase nor the clause is complete, it leaves the mind in suspense. We ask, "Well, what then?" and wait for some conclusion. But the sentence, "Man is mortal," is complete. All is said, and the mind rests.

Subject and Predicate

The sentence is composed of two parts: the *subject* and the *predicate*.

The **subject** is the part of the sentence about which an assertion is made by the use of a finite verb: *The Romans* conquered Britain.

The **predicate** is the part of the sentence that makes an assertion about the subject by using a finite verb: The Romans *conquered Britain*.

REMARKS.—See PART I, p. 87. The *finite verb* is essential to the sentence. It is the finite verb that really completes the sentence, binding it together as the keystone binds the arch. Neither the infinitive nor the participle can complete a sentence. "The man *being* good" (present participle) is not a sentence. "The man *to be* good" (infinitive) is not a sentence. But "The man *is* good" (finite verb) is a sentence. There can be no predicate and no complete assertion without a finite verb.

For complete predication, however, the finite verb must be used in a simple sentence or an independent clause. A *dependent clause* contains a finite verb, but is not complete: If the man *is* good. Despite the finite verb *is,* this statement is incomplete because of the subordinating conjunction *if.* "If the man is good," we ask, "what then?" For a complete thought we must have a simple sentence with a finite verb: The man is good. Or the dependent clause with a finite verb must be related to an independent clause that completes the thought: If the man is good, *he will be rewarded.* (For full explanation of the terms used above, see THE SIMPLE SENTENCE, pp. 167–170 and THE COMPLEX SENTENCE, p. 228.)

CLASSES OF SENTENCES

Sentences are divided along two different lines according to their *manner of expressing thought* and their *structure.*

A. As to their *manner of expressing thought,* sentences are divided into four classes:

1. **Declarative.**—A declarative sentence affirms that something is or is not a fact or a possibility: The sun shines. The earth moves. The sun has not set.

2. **Interrogative.**—An interrogative sentence asks whether something is or is not a fact: Is this your home? Is not that reasonable?

3. **Imperative.**—An imperative sentence commands or forbids something: Listen to me. Do not neglect your lessons.

4. **Exclamatory.**—An exclamatory sentence expresses a thought as an exclamation, either with or without an interjection: Oh, give me my lowly thatched cottage again! How brightly the sun shines!

REMARKS.—The first of these *exclamatory* sentences is also *imperative*—"give me, etc." The second is *declarative* as well as *exclamatory*—"the sun shines." But the command or the declaration is uttered as an exclamation and therefore such sentences are preferably called *exclamatory*.

The exclamation point does not make the exclamatory sentence, but merely indicates its essential character. It is a blemish of style to use an exclamation point with an imperative sentence or with any other kind of sentence which is *not* exclamatory.

EXERCISE

Tell which of the following sentences are declarative, interrogative, imperative, or exclamatory; tell which are also negative.

(1)   Endurance is the crowning quality,
        And patience all the passion of great hearts.
                              LOWELL *Columbus,* l. 237.

(2)   Swiftly walk over the western wave,
            Spirit of Night!
                              SHELLEY *To Night.*

(3)   There is no knowledge that is not power.
            EMERSON *Society and Solitude,* "Old Age."

(4)   Parliament is not a congress of ambassadors from different and hostile interests; which interests each must maintain, as an agent and advocate, against other agents and advocates. . . . —EDMUND BURKE *To The Electors of Bristol, 1774.*

(5)   And, all this, from the apparently insignificant affair of shaving! How many a piece of important business has failed from a short delay! And how many thousand of such delays daily proceed from this unworthy cause!—WILLIAM COBBETT *Advice to Young Men.*

(6)   The Germans, like the Welsh, can sing perfectly serious songs perfectly seriously in chorus: can with clear eyes and clear voices join together in words of innocent and beautiful personal passion, for a false maiden or a dead child.—G. K. CHESTERTON *The Victorian Compromise.*

(7)   How much better, I say, is it for the active and thoughtful intellect, where such is to be found, to eschew the College and the University altogether, than to submit to a drudgery so ignoble, a mockery so contumelious!—NEWMAN *Liberal Knowledge Viewed in Relation to Learning.*

(8)   What is it the birds sing among the trees in pairing time? What means the sound of the rain falling far and wide upon the leafy forest? To what tune does the fisherman whistle, as he hauls in his net at morning, and the bright fish are heaped inside the boat?—ROBERT LOUIS STEVENSON *Pan's Pipes.*

(9)   Whenever in your reading you come across one of these words, *case, instance, character, nature, condition, persuasion, degree,* whenever in writing your pen betrays you to one or another of them—pull yourself up and take thought. —A. QUILLER-COUCH *On Jargon.*

(10)   Poor Mr. Cox! Left gasping in his aquarium!—A. QUILLER-COUCH *On Jargon.*

(11)   What has become of the elaborate argument that they were so learnedly developing scarcely a century ago proving that general overproduction is an impossibility, and which is still the stock in trade of most of the teachers of conventional economics to-day?—HENRY PRATT FAIRCHILD *Exit the Gospel of Work.*

(12)   But with the coming of Christianity, luxury, though still practiced, was no longer preached.—J. B. S. HALDANE *In Defense of Luxury.*

(13)   Consider initially the simple and widespread practice of yesing the boss—to use the current phrase.—STUART CHASE *The Luxury of Integrity.*

(14)   It was an interesting idea to deposit the body of an unrecognized soldier in the national memorial of the Great War, and yet, when one stops to think of it, how strange it is! —HARRY EMERSON FOSDICK *The Unknown Soldier.*

(15)   For there is not a single one of the fashionable forms of scientific scepticism, or determinism, that does not end in a stark paralysis, touching the practical conduct of human life. —G. K. CHESTERTON *The Return to Religion.*

B. According to *structure* sentences are divided into four classes:

1. **The Simple Sentence.**—A *simple sentence* contains only one subject and one predicate: Life is short. Flowers bloom in the spring. A good man is at peace with himself and the world.

REMARKS.—A simple sentence may be long or short. A very long sentence may be simple if it contains only one subject and one predicate. Two or more nouns or pronouns may be joined to form *one compound subject,* and two or more verbs may be joined to form *one compound predicate,* but the sentence will still be a simple sentence if there is only *one compound subject* and *one compound predicate: John and James* study together. John and James *study and recite and play* together. Each of these sentences is a simple sentence. (See pp. 167–170; 172–173.)

2. **The Complex Sentence.**—One or more dependent clauses may be joined to a simple sentence to form a *complex sentence:* When I signal, you must run. (See THE COMPLEX SENTENCE, pp. 228–229.)

3. **The Compound Sentence.**—Two or more simple sentences may be combined to form a *compound sentence:* The temperature is high, but the humidity is low. (See THE COMPOUND SENTENCE, p. 236.)

4. **The Compound-Complex Sentence.**—One or more dependent clauses may be combined with two or more simple sentences to form a *compound-complex sentence:* The man who made the offer is here, but he is too late. (See THE COMPOUND-COMPLEX SENTENCE, p. 237.)

Various Terms Used in Discussing the Sentence

Adjuncts.—An *adjunct* is something joined to or connected with another thing, but holding a subordinate place. For example, a set of doorsteps is an *adjunct* to a house. Grammatically, an adjunct may be a direct modifier, as an adjective or adverb; or it may be an infinitive or prepositional phrase, etc., quite loosely connected with the sentence.

Analysis.—Separating a sentence into parts and determining their definite relations to each other and to the whole sentence is called *analysis.* (Compare SYNTHESIS, p. 167.) To subdivide a sentence into clauses, phrases, or elements is to *analyze* the sentence.

Clauses.—A *clause* is a group of words that contains a subject and predicate and that is used as *part of a sentence.* An *independent clause* makes a complete predication. A *dependent clause* does not make a complete predication and can not be written as a sentence. (Compare PHRASES, p. 167.) A *clause* is always part of a sentence.

Connectives.—Words that connect words, phrases, or clauses are called *connectives.* The chief connectives are:

1. Conjunctions, connecting words, phrases, or clauses: *as, and, but, if, or,* etc.

2. Prepositions, connecting words: *at, by, in, to,* etc.

3. Relative pronouns, connecting clauses or phrases: *who, which, what,* and *that.*

4. Conjunctive or relative adverbs, connecting clauses or phrases: *hence, when, whence, where, why,* etc.

Construction.—To *construct* is to build or shape out of materials given. *Construction* in grammar may be either the process of building a phrase, clause, or sentence, or it may be that which is so built: A group of combined words may be a correct or an incorrect *construction.*

Elements.—Any part of a sentence which is capable of being considered by itself as helping to make up the sentence is called an *element* of the sentence. An element may be a single word or a group of words. An element used as a noun is called a *noun-element,* used as an adjective, an *adjective-element,* as an adverb, an *adverb-element,* etc.; but these names are of no special importance. (See also INDEPENDENT ELEMENTS, pp. 221–224.)

Members.—The clauses which are united to form a compound or complex sentence are called the *members* of the sentence. They are sometimes less strictly called *elements* of the compound or complex sentence. (See pp. 233–234.)

Modifiers.—A *modifier* is an element used to qualify a word or phrase so as to affect or change its meaning. An adjective is a *modifier* of a noun; an adverb is a *modifier* of a verb, etc. We say the adjective *modifies* the noun, the adverb *modifies* the verb, etc.

Phrases.—A group of two or more associated words *not containing a subject and predicate* is called a *phrase:* the boy; changeable weather; the sun having risen. But "The sun *has risen"* (a finite verb substituted for the participle *having risen*) may be a clause or a simple sentence. (Compare CLAUSES, p. 166.)

A phrase often consists of only two or three associated words: in truth; according to; as well as, and numerous other combinations. A *phrase* is never a *sentence,* and never a *clause.*

Synthesis.—*Synthesis* is the opposite of *analysis, viz.:* the putting together of words, phrases, or clauses, so as to form a grammatical unity. (See ANALYSIS, p. 166.) Analysis enables us to explain a sentence already formed; synthesis enables us to form a sentence out of elements given or thought of.

THE SIMPLE SENTENCE

The **simple sentence** is a sentence that contains only one subject and one predicate. In other words the simple sentence contains no clauses.

A simple sentence may consist of only two words, a noun (or pronoun) and a verb: John runs. Time flies. He lives. I go. Or a simple sentence may contain many words in both subject and predicate as long as we do not bring in a *new* subject or a *new* predicate. Thus: John, the youngest boy in the class, runs faster than any of the others. Here *John* is still the essential subject, the related words merely describing him. *Runs* is still the essential predicate, the added words merely describing how he runs.

The simple sentence is the basis of all sentence construction. One who has completely mastered the simple sentence can understand any sentence that can be made, for the most involved complex or compound sentences are only combinations of elements in the simple sentence.

The Essential Subject

The noun (or noun element) which is essential as the subject of the verb is called the **essential subject**: *Love* conquers all. A *word* to the wise is sufficient. A remarkably pretty little *girl* was knocking at our door.

The essential subject may be:

1. A noun: *Rain* is falling.

2. A pronoun: *He* is here.

3. An adjective used as a noun: The *good* are the happy.

4. An infinitive used as a noun: *To work* is the way to win.

5. A gerund: *Working* strengthens the worker.

6. A phrase used as a noun: *To be first* in class was his ambition.

7. Any part of speech treated simply as a name and thus used as a noun: *If* often brings failure.

The Complete Subject

The **complete subject** consists of the essential subject together with all of its modifiers: *The best of their houses* is covered with bark. In this sentence *best* is the essential subject; the complete subject is *the best of their houses.*

The Simple and Compound Subject

The essential subject may be either *simple* or *compound.*

A **simple essential subject** consists of a single noun or noun-element: All *men* are created equal. The *pen* is mightier than the sword.

A **compound essential subject** consists of two or more nouns or pronouns united by a conjunction: *John* and *James* sit together. Here we do not have two sentences, for we could not say, "*John* sit together and *James* sit together." *John and James* must be treated as the compound essential subject of the sentence, usually called simply the *compound subject.*

A great number of nouns or pronouns may be connected to form one compound essential subject:

> The *Goth,* the *Christian, time, war, flood* and *fire,*
> Have dealt upon the Seven Hilled City's pride.
> > BYRON *Childe Harold,* can. iv.

Where several nouns (or pronouns) are thus connected to form a compound subject, the conjunction is often omitted before each of the nouns except the last, the place of the omitted nouns being supplied by a comma, as in the extract given above.

The Essential Predicate

The finite verb which makes the principal assertion about the subject and is therefore essential to the construction of the sentence is called the **essential predicate**: Good wits *jump.* A stitch in time *saves* nine. Polly *put* the kettle on.

The Complete Predicate

The essential predicate and the entire group of words associated with it is called the **complete predicate**: Polly *put the
copper kettle on the stove.*

In the sentence above *put* is the essential predicate, and *put
the copper kettle on the stove* is the complete predicate. The
complete predicate always includes the essential predicate. The
complete predicate may consist of the essential predicate alone:
John *sings.* Or the complete predicate may consist of the essential predicate and its modifiers: John *sings German lieder very
well.*

EXERCISE A

Point out the essential subject and the essential predicate in
each of the following sentences, also the complete subject and
the complete predicate.

(1)   So may a glory from defect arise.
                          BROWNING *Deaf and Dumb.*

(2)   Earth, with her thousand voices, praises God.—COLERIDGE
Hymn Before Sunrise in the Vale of Chamouni.

(3)   The child is father of the man.
                          WORDSWORTH *My Heart Leaps Up.*

(4)   He shall have merely justice and his bond.
        SHAKESPEARE *Merchant of Venice,* act iv. sc. i, l. 339.

(5)   The wisdom of the wise and the experience of ages may
be preserved by quotation.—DISRAELI *Curiosities of Literature. Quotation.*

(6)   That fellow would vulgarize the day of judgment.
                          DOUGLAS JERROLD *A Comic Author.*

(7)   Men are more satirical from vanity than from malice.
                          LA ROCHEFOUCAULD *Maxims.* No. 508.

(8)   Violets spring in the soft May shower.
                          BRYANT *The Maiden's Sorrow.*

(9)   Justice, sir, is the great interest of man on earth.
                WEBSTER *On Mr. Justice Story*, 1845.

(10)   A sound Mind in a sound Body, is a short but full description of a happy State in this World.—LOCKE *Thoughts Concerning Education.*

(11)   At one time, during several weeks, her vituperation descended upon the head of Sidney Herbert himself.—LYTTON STRACHEY *Florence Nightingale.*

(12)   I found an endless pattern and endless complication of small objects hung like a curtain of fine links between me and my desire.—G. K. CHESTERTON *On Lying in Bed.*

(13)   In the neighborhood of latitude fifty north and for the last hundred years or thereabouts it has been an axiom that nature is divine and morally uplifting.—ALDOUS HUXLEY *Wordsworth in the Tropics.*

(14)   You may, from sheer perversity, utter them in a rich baritone or bass.—MAX BEERBOHM *A Clergyman.*

(15)   To regard all things and principles of things as inconstant modes or fashions has more and more become the tendency of modern thought.—WALTER PATER *Studies in the History of the Renaissance*, "Conclusion."

EXERCISE B

Select and explain the compound subject or compound predicate in each of the following sentences:

(1)   The genius, wit, and spirit of a nation are discovered in its proverbs.—BACON.

[Here three things "are discovered"—*genius, wit, and spirit* —which together form the *compound subject* of the one predicate verb.]

(2)   My brother wears a martial plume,
                And serves within a distant land.

[Here two acts are stated in the predicate—*wears* and *serves* —each ascribed to the one subject, *brother*. Therefore these two verbs form the *compound essential predicate* of the sentence. All the words after *brother* form the *complete predicate*.]

(3)   Thus can the Professor, at least in lucid intervals, look away from his own sorrows, over the many-coloured world, and pertinently enough note what is passing there.—CARLYLE *Sartor Resartus*, bk. ii, ch. 8.

(4)   He was always earning some ridiculous nickname, and then "binding it as a crown unto him," not merely in metaphor, but literally.—MACAULAY *Boswell*.

(5)   The Greek divinities and demigods, as the statuary has molded them, with their symmetry of figure, and their high forehead and their regular features, are the perfection of physical beauty.—NEWMAN *The Idea of a University*, Discourse 5.

(6)   Population, again, and bodily health and vigor, are things which are nowhere treated in such an unintelligent, misleading, exaggerated way as in England.—ARNOLD *Sweetness and Light*.

(7)   A man may be a better scholar than Erasmus, and know no more of the chief causes of the present intellectual fermentation than Erasmus did.—T. H. HUXLEY *Science and Culture*.

(8)   I wake and feel the fell of dark, not day.
             G. M. HOPKINS *I Wake and Feel*.

(9)   In the fell clutch of circumstance
        I have not winced nor cried aloud.
             W. E. HENLEY *Invictus*.

(10)   Yonder a maid and her wight
        Come whispering by.
             THOMAS HARDY *In Time "Of the Breaking
                                     Of Nations."*

(11)   The tumult and the shouting dies—
        The captains and the kings depart—
             KIPLING *Recessional*.

(12)   Boot, saddle, to horse, and away!
             BROWNING *Boot and Saddle*.

THE SIMPLE SENTENCE RECAPITULATED

A simple sentence consists of *one essential subject* and *one essential predicate*, with any modifiers or adjuncts of either.

A simple sentence must contain:

1. An essential subject (simple or compound);
2. An essential predicate (simple or compound).

Because the simple sentence is limited to one essential subject and predicate, it cannot contain a clause. The correct framing of the sentence depends absolutely on recognizing the essential subject and the essential predicate, and uniting them in proper agreement.

The number of adjuncts or modifiers in the *complete subject* or the *complete predicate* does not change the character of the sentence; it is a *simple sentence,* so long as it contains but *one essential subject* and *one essential predicate.* Thus:

> The good, wise, noble *man,* honored and beloved by all, *lives* simply and quietly in a small, plain house, in that great city.

Here *man* is the essential subject and *lives* is the essential predicate. All the parts of that long sentence are built around those two little words *man* and *lives,* which are essential to the sentence, one as the essential subject, and the other as the essential predicate.

If we were to change the essential subject of the sentence given above from *man* to *men,* we should at once have to change the essential predicate from *lives* to *live* since the verb must agree with its subject in person and number, but not another word in the sentence would need to be changed. The sentence would then read:

> The good, wise, noble *men* honored and beloved by all, *live* simply and quietly in a small, plain house in that great city.

But any number of words we might add would still leave the sentence a *simple sentence* so long as we do not introduce a new subject and a new predicate. (Compare COMPOUND AND COMPLEX SENTENCES, pp. 226–228.)

THE SUBJECT

PARTS OF SPEECH IN THE COMPLETE SUBJECT

Any part of speech, except a finite verb, may be joined to the essential subject as an adjunct or modifier, to make up the complete subject.

1. THE NOUN

A noun may be used in the complete subject in either one of the three cases.

The Nominative Case

1. **The Essential Subject.**—In the subject of a simple sentence, the noun is used chiefly as the essential subject: The *time* has come. A noun used as the essential subject is in the nominative case. Where two or more nouns form a compound essential subject, each of the nouns is in the nominative case: *Time* and *tide* wait for no man.

2. **An Appositive of the Essential Subject.**—Since the essential subject is always in the nominative case, any noun in apposition with the essential subject is also in the nominative case: Washington, *the general,* was present. (See APPOSITION under NOUN, Part I, p. 23.)

Personal names, titles, and designations of office or honor are treated as appositives or part of the appositive: *Mr.* Brown; *Dr.* Sweet; *the Reverend Mr.* Hyssop; *George* Washington; *General* Washington; *Lord* Bacon; *John Paul* Jones.

A noun in apposition with the subject is *not* an added subject, but a modifier, modifying the subject very much as an adjective might. A simple subject does not become compound when an appositive is added, but remains the single subject of the verb. A number of appositives may be added to a single subject: *George Washington,* the *citizen, soldier, statesman,* and *patriot,* was present.

The Possessive Case

3. A Possessive Modifying the Essential Subject.—The *child's* hands were cold. Here the noun *hands* is the essential subject, and being in the plural number takes a plural verb, *were*. The noun *child's* is in the possessive case, modifying the essential subject *hands*. *The child's hands* is the complete subject.

CAUTION.—A possessive modifier has no effect upon the number of the predicate verb, which is determined wholly by the essential subject.

The *child's* HOME *was* pleasant.

The *children's* HOME *was* pleasant.

4. A Possessive Modifying an Adjunct of the Essential Subject: The shoes covering the *child's* feet were old and worn.

The Objective Case

5. The Object of a Participle: The teacher, seeing the *difficulty,* changed the question. (See THE PARTICIPLE IN THE SUBJECT, p. 185.) The noun *difficulty* is the object of the participle *seeing,* which modifies *teacher,* the essential subject.

6. The Subject or Object of an Infinitive: For *fishes* to swim is easy. The time to gain *education* is in youth. (See THE INFINITIVE IN THE SUBJECT, pp. 184–185.)

7. The Object of a Preposition.—This occurs in a prepositional phrase modifying the essential subject. The lady at the *desk* is the teacher. (See PREPOSITIONAL PHRASE, p. 20; also, pp. 189–190, CAUTION.)

Thus a noun in either of the three cases may be part of the complete subject:

The *nominative case* (1), (2);
The *possessive case* (3), (4);
The *objective case* (5), (6), (7).

How to Determine the Essential Subject.—When various nouns make up the complete subject, we may at once set aside those in the possessive and objective case (numbers 3, 4, 5, 6, and 7) since neither the possessive nor the objective case can be the essential subject of a predicate verb or a sentence.

We then have left only principal nouns and appositives, both in the nominative case (numbers 1 and 2), and between them there is rarely any confusion. The essential subject is usually distinguished at once from the appositive by its prominence as the chief thing spoken of. Usually, too, the essential subject comes before the appositive, which is added to explain or emphasize it. Take, for instance, the following sentence:

> New York, the center of America's commerce and one of the most famous cities of the world, is situated at the mouth of the Hudson.

The complete subject, including all of the words down to the verb *is situated,* contains six nouns and a pronoun. Of these, which is the essential subject? None of the following can be because of the reasons given: *Center* and the pronoun *one,* because they are appositives; *America's,* because it is in the possessive case; *commerce, cities,* and *world* because they are objects of the preposition *of.* The only noun left is *New York. New York,* which is nominative, must therefore be the essential subject, a fact which is signaled at the outset by its position at the beginning of the sentence.

EXERCISE

Identify the essential subject of each of the following sentences and explain the use of every noun in the complete subject of each.

(1)   Most people would succeed in small things if they were not troubled with great ambitions.—LONGFELLOW *Driftwood,* "Table-Talk."

(2) A wild boar, a devourer of Tuscan acorns, and heavy with the fruit of many an oak, second in fame only to the monster of Ætolia, lies an envied prey for my kitchen fire.—MARTIAL *Epigrams*, bk. vii, ep. 27.

(3) The living-room walls were brown bare boards without a picture or scrap of wall-paper.—RING LARDNER *Ex Parte*.

(4) Elmer's big new Buick, mud-splashed but imposing, stood tilted on the uneven road.—RUTH SUCKOW *A Start in Life*.

(5) Four men in their shirt sleeves stood grouped together on the garden path.—KATHERINE MANSFIELD *The Garden Party*.

(6) A wet wind of autumn, smelling of sodden garden, blew in her face and tilted her hat.—ELIZABETH BOWEN *A Queer Heart*.

(7) Mrs. Ray, the mother of Charles, suddenly knelt down by his wife and put an arm round her shoulders without saying a word.—ELIZABETH BOWEN *Joining Charles*.

(8) After one Fourth of July, Nick, driving home late from town in the big wagon with Joe Garner and his family, passed nine drunken Indians along the road.—ERNEST HEMINGWAY *Ten Indians*.

(9) On a chicken farm where hundreds and even thousands of chickens come out of eggs surprising things sometimes happen.—SHERWOOD ANDERSON *The Egg*.

(10) The long planks set on trestles rose one above the other to a monstrous height and stretched dizzyingly in a wide oval ring.—KATHERINE ANNE PORTER *The Circus*.

(11) The practical nurse, sitting in a straight chair busy at her needlework, looked over her glasses to give me some little instruction in the arrangement of my mother's pillows. —PETER TAYLOR *A Spinster's Tale*.

(12) The grass-green cart, with "J. Jones, Gorsshill" painted shakily on it, stopped in the cobblestone passage between "The Hare's Foot" and "The Pure Drop."—DYLAN THOMAS *Peaches*.

2. THE PRONOUN

The use of the pronoun in the subject of a simple sentence is for the most part the same as that of the noun.

The Nominative Case

1. The Essential Subject.—A pronoun may be the essential subject: *He* is attentive. *They* are absent. Two or more pronouns may be united in a compound essential subject: *You* and *I* will go. *This, that* or the *other* will interrupt.

A pronoun may be joined with a noun to form a compound essential subject: George and *I* will go. *He* and his lawyer contrived the plan. An indefinite number of nouns or pronouns, or both, may be thus combined in a compound essential subject. When the pronoun *I* is one of these, the *I* comes last in the series: He and *I* met at the train. John, James, and *I* were present.

RULE.—A pronoun used as the essential subject must be in the nominative case. This case is indicated by the form of the pronoun in the personal pronouns: *I, thou, he, she, we, you, they,* and in the interrogative or relative *who.*

ERRORS.—Hence, to say "You and *him* may go" is a complete error. To say *"Me* and you will go" violates two rules of grammar at once; the *Me* is wrong both by case and position. The expression should be "you and *I.*" (For a common misuse of the objective *whom* see THE COMPLEX SENTENCE, pp. 231–232.)

It as an Apparent Subject.—The pronoun *it* is often used merely as an introductory word: *It* rains. *It* is cold. Here *it* does not represent any definite person or thing, either expressed or understood, but is an introductory word used as the apparent subject to give sentence-form to the idea expressed by the verb. *It* is the apparent essential subject of the verb. *It* fills out the grammatical frame, giving the thought that "rain is falling" the briefest possible sentence form, "It rains." A verb so used is often called impersonal.

It as an introductory word may refer to a following phrase or clause: *It* is evident that a mistake was made. *It* is necessary to study the lesson. The true essential subjects of these sentences are *that a mistake was made* and *to study the lesson,* respectively. The introductory *it,* serving as the apparent subject of these sentences, is frequently called an *expletive.* (See THE INDEFINITE IT, p. 33; for the adverb *there* as an introductory word, see ADVERB, p. 187.)

By inverting the sentences above, we may dispense with *it* and yet express the same thought: *That a mistake was made* is evident. *To study the lesson* is necessary. The introductory *it* is an ingenious device to carry over the really important subject of thought to the emphatic place at the end of the sentence; thus *that a mistake has been made* or *to study the lesson* becomes the final and impressive thought.

The Plural Following Introductory It.—*It* as an introductory subject may represent a noun or pronoun of any gender or person, or of either number.

It was *Milton* who wrote Paradise Lost.

It was government *bonds* that I purchased.

It has been *years* since I met him.

It is *these* that I want.

It was *they* who told me.

Such forms are well established in English usage.

2. **The Pronoun Not an Appositive.**—The pronoun is rarely if ever used as the appositive of a noun or of another pronoun, but may take a noun in apposition with itself: *We,* the people of the United States . . . do ordain and establish this Constitution. Here it will be seen that the noun is explanatory of the pronoun, which might stand alone as the essential subject; *the*

people explains who are the *we* (who "ordain and establish this Constitution"). For the *nominative absolute,* see INDEPENDENT ELEMENTS, pp. 222–223.

The Possessive Case

3. A Possessive, Modifying the Essential Subject: *My* book is on the table. *His* note is now due. This case is exactly like that of a noun in the possessive case modifying the essential subject.

4. A Possessive Used as the Essential Subject: *Yours* has already been received. In this sentence we can not supply a noun without changing the form of the possessive; we should have to write "*your* letter," or the like. If we use *yours,* we must use it without a noun, and as itself the essential subject. This form of the pronoun is a secondary possessive *used as a noun.* (See CASE IN PERSONAL PRONOUNS (3) Part I, p. 37.)

5. A Possessive as Modifier of any Adjunct.—A possessive may be used as a modifier in any phrase modifying the essential subject: The way to learn *your* lessons is to study. Trusting *his* honesty I went with him.

The Objective Case

A pronoun in the objective case may be used in the complete subject as follows:

6. The Object of a Participle: Trusting *him,* I did as he asked.

7. The Subject or Object of an Infinitive: Trusting *me* to lead them, they advanced. The attempt to relieve *them* failed.

8. The Object of a Preposition: Doubt about *him* gave way to certainty.

EXERCISE

Give the essential subject of each of the following extracts. Then select all of the pronouns in the complete subject of each

extract and explain how each pronoun is related to the essential
subject and to the predicate.

(1)   She in beauty, education, blood,
        Holds hand with any princess of the world.
                SHAKESPEARE *King John,* act iv. sc. 1.

(2)   It is a poor sport that is not worth the candle.—HERBERT
Jacula Prudentium.

(3)   I am a part of all that I have met.—TENNYSON *Ulysses.*

(4)   On the light of Liberty you saw arise the light of Peace.
—WEBSTER *The Bunker Hill Monument, 1825.*

(5)   The former tenant of our house, a priest, had died in the
back drawing-room.—JAMES JOYCE *Araby.*

(6)   As for Warner, the unexpected advent of the girl, her
youth and seductiveness, the aura of wealth and power about
her, dazzled him. . . .—ABBEY C. GOODLOE *Claustrophobia.*

(7)   To take off her boots or to put them on was an agony to
her. . . .—KATHERINE MANSFIELD *Life of Ma Parker.*

(8)   None of them knew the color of the sky.—STEPHEN
CRANE *The Open Boat.*

(9)   She is all so slight
            And tender and white
            As a May morning.
                RICHARD ALDINGTON *After Two Years.*

(10)   All passions that suffer themselves to be relished and
digested are but moderate.—MONTAIGNE *Of Sorrows.*

(11)   The general himself ought to be such a one as can at the
same time see forward and backward.—PLUTARCH *Whether
an Aged Man Ought to Meddle in State Affairs.*

(12)   For my part, I had rather be the first man among these
fellows than the second man in Rome.—PLUTARCH *Life of
Caesar.*

3. THE ADJECTIVE

The English adjective has neither gender, person, number,
nor case. (See THE ADJECTIVE, Part. I, pp. 62–73.) We have only

to know the common form of the adjective and then apply that to any noun or pronoun. Wherever a noun is used in the complete subject of a sentence an adjective may be used as a modifier of that noun.

The adjective in the subject of a sentence may be used as:

1. **The Essential Subject.**—This occurs when the adjective preceded by the definite article is used as a noun: The *best* is the cheapest. The *good* are blessed.

Some words originally adjectives have come to be definitely used as nouns, as *right* and *good,* which have regular plurals: the *rights* of man; *goods* and chattels. Except in such cases an adjective with the definite article *the* is to be classed as an adjective used as a noun.

2. **A Modifier of the Essential Subject.**—This is the most common use of the adjective: A *busy* day awaited me. A *harder* task remained. The *best* news came at last.

3. **A Modifier of an Adjunct.**—An adjective may modify an appositive of the essential subject or any noun used in a participial phrase, a prepositional phrase, or any other phrase forming part of the complete subject: Grant, the *great* soldier, was a lover of peace. To make an *early* start was our plan. The orator, telling a *funny* story, put his audience in good humor.

EXERCISE

Identify the essential subject of each of the following extracts. Then select all adjectives in every complete subject and explain the use of each adjective.

(1)   The awful shadow of some unseen Power
        Floats, tho unseen, amongst us.
                SHELLEY *Hymn to Intellectual Beauty.*

(2)   In his days shall the righteous flourish.—*Psalm 72:7.*

(3)   All her gestures were liquid and possessed of an inner rhythm that flowed to inevitable completion with the finality

of architecture or music.—AGNES DEMILLE *Dance to the Piper*.

(4)   The know-it-all state of mind is just the result of being outside the mucose-paper wrapping of civilization.—D. H. LAWRENCE *Phoenix*.

(5)   The vast mythology of Scottish education is full of stories about the crofter's son who lived all term in half a room on a barrel of oatmeal and a barrel of herring brought from home. . . .—GILBERT HIGHET *The American Student As I See Him*.

(6)   Any consideration of the responsibilities of education at any level in America must begin with a basic consideration of the total relationship of our educational system.—WILLIAM H. CORNOG *Bread and Hyacinths*.

(7)   The brisk little man came into my office and said he wanted to study philosophy because he needed it in his profession.—IRWIN EDMAN *Under Whatever Sky*.

(8)   The language of the Bible, now simple and direct in its homely vigor, now sonorous and stately in its richness, has placed its indelible stamp upon our best writers from Bacon to Lincoln and even to the present day.—MARY ELLEN CHASE *The Bible and the Common Reader*.

(9)   Sea caves in cliffs now high above the battering assault and the flung spray of the waves . . . are eloquent of the changed relations of sea and land.—RACHEL CARSON *The Sea Around Us*.

(10)   The astonishing thing, considering the trifling number of anthropologists and the minute fraction of the population that has been exposed to formal instruction in the subject is that during the last decade or so the word "anthropology" and some of its terms have come out of hiding in recondite literature to appear with increasing frequency in *The New Yorker, The Saturday Evening Post*, and even in moving pictures.—CLYDE KLUCKHOHN *The Mirror for Man*.

(11)   On a courtship flight a male Empis cuts quite a figure now. . . .—JAMES THURBER *My World—and Welcome to It*.

(12)   Vast numbers of persons, many of them highly intelligent, derive no pleasure at all from organized sound.—VIRGIL THOMSON *The Musical Scene*.

4. THE VERB

A finite verb can not be part of the subject of a simple sentence.* If we say, for instance, *"The man who is at the gate may enter,"* we have not a *simple* but a complex sentence. (See COMPLEX SENTENCE, p. 228.)

There are, however, two verbal forms, the *infinitive* and the *participle,* either of which may be used in the subject of a simple sentence.

The Infinitive in the Subject †

An infinitive or an infinitive phrase (see pp. 85–87) may be:

1. **The Essential Subject:** *To lie* is base. *To learn* all the facts of the case is a necessity.

The infinitive denoting purpose is often the object of the preposition *for,* having a subject in the objective case: for *them* to *go.* An infinitive phrase with *for* may be:

(*a*) The essential subject: *For him to escape* is impossible. Here the infinitive phrase *For him to escape* is a *noun-element,* the subject of the verb *is.*

(*b*) An adjunct of the essential subject: The plan *for him to escape* was craftily formed. Here the infinitive phrase *for him to escape* is an *adjective-element,* modifying the noun *plan.*

2. **A Modifier of the Essential Subject:** The time *to learn* is while we are young. In such use the infinitive or infinitive phrase is classed as an adjective-element.

---

* NOTE.—The only exception is when a verb is used as a mere *word* (p. 168): That *is* is incorrect.

† NOTE.—For the use of the infinitive as an independent element, see under INDEPENDENT ELEMENTS, p. 223.

3. **A Modifier of an Adjunct of the Essential Subject:** The children, eager *to go,* crowded to the door.

The Participle in the Subject

A participle or participial phrase may form part of the complete subject as follows:

1. **A Modifier of the Essential Subject:** The children, *seeing the door open,* ran out.*

2. **A Modifier of an Adjunct of the Essential Subject:** *Angry at being detained,* he became silent.

Here the participial phrase *at being detained* is an adverb element modifying the adjective *angry; he, angry at being detained* is the complete subject, of which the participial phrase *at being detained* is a part.

The Gerund in the Subject

A gerund (scc GERUND, p. 93) may be used in the complete subject of a sentence as follows:

1. **As the Essential Subject:** *Seeing* is believing. *Lying* is reprehensible.

The Gerund with the Possessive.—A gerund may be preceded by a noun or pronoun in the possessive case: The *man's* leaving home was a surprise. *His* buying the property was a mistake. *My* going there was a necessity. The same construction is used in the predicate: What do you think of *his* selling the property? (Not of *him* selling the property.)

2. **As an Appositive of the Essential Subject:** His favorite sport, *swimming,* is healthful. My current hobby, *collecting stamps,* is educational.

---

* NOTE.—For the absolute construction of the participle with a noun (The hour *being* late, we started at once.) see the NOMINATIVE ABSOLUTE, under INDEPENDENT ELEMENTS, p. 222–223.

EXERCISE

In each of the following extracts, select every gerund, every infinitive or infinitive phrase, and every participle or participial phrase, forming part of the *complete subject,* and show how each is related to the *essential subject* and to other elements of the sentence. Give the *essential subject* of each extract.

(1)   To blow and swallow at the same moment isn't easy to be done.—PLAUTUS *Mostellaria,* act iii, sc. 2. Riley's trans.

(2)   To live by one man's will became the cause of all men's misery.—RICHARD HOOKER *Ecclesiastical Polity,* bk. i, ch. x, 5.

(3)   Reputation being essentially contemporaneous, is always at the mercy of the envious and the ignorant.—MRS. JAMESON *Memoirs and Essays,* "Washington Allston."

(4)   A house divided against itself can not stand. I believe this government can not endure permanently half-slave and half-free.—ABRAHAM LINCOLN *Speech,* June 17, 1858.

(5)   To be conscious that you are ignorant is a great step to knowledge.—DISRAELI *Sybil,* bk. i, ch. v.

(6)   To be prepared for war is one of the most effectual means of preserving peace.—GEORGE WASHINGTON *Speech to Both Houses of Congress,* Jan. 8, 1790.

(7)   To execute laws is a royal office; to execute orders is not to be a king.—BURKE *Reflections on the Revolution in France,* vol. iii, p. 497.

(8)   To take Macaulay out of literature and society and put him in the House of Commons, is like taking the chief physician out of London during a pestilence.—SYDNEY SMITH *Memoir,* vol. i, p. 265.

(9)   A loving heart is the beginning of all knowledge.—CARLYLE *Article on Biography.*

(10)   To be great is to be misunderstood.—EMERSON *Self-Reliance.*

(11)   The hearing ear is always found close to the speaking tongue.—EMERSON *English Traits.*

(12)   To be seventy years young is sometimes far more cheerful
and hopeful than to be forty years old.—HOLMES *On the
Seventieth Birthday of Julia Ward Howe.*

5. THE ADVERB

The adverb may form part of the complete subject by
modifying:

1. The Essential Subject: *Almost* everything was recovered.

> *Not* walls nor hills could guard so well
> Old Salem's happy ground.

(See ADVERBS MODIFYING NOUNS, etc., Part I, pp. 135–136.)

2. Any Adjunct of the Essential Subject: Your *highly*
esteemed favor is received. This *very* important matter must
have attention. The point to be *carefully* considered is his
honesty.

There as an Introductory Adverb.—The adverb *there* is used,
much like *it* (see *It* AS INTRODUCTORY SUBJECT, pp. 178–179),
as an introductory word or *expletive* serving to carry the real
subject to the close of the sentence: *There* is time enough. *There*
is no opportunity.

In such cases, to say, "Time enough is," or "No opportunity
is," would be both feeble and harsh. *There,* as an introductory
adverb, is often called an *expletive*. The real subject of such a
sentence is the nominative following the verb: There *is a* MAN
present. There *are* MEN present. The introductory *there* so
loses its meaning as an adverb of place that another *there,* with
place-meaning may be used in the same sentence: "Because
there was much water THERE." *John* 3:23. Also *here* may be
used in the same sentence without contradiction: *There* is a lad
HERE.

The as an Adverb.—*The,* preceding a comparative, in such
expressions as *"the* more, *the* less," *"the* sooner *the* better," is
not the definite article, but an adverb. (See COMPARATIVES WITH

The, p. 140.) *The,* in this use, signifies *by that, by as much, by so much,* or the like. The phrase, *"the* sooner *the* better," thus signifies *"by as much as* (it is) sooner, *by so much* (it will be) better." (For adverbs used independently, see under INDEPEND-ENT ELEMENTS, p. 223.)

EXERCISE

Select every adverb included in the *complete subject* of each of the following extracts, and explain the relation of the adverb to any other word or words of the subject. Give the *essential* subject of each extract.

(1)   The poem now offered to the public is intended to illus-trate the customs and manners which anciently prevailed on the borders of England and Scotland.—Sir Walter Scott *Lay of the Last Minstrel,* Preface.

(2)   Small habits, well pursued betimes,
           May reach the dignity of crimes.
                              Hannah More *Florio,* pt. i.

(3)   How slight a chance may raise or sink a soul!
                    Bailey *Festus,* "A Country Town."

(4)   A very great multitude spread their garments in the way. *Matt.* 21:8.

(5)   Heaven's ebon vault,
           Studded with stars unutterably bright,

           . . . .

           Seems like a canopy which love has spread
           To curtain her sleeping world.
                         Shelley *Queen Mab,* pt. iv.

(6)   How many a rustic Milton has passed by,
           Stifling the speechless longings of his heart,
           In unremitting drudgery and care!
                    Shelley *Queen Mab,* pt. v, st. 9.

(7)   There are truths which are not for all men, nor for all times.—Voltaire *Letter to Cardinal de Bernis, April 23, 1761.*

(8)   Here is the devil and all to pay.—Cervantes *Don Qui-xote,* pt. i, bk. iii, ch. ix.

(9)   The expression often used by Mr. Herbert Spencer of the Survival of the Fittest is more accurate, and is sometimes equally convenient.—DARWIN *Origin of the Species,* ch. iii.

(10)   With their beaks still loaded, they move around with a frightened look. . . . —JOHN BURROUGHS *Birds'-Nests.*

(11)   That [building material] most freely used is a sort of cotton-bearing plant, which grows in old, worn-out fields. —JOHN BURROUGHS *Birds'-Nests.*

(12)   Innumerable peaks and spires but little lower than its own storm-beaten crags rise in groups like forest trees. . . . —JOHN MUIR *The Mountains of California* "The Sierra Nevadas."

6. THE PREPOSITION

The Prepositional Phrase.—A preposition with its object and any adjunct or adjuncts of the object forms *a prepositional phrase.* A prepositional phrase may be part of the complete subject of a sentence as follows:

1. **The Essential Subject:** *For him to fail* would be shameful. (See THE INFINITIVE PHRASE, pp. 86–87.)

2. **An Adjective Element Modifying the Essential Subject:** The hour *of meeting* had arrived.

CAUTION 1.—A prepositional phrase must not be mistaken for a member of a compound essential subject. Compare the following sentences:

The man *and his son* WERE present.

The man *with his son* WAS present.

In the first sentence *son* is in the nominative case as a member of the compound subject *man and son* with which the plural verb *were* agrees. In the second sentence *son* is the object of the preposition *with* and is therefore in the objective case; thus it can not be the subject of a verb. This leaves *man* as the only subject with which the verb can agree, and we must therefore use the singular verb *was.*

CAUTION 2.—When a prepositional phrase is used as a subject modifier, the object of the preposition has no effect on the predicate verb.

The man *with his two sons* WAS present. (*Was* agrees with the singular subject *man,* and not with the plural noun *sons,* object of *with.*)

Every one *of us* IS here. (*Is* agrees with the singular subject *one,* and not with the plural pronoun *us,* object of the preposition *of.*)

Not one *of them* HAS come.

The speaker, *with a party of friends,* HAS arrived.

The president, *with the advice and consent of* the senate, appoints. . . .

The house *in the midst of fields and orchards* is a beautiful object.

I, *with the approval of my friends,* am determined to remain.

RULE.—To determine what verb should be used when an essential subject is modified by a prepositional phrase, *drop the prepositional phrase wholly out of sight* and make the verb agree with the essential subject just as if the prepositional phrase did not exist. Use the sentences above as guides.

3. A Modifier of Any Adjunct of the Essential Subject.— So used, a prepositional phrase may be:

(*a*) An adjective element modifying a noun or noun element of the complete subject: Nelson, the hero *of many battles,* was killed at Trafalgar. Here the prepositional phrase *of many battles* is used as an adjective element and modifies the noun *hero* which is an appositive of the essential subject, *Nelson.*

(*b*) An adverb element modifying an adjective, participle, infinitive, etc. of the complete subject: The children, *eager for play,* ran out. The books, *guarded with care,* are well preserved.

4. Appositive Use.—The prepositional phrase with *of* is often equivalent to an appositive: The city *of London*. He was known by the name *of Augustus*.

EXERCISE

Select every prepositional phrase in the *complete subject* in each of the following extracts and show its relation to the other words of the complete subject. Give the *essential subject* of each sentence.

(1)   The progress of rivers to the ocean is not so rapid as that of man to error.—VOLTAIRE *A Philosophical Dictionary*, "Rivers."

(2)   The thing in the world I am most afraid of is fear.—MONTAIGNE *Essays*, "Fear."

(3)   The flower of sweetest smell is shy and lowly.
          WORDSWORTH *Sonnet. Not Love, Not War, etc.*

(4)   Nothing except a battle lost can be half so melancholy as a battle won.—DUKE OF WELLINGTON *Despatch*. 1815.

(5)   The reward of one duty is the power to fulfil another.—GEORGE ELIOT *Daniel Deronda*, bk. vi, ch. 46.

(6)   The fear of some divine and supreme powers keeps men in obedience.—BURTON *Anatomy of Melancholy*, pt. iii, sec. 4, Memb. 1. Subsec. 2.

(7)   The course of my long life hath reached at last,
          In fragile bark o'er a tempestuous sea,
          The common harbor.
                            LONGFELLOW *Old Age.*

(8)   Nothing can bring you peace but the triumph of principles.—EMERSON *Essays*, "Of Self-Reliance."

(9)   The hand of little employment hath the daintier sense.
          SHAKESPEARE *Hamlet*, act v, sc. 1, l. 77.

(10)   Passing by the Phibsbora Church, its Vincentian spire thrusting into the deep-blue of the sky, looking like a huge spear left behind on the field of one of heaven's battles with Lucifer and his lost angels, he crossed Blaquiere Bridge to

enter into the lower part of the thoroughfare.—SEAN O'CASEY *Inishfallen, Fare Thee Well*, "The Raid."

(11)   An extravagance of electricity, with almost every light in the house on, swelled the significance of the evening in the Lonigan household.—JAMES T. FARRELL *Young Lonigan*, ch. ii.

(12)   Sitting on the bed, holding the cheap florid candy box in her hand, she sat as she had sat while the blonde woman talked to her.—WILLIAM FAULKNER *Light in August*, ch. viii.

(13)   The most famous school of law in Italy was the one at Bologna.—ANGUS ARMITAGE *The World of Copernicus*, ch. xvi.

7. THE CONJUNCTION

Conjunctions connect words, phrases, or clauses. In the simple sentence, conjunctions are used only to connect words or phrases. For conjunctions connecting clauses, see THE COMPOUND SENTENCE, p. 236, and THE COMPLEX SENTENCE, pp. 228–230.

Conjunctive Phrases.—Certain combinations of words having the force of conjunctions are best parsed as conjunctive phrases: *and also, and likewise, as if, as well as*. In this class are also the correlatives *although—still; although—yet; both—and; not —but; not only—but; not only—but also; not only—but likewise.*

A conjunction or conjunctive phrase may be used as part of the complete subject of a sentence as follows:

1. To Connect the Parts of a Compound Essential Subject: Sun *and* rain have melted the snow. *Either* the brother *or* the sister will come.

REMARKS

(1) If the nouns or pronouns of a compound subject are connected by *and,* the verb of the predicate agrees with them jointly and is in the plural number: Storm *and* darkness *have* their uses.

(2) If the nouns or pronouns of a compound subject are connected by any conjunction except *and,* the verb agrees with each singly and is singular if all the nouns or pronouns are singular, or plural if all are plural: Money *or* credit *is* necessary. *Neither* soldiers *nor* citizens *were* ready. If the members of the compound subject are singular and plural, the verb agrees with the nearer: Neither the pupils nor the *teacher was* injured. BUT: Neither the teacher nor the *pupils were* injured. (For exceptional uses, see under PREDICATE, pp. 211–212.)

When more than two nouns or pronouns are connected by the same conjunction, that conjunction is usually omitted before every member of the series except the last: Men, women, *and* children attended the service. *Neither* sun, moon, *nor* star appeared. The conjunction may, however, be retained throughout, having then the effect of separating the connected words and emphasizing them by compelling the mind to move from one to the other more slowly; thus:

> O night
> *And* storm *and* darkness, ye are wondrous strong,
> Yet lovely in your strength.
> > BYRON *Childe Harold,* can. iii, st. 92.

All the conjunctions may be omitted, with the effect of crowding and hurrying the enumeration: The sun, the moon, the planets, the stars, are all in motion.

2. **To Connect Adjuncts of the Essential Subject,** or any modifiers of such adjuncts: Earnest *and* diligent students will succeed. The soil, rich *and* fertile, favors agriculture. Money well *and* honestly earned is a worthy possession.

Or and Nor in Negative Statements.—After *neither, nor* must be used: *Neither* the one *nor* the other will answer. After *not,* either *or* or *nor* may be used: Not a book *or* (*nor*) paper was missing. The rhetorical distinction that formerly existed between *or* and *nor* after *not* is no longer observed.

As and Or with Appositive Force: Lincoln, *as* president, made the address. The Sequoia, *or* redwood, grows to an immense height.

Elements of the Same Class Connected

Conjunctions connecting words, phrases, or clauses must connect those of the same class, as nouns with nouns, adjectives with adjectives, etc.

Correlative conjunctions or conjunctive phrases should be so placed as to apply directly to the words that are to be connected. To say, *"Not only* a man rich *but* influential is required"* is both awkward and obscure; the sentence becomes clear when the conjunctive phrase *not only* is correctly placed: A man *not only* rich *but* influential is required. Both correlatives now clearly modify the adjectives *rich* and *influential*.

EXERCISE

Select every conjunction or conjunctive phrase included in the *complete subject* in each sentence of the following extracts, and show its relation to other words of the subject. Also note and explain the omission of conjunctions. (Compare pp. 152–153; 229–230.) Give the *essential subject* of every sentence.

(1)   Plenty, as well as Want, can separate friends.—COWLEY *Davideis,* bk. iii, l. 205.

(2)   A scar nobly got, or a noble scar, is a good livery of honor.
         SHAKESPEARE *All's Well That Ends Well,*
                 act iv, sc. 5, l. 105.

(3)   Sleep, riches, and health, to be truly enjoyed, must be interrupted.—RICHTER *Flower, Fruit, and Thorn Pieces,* ch. 8.

(4)   No mighty trance, or breathèd spell
Inspires the pale-eyed priest from the prophetic cell.
         MILTON *Hymn on Christ's Nativity,* l. 173.

(5)   The genius, wit, and spirit of a nation are discovered in its proverbs.—BACON

(6)   Shall ignorance of good and ill
                Dare to direct the eternal will?
                            GAY *The Father and Jupiter.*

(7)   Nothing in history or fiction approaches the horrors . . .
        of that night.—MACAULAY *Essay on Lord Clive.*

(8)   The sound of a boy's whoop or a man's hearty halloo
        drove him deeper into the shade.—MARY HALLOCK FOOTE
        How the Pump Stopped at the Morning Watch.

(9)   They sat as if they were frozen.—LAURA I. WILDER
        Little Town on the Prairie, ch. 1.

(10)   The simplicity and innocence and unconsciousness of the
        old farmer are perfectly simulated, and the result is a per-
        formance which is thoroughly charming and delicious.
        —MARK TWAIN *How to Tell a Story.*

(11)   The tracing of a line to be followed, of a tone to be taken,
        of a form to be filled out, is a limitation of that freedom
        and a suppression of the very thing that we are most curious
        about.—HENRY JAMES *The Art of Fiction.*

(12)   "The mass of creatures and of qualities are still hid and
        expectant," and to break new ground is still one of the un-
        commonest and most heroic of virtues.—WILLIAM DEAN
        HOWELLS *Criticism and Fiction.*

8. THE INTERJECTION

The interjection is not grammatically included in the subject
of a sentence unless as a quotation: *"Alas!"* was his cry. (See
INDEPENDENT ELEMENTS, p. 223.)

REVIEW: SELECTING THE ESSENTIAL SUBJECT

The essential subject must be (1) a noun, (2) a pronoun,
or (3) some word or phrase used as a noun.

1. The *president* is the chief executive. (A noun as essential subject.)

2. *She* walks in beauty. (A pronoun as essential subject.)

3. *Authoritarian* is a harsh word to use in this context. (A word used as essential subject.)

Telling romances at short notice was her specialty. (A gerund phrase as essential subject.)

The essential subject *can not* be a noun, pronoun, or noun element which is itself the object of (1) a participle or gerund, (2) an infinitive, or (3) a preposition.

1. Opening the *door,* the man entered the room. (As the object of the participle *opening,* the noun *door* can not be the essential subject.)

2. To gain the *advantage* the boy resorted to a trick. (As the object of the infinitive *to gain,* the noun *advantage* can not be the essential subject.)

3. For this *reason,* the lawyer undertook the case. (As the object of the preposition *for,* the noun *reason* can not be the essential subject.)

A company *of soldiers* is quartered on the green. (As object of the preposition *of,* the noun *soldiers* can not be the essential subject. The prepositional phrase *of soldiers* is a *subject modifier,* and a subject modifier can never be the essential subject.)

The essential subject can not be a word or phrase that is used for some other purpose. Hence by the process of elimination, many words or phrases may be discarded, leaving the essential subject distinct as the only word that can be so used.

EXAMPLE.—In the following long and complicated sentence, the subject, extending to the verb *was divided,* contains seven singular or plural nouns, which are printed in italics.

Fringed by the rapid *Meuse* and enclosed by gently rolling *hills* cultivated to their *crests,* or by abrupt *precipices* of *limestone* crowned with *verdure,* the broad, crescent-shaped *plain* was divided by numerous hedgerows.

Which of these nouns is the essential subject? We can find out by determing their use.

Meuse:	object of the preposition *by*
hills:	object of the preposition *by*
crests:	object of the preposition *to*
precipices:	object of the preposition *by*
limestone:	object of the preposition *of*
verdure:	object of the preposition *with*

Since these six nouns are objects, no one of them can be the essential subject. The only noun left is *plain; plain* is the essential subject of the verb *was divided.* Basically the sentence is a very simple one: The plain was divided by hedgerows. All of the other words in the sentence are merely descriptive modifiers. (For the COMPOUND ESSENTIAL SUBJECT, see p. 169.)

THE PREDICATE

Review

The *predicate* is the part of the sentence that makes an assertion about the *subject:* John *runs.*

The predicate must contain a finite verb. The finite verb is the *essential predicate:* The boy *speaks* French.

The predicate, in addition to the finite verb, may contain all of the other parts of speech: The boy *speaks French with the fluency of one who has lived in France for many years.*

The *complete predicate* is the *essential predicate* (finite verb) plus all of the words associated with it. In the sentence above, the essential predicate is *speaks;* the complete predicate is *speaks* plus all that follows.

A *compound predicate* is one that contains two or more essential predicates joined by *and* or some other conjunction. The child *runs and skips.* In addition a compound predicate may contain any number of words modifying the compound predicate: The child *runs and skips gayly down the street.* (See pp. 169–170.)

PARTS OF SPEECH IN THE COMPLETE PREDICATE

1. THE NOUN

The noun may be used in the predicate in either one of the three cases.

The Nominative Case

1. The Predicate Nominative: Daniel Webster was a great *orator.* (See RULES OF CASE IN NOUNS, (2), Part I, p. 19.)

2. The Nominative after an Infinitive or Gerund.—The infinitive or gerund of any *copulative* verb (as *appear, be, seem,* etc.) may be followed by a noun in the nominative case: He was shy on account of being a *stranger.* He seems to be the *culprit.* (Compare PRONOUN, p. 202, (2).)

EXCEPTION.—If the infinitive has a subject in the objective case, or if the participle is modifier of a noun or pronoun in the objective case, the noun following the infinitive or participle is also in the objective case: I expect HIM to be a *candidate*: I saw THEM made *prisoners.*

3. The Nominative by Apposition.—A noun in apposition with the predicate nominative, or with any other nominative included in the complete predicate, must also be in the nominative case: The prisoner was Columbus, the *discoverer* of America. *Discoverer* is nominative because it is in apposition to the predicate nominative *Columbus.* (For the *nominative absolute,* see under INDEPENDENT ELEMENTS, pp. 222–223.)

The Possessive Case

4. As a Modifier.—A noun in the possessive case may be used in the predicate when it modifies another noun or a gerund of the complete predicate: The son lives in his *father's* house. Everything depends on the *man's* keeping the appointment.

The Objective Case

A noun in the objective case may be used in the complete predicate as:

5. The Direct Object of the Predicate Verb: Alexander conquered *Persia.*

When the subject and the direct object are both nouns, the regular order of words is—*subject, verb, object.*

6. The Indirect Object.—Verbs of *giving, telling, providing,* and the like, as *allow, buy, deny, find, give, grant, hand, make, obtain, offer, pass, pay, procure, promise, provide, secure, send, telegraph, telephone, tell, write,* and some others, take an *indirect object* denoting the person to or for whom something is done. The indirect object is the ultimate goal of the action of the verb. Buy the *boy* a set of tools. (*Tools* is the direct object of *buy; boy* is the indirect object, with the force of *for the boy.*) Give the *men* my orders. (*Orders* is the direct object of give; *men* is the indirect object with the force of *to the men.*) Telegraph the *agent* the price.

REMARKS

(1) The indirect object, when used without a preposition, always *precedes* the direct object: Hand *me* the *book.*

(2) The indirect object is the object of a preposition understood. This will be seen by changing the order, as in the examples above.

(3) *When the indirect object follows the direct object, the preposition must be expressed:* Buy a set of tools *for* the boy. Give my orders *to* the men. Telegraph the price *to* the agent.

7. The Secondary Object.—Verbs of *making* or *naming,* as *appoint, call, choose, constitute, elect, find, make, name, ordain,* and the like, may take a *secondary* object denoting office, rank, name, title, etc. The secondary object *follows* the direct object: The people elected Washington *president*. They named the child *John*.

CAUTION.—*Make* in the sense of *construct* takes an **indirect object**, which (when used without a preposition) always *precedes* the direct object: Make the *customer* a suit of clothes.

Make in the sense of *appoint or constitute* takes a **secondary object**, which always *follows* the direct object *without a preposition:* They made John *captain*.

8. **The Cognate Object.**—Some intransitive verbs take as an object a noun whose meaning is similar (cognate) to that of the verb; this is called the *cognate object:* He LIVED a wretched *life*. He SLEPT a dreamless *sleep*.

9. **The Object of an Infinitive, Gerund, or Participle:** Tell the pupils to bring *pencils*. Be faithful in learning your *lessons*.

10. **The Subject of an Infinitive:** I believe the *man* to be honest. (SEE RULES OF CASE IN NOUNS, p. 19, (3); also, USES OF THE INFINITIVE, pp. 85–87.)

11. **The Object of a Preposition:** He paid a high price for the *property*.

12. **The Objective Denoting Weight, Measure, etc.**—Nouns denoting *distance, measure, time, value, weight,* etc., are often used in the objective case without a preposition: He ran a *mile*. She is ten *years* old. The chimney is two hundred *feet* high.

13. **In the Passive Construction.**—The direct object of an active verb becomes the subject of a passive verb:

Active   That man sold a *horse*.

Passive   A *horse* was sold by that man.

Note that in the passive voice *man* is the object of the preposition *by*.

In the passive an indirect object is governed by a preposition, expressed or understood.

Active That man sold the *stranger* a horse.

Passive The horse was sold *to* the *stranger* by that man.

After verbs of making or naming (pp. 199–200) a secondary object of the active voice becomes the predicate nominative in the passive voice.

Active The voters elected McKinley *president* (Secondary object)

Passive McKinley was elected *president* by the voters. (Predicate nominative)

The Retained Object.—The direct object of a verb in the active voice frequently becomes the *retained object* in the passive voice.

Active The teacher gave the boy a *book*. (Object of *gave*)

Passive The boy was given a *book* by the teacher. (Retained object)

Note that *book,* which is carried over from the active construction, can not be the subject of *was given* (*boy* is subject), nor the object, because a passive form does not take an object. Nor can *book* be governed by a preposition. Hence we explain *book* by saying that it is carried over from the active construction, and we call it a *retained object*. The active construction can be changed to the passive so as to eliminate the retained object: A *book* was given to the boy by the teacher. Here *book* is the subject of *was given,* and *boy* and *teacher* are governed by the prepositions *to* and *by*. However, this is an awkward, wordy construction.

2. THE PRONOUN

The uses of the pronoun in the predicate are in nearly all respects the same as those of the noun, and for the most part the same rules apply to both. Some differences may be noted at certain points. (For full explanations of the various terms, compare the following numbered sections with the corresponding ones under THE NOUN, pp. 198–201.)

The Nominative Case

1. **The Predicate Nominative:** This is *he*. It is *I*.

NOTE: The forms *it's me, that's him,* etc., are now acceptable in informal discourse, but the nominative forms are still preferred in formal discourse:

Formal Who is there? It is *I*.

Informal Who's there? It's *me*.

An introductory relative or interrogative pronoun in the nominative case is really a predicate nominative. Hence the verb agrees with the noun or pronoun following the verb: Who *are* you? Which *are* the strangers? Who *am* I. (See INVERSION, pp. 224–226; compare pp. 203–204.)

2. **The Nominative After an Infinitive, Gerund, or Participle** is often harsh and clumsy and is therefore rarely used: I could wish to be *he*. I did not think of its being *I*.

CAUTION.—After an infinitive with a subject in the objective case, or after a participle agreeing with a noun or pronoun in the objective case, the following pronoun must be in the objective case: I understood *it* to be *him*.

3. **The Nominative by Apposition:** It is your father, *I*, the king. This use is also rare, since a pronoun is seldom used as an appositive.

The Possessive Case

4. **As a Modifier.**—A pronoun in the possessive case may be used to modify any noun or participle in the complete predicate: Did any one take *my* book? I had no idea of *his* coming.

The possessives *mine, thine, his, hers, its, ours, yours,* and *theirs* are *used as nouns* in the predicate, as in the subject. (See under SUBJECT, p. 180.)

The Objective Case

5. The Direct Object.—A pronoun in the complete predicate may be the *direct object* of the predicate verb. When used as the direct object, the pronoun usually follows the verb. His father sent *him.* I want no money from *them.*

EXCEPTIONS

(1) As the personal pronouns, and the pronoun *who,* have special forms in the objective case, they are not necessarily limited to the place after the verb, but may be used in some other position in the sentence in order to gain emphasis or some other rhetorical effect.

Me he restored unto mine office.—*Gen.* 41:13.

Whom he would he slew; and *whom* he would he kept alive; and *whom* he would he set up; and *whom* he would he put down.—*Dan.* 5:19.

(2) The relative or interrogative pronouns *whom, which,* and *what* regularly precede the verb by which they are governed, standing usually at the beginning of the clause or sentence: *Whom* did you meet? *Which* will you take? *What* did they pay him? Here the pronouns *whom, which,* and *what* are in the objective after the verbs *meet, take,* and *pay.* (Compare p. 202.)

CAUTION.—Such expressions as *"Who* did you meet?" (though sometimes used colloquially even by educated people) are inaccurate. We may say:

Whom did you meet at the door? (Object of *meet*)

Who was at the door? (Subject of *was*)

Who was employed by you? (Subject of *was employed*)

Whom did you employ? (Object of *did employ*)

As the case of a personal pronoun is *shown by its form,* it may take almost any position in the sentence, the nominative coming at times after the direct object of the verb: That messenger *I* sent to you.

6. The Indirect Object.—The pronoun is very frequently used as the *indirect object* after verbs of giving, sending, etc., and is treated in all respects like the noun in similar use.

> Buy *him* a set of tools.
>
> Find *her* a home.
>
> Give *them* my orders.
>
> He told *them* a story.

Like the noun, a pronoun used as an *indirect object* without a preposition must *precede* the direct object; if it *follows* the *direct object,* it must take a preposition, *to* or *for:*

> Buy a set of tools *for* him.
>
> Find a home *for* her.
>
> Give my orders *to* them.
>
> He told a story *to* them.

7–8. The Secondary Object; The Cognate Object.—A pronoun is rarely, if ever, used as the *secondary object,* and never as the *cognate object* of a verb.

9. The Object of an Infinitive, Participle or Gerund: My father promised to send *them.* I have not known of his meeting *her.* You should stop making *promises* you can not keep.

10. The Subject of an Infinitive: I believe *him* to be honest. (See USES OF THE INFINITIVE, p. 87.)

11. The Object of a Preposition: These books belong to *me.*

12. (No use of pronoun corresponding to 12 of NOUN.)

13. **The Passive Construction; The Retained Object.**—The rules and explanations for these items given under the NOUN (p. 201) apply directly to the pronoun, also. Thus:

Active Form   That man sold *him* a horse.

Passive Form   A horse was sold to *him* by that man.

Active Form   The teacher gave *him* a BOOK.

Passive Form   *He* was given a BOOK by the teacher.

EXERCISE

Find and parse every noun and pronoun in the complete predicate of each sentence of the following extracts, explaining the construction of each.

(1)   Where'er I roam, whatever realms to see,
        My heart untraveled, fondly turns to thee.
                              GOLDSMITH *Traveler*, l. 7.

(2)   The best way to keep good acts in memory is to refresh them with new.—*Attributed to* CATO *by* BACON *Apothegms*, No. 247.

(3)   And they three passed over the white sands, between the rocks, silent as the shadows.—COLERIDGE *The Wanderings of Cain.*

(4)   For every social wrong there must be a remedy. But the remedy can be nothing less than the abolition of the wrong. —HENRY GEORGE *Social Problems*, ch. 9.

(5)   Those who think must govern those that toil.—GOLDSMITH *The Traveler*, l. 372.

(6)   Our bugles sang truce, for the night-cloud had lowered,
        And the sentinel stars set their watch in the sky.
                        CAMPBELL *The Soldier's Dream.*

(7)   A people is but the attempt of many
        To rise to the completer life of one.
                    BROWNING *Luria*, act v, l. 334.

(8)   There was no other soul on that hill or on the shoveled walks, nor, so far as I could see, in the entire neighborhood. —SAUL BELLOW *Henderson the Rain King,* ch. 2.

(9)   There is maybe a small sign of uneasiness in the pugnacious assertion of high breeding in this and in the methodical brutality of their common behavior towards the travelers who must pass through their hands to reach the temporary haven of some ship in the harbor.—KATHERINE ANNE PORTER *Ship of Fools,* ch. 1.

(10)   This morning he had walked up the stairs slowly, a dark-blue mohair overcoat over his gray suit, bare-headed, slightly stooped.—THEODORE H. WHITE *The Making of the President 1960,* ch. 1.

(11)   He drove the hundred yards to the Kaiserhof and was soon with his old cronies, Goebbels, Goering, Roehm and the other Brownshirts who had helped him along the rocky, brawling path to power.—WILLIAM L. SHIRER *The Rise and Fall of the Third Reich,* ch. 1.

(12)   Hence the sixteenth century sees a collision, not only between different schools of religious thought, but between the changed economic environment and the accepted theory of society.—R. H. TAWNEY *Religion and the Rise of Capitalism,* ch. i.

3. THE ADJECTIVE

The adjective may be used in the predicate as:

1. **The Predicate Adjective to Modify the Subject,** after an intransitive or a passive verb (p. 65): Money is *useful.* The light is *bright.* The weather grows *cold.* The plan seems *wise.* He was considered *prosperous.* He was called *great.*

REMARKS

(1) The *predicate adjective* exactly corresponds in use to the predicate noun (see THE PREDICATE NOMINATIVE, p. 19, 2). The predicate adjective follows the predicate verb and adds something that applies to the *subject* of that verb. Using the

predicate noun, we say, "He seemed a *hero"*; using the *predicate adjective,* we say, "He seemed *heroic."*

(2) The predicate adjective is to be distinguished from other adjectives in the predicate. The predicate adjective modifies the subject: The *man* was *late.* Other adjectives in the predicate modify nouns or pronouns *in the predicate:* The man came at a *late* hour. Here *late* modifies *hour* (a noun in the predicate) and not the subject, *man.* Thus the predicate adjective stands in the predicate, but modifies the subject.

Adjective or Adverb.—To determine when a predicate adjective should be used, and when an adverb, see THE PREDICATE ADVERB, pp. 213–214.

2. **An Indefinite Modifier After an Infinitive, Participle, or Gerund:** He wished to be *good.* He believed in being *good.* Being *good* was too hard for him.

REMARKS.—Here the adjective may be said to be used *indefinitely,* not modifying any definite noun. It is sufficient in such cases to call the adjective an *indefinite modifier* or an *adjective used indefinitely.*

3. **A Modifier After a Verb of Calling, Naming, etc.**—After verbs of *making, calling, choosing,* etc. (called *factitive* verbs), an adjective is used precisely as a noun is used when it is the *secondary object* (see SECONDARY OBJECT under NOUN, p. 199): They made him *angry.* They called him *wise.* When the active form is changed to the passive, such an adjective is retained: He was made *angry.* Here *angry* becomes a *predicate adjective* modifying the subject.

4. **A Modifier of Any Noun or Pronoun.**—Any noun or pronoun included in the complete predicate may be modified by an adjective: This is the *same* man. He loved the *faithful* student. (Compare THE PREDICATE ADJECTIVE, above, Remark 2.)

4. THE VERB

The essential predicate of a sentence is always a finite verb or a series of finite verbs agreeing with the same essential subject (see THE COMPOUND ESSENTIAL PREDICATE, pp. 169–170): The boys *runs*. The boy *runs* and *slides*. The sky *is* blue. The owner *sold* the house.

Verbs of Complete and of Incomplete Predication

In sentence-construction verbs are divided into:

1. **Verbs of Complete Predication,** any one of which can by itself make a complete predicate: The boy *runs*. The child *sleeps*.

2. **Verbs of Incomplete Predication,** no one of which can by itself make a logically complete predicate: That *seems*—; The Romans *destroyed*—. We at once ask for something to complete the thought of the sentence: What or how does that *seem?* What did the Romans *destroy?*

Thus all transitive verbs, since they require an object to complete the sense of the sentence, are verbs of incomplete logical predication; so are the many verbs that require a predicate nominative, a predicate adjective, etc. Some of these that have received special names are:

(*a*) **The Copula.**—The verb *be,* because of its connective use, has been often called the *copula* or *link,* linking the essential subject with the predicate nominative or predicate adjective: John *is* the president.

The verb *be,* when called the *copula,* is still the *predicate verb;* it is the *essential predicate,* the one verb *essential* to make the construction of a sentence complete. Thus in the sentence "Time *is* money," the verb *is* is the *essential predicate*—the one finite verb by which the group of words becomes a sentence; *is money* is the *complete predicate*.

(*b*) **Copulative Verbs.**—There are many other intransitive verbs, such as *appear, become, seem,* etc., which connect the subject with a predicate nominative or a predicate adjective, and are hence called *copulative verbs*. Among intransitive verbs used in a weakened sense, approaching that of *be* or *become,* are the following:

come	keep	sit
continue	lie	sound
feel	look	stay
get	prove	turn
go	remain	wax
grow	run	

These verbs are used with predicate adjectives as follows:

to *come* true (as a prediction)	to *prove* false
to *continue* faithful	to *remain* unanswered
to *feel* tired	to *run* mad
to *get* rested	to *sit* mute
to *go* lame	to *sound* fair
to *grow* weary	to *stand* opposed
to *keep* busy	to *stay* settled
to *lie* hid	to *turn* traitor
to *look* pale	to *wax* great

The Complement.—The word or phrase used after a verb of incomplete predication to fill up the meaning of the sentence is often called the *complement* (from the Latin *compleo,* "fill up" complete). Thus the direct object, the predicate nominative, and the predicate adjective are different kinds of complements.

Agreement of the Verb

A finite verb must agree with its subject in person and number. This rule covers all ordinary cases; only matters requiring special notice will here be considered.

A. Person

When the elements of a compound subject joined by *or, nor, but* or by the correlatives *either—or, neither—nor* are of *different persons,* the verb agrees with the nearer element: Either you or I *am* in error. Either you or he *is* to blame.

If such constructions are awkward, they should be revised: Either you *are* in error, or I *am*. Either you *are* to blame, or he *is*.

For the person of a verb with an *interrogative pronoun,* see under NUMBER (pp. 211–212). For the person of a verb with a *relative pronoun,* see COMPLEX SENTENCE, VERBS IN RELATIVE CLAUSES (p. 231).

B. Number

1. A collective noun (Part I, p. 4), though singular in form, may take either a singular or plural verb. If the collective noun refers to a group as a *unit,* it takes a singular verb: The audience *was* large. If the collective noun refers to a group as separate entities, it takes a plural verb: The audience *were divided* in their opinion.

2. Certain nouns plural in form are singular in meaning and take singular verbs: The *news is* good tonight. (See PLURALS TREATED AS SINGULARS, p. 15.)

3. Two or more singular nominatives connected by *and* in a compound subject form a *plural* subject and take a verb in the plural: * A *lake and* a *boat are* all I need for a good vacation. (See p. 193.)

* NOTE.—A singular noun modified by two or more adjectives denoting different aspects or varieties of an object may take a plural verb: *Greek* and *Roman* ARCHITECTURE *were* different in type.

EXCEPTIONS

(1) When two or more singular nominatives connected by *and* denote the same person or thing, they take a verb in the singular: The husband *and* father *was devoted* to his family.

(2) When two or more singular nominatives connected by *and* are modified by *each, every,* or *no,* they are taken separately and have a verb in the singular number: EACH officer *and* [EACH] soldier *was* at his post. EVERY teacher *and* [EVERY] pupil *was* ready. No sentence *and* NO word *is* to be neglected.

(3) When two or more singular nominatives connected by *and* are emphatically distinguished by some added word or words such as *also, as well as, commonly, even, not, often, oftentimes, perhaps, too, usually,* or the like, they are as a rule taken separately with a verb in the singular: Famine, *and* ALSO pestilence, *threatens* the besieged city. Pity, *and* NOT fear, *makes* me pause.

4. Two or more singular nominatives connected by any conjunction except *and* (as *or, nor,* etc.) are considered separately and take a verb in the singular: John *or* Robert *is* calling us.

5. When the compound essential subject is made up of nouns or pronouns *different in number,* the verb agrees with *the noun or pronoun nearest to it,* whatever the connecting conjunction may be: The president or his advisors *are* to blame. The president's advisors or the president himself *is* to blame.

6. The introductory word *it* is always followed by a singular verb. This rule applies even when the predicate nominative is plural: IT *is* the philosophers who have taught the worth of patience.

7. An *interrogative pronoun* commonly takes a verb in the third person singular: Who *is* there?

But a verb in the same construction agrees in person and

number with the following noun or pronoun: Who *am* I? Which *are* the specimens? What *are* we against that host?

The reason for this is that the interrogative pronoun in such use is a *predicate nominative* placed at the beginning of the sentence by inversion. (See THE PREDICATE NOMINATIVE, p. 198.)

The Infinitive in the Predicate

See USES OF THE INFINITIVE, (2), (3), (4), (5), (6), pp. 85–86. An *infinitive phrase* may be used as:

1. **The Predicate Nominative:** To love is *to be loved*.

2. **The Object of a Verb or of a Participle:** Athletes love *to win*. Striving *to win* our approval, the children washed the dishes.

3. **An Adverbial Modifier** of the essential predicate or of any verb, adjective, or adverb contained in the complete predicate: He shouted *in order to alarm the camp*. This is important *for you to know*. We arrived early enough *to be admitted*.

4. **An Adjective Element** modifying any noun or pronoun in the complete predicate: He formed a scheme *to defraud his creditors*.

The Gerund in the Predicate

In the predicate of a sentence, the gerund may be:

1. **The Predicate Nominative:** Seeing is *believing*.

2. **The Direct Object** of the predicate verb or of a preposition: I hate *lying*. He was ruined by *speculating*.

The Participle in the Predicate

In the predicate of a sentence, the participle may be a modifier of any noun or pronoun included in the complete predicate: We found him *trying* to open the door.

A **Participial Phrase** is often used as an adverb-element modifying the essential predicate or any adjective or adverb included in the complete predicate: He failed *by attempting the impossible*. The traitor was skillful *in framing excuses*.

5. THE ADVERB

An adverb may be used in the complete predicate (1) as a modifier of the predicate verb; or, (2) as a modifier of any adjective, infinitive, participle, or adverb; or, (3) as an adjunct of a noun or pronoun of the complete predicate. (See THE ADVERB, Part I, pp. 134–142.)

The Predicate Adverb (often called the **Adverb Complement**).—An intransitive verb may take an adverb as a complement to complete the sense. The man is *here*. The letter is *there*.

In such use the adverb is often closely parallel in effect to the predicate adjective (p. 206), so that it may be called the *predicate adverb*. Thus we may say with the adjective, "The man is *present*," or with the adverb, "The man is *here*," and the two statements are almost identical.

Adjective or Adverb.—Whether to use a predicate adjective or adverb at the close of a sentence is often a perplexing question. Depending on the intended meaning, either may be used.

If something in the subject is to be described or modified, an adjective must be used:

> They escaped *safe* to shore. [The adjective *safe* modifies the pronoun *they* in the subject, expressing their condition after the escape.]

> The children sat *quiet* through the long ceremony. [The adjective *quiet* modifies the noun *children* in the subject, the *quiet children*.]

If, however, the *action* is qualified, an adverb must be used:

> They escaped *safely* to shore. [The adverb *safely* modifies the verb *escape*, expressing the *manner of escape*.]

The children sat *quietly* through the long ceremony. [The adverb *quietly* modifies the verb *sat,* expressing the manner in which they *sat.*]

With such verbs as *look, smell,* and *taste,* we must note carefully whether the reference is to the subject or the verb:

The rose smells *sweet.*

The butter tastes *bad.*

He looked *sad.*

He looked *sadly* about him.

I feel *bad.*

The boy is *bad* in school.

The boy does *badly* in school.

6. THE PREPOSITION

Prepositions and prepositional phrases, as used in the complete predicate, are subject to essentially the same rules as when used in the complete subject. (See SUBJECT, pp. 189–190.)

Prepositional Phrases as Adverbs.—Prepositional phrases used adverbially are very numerous, and often more explicit than adverbs of similar meaning. Thus, "I arrived *at that very instant*" is far more precise, as well as more emphatic, than "I arrived *then.*"

7. THE CONJUNCTION

The use of conjunctions as connecting elements of the predicate is precisely similar to their use as connecting elements of the subject. (See under SUBJECT, pp. 192–193.)

8. THE INTERJECTION

The interjection can be a part of the complete predicate only in some rare case when it is used as a quotation, being the predicate nominative or the direct object of the verb: His cry was *"Alas!"* He cried *"Alas!"*

TO SELECT THE ESSENTIAL PREDICATE

In Analysis

1. When there is *but one finite verb in the sentence,* that verb is the essential predicate.

Thus, turn to the sentence given for analysis under the ESSENTIAL SUBJECT, p. 196.

> Fringed by the rapid Meuse and enclosed by gently rolling hills cultivated to their crests, or by abrupt precipices of limestone crowned with verdure, the broad, crescent-shaped plain‖*was divided* by numerous hedgerows.

In this sentence of thirty-three words, there is only one finite verb, *was divided,* which is accordingly the *essential predicate* of the sentence and which agrees with *plain,* the essential subject. The words *by numerous hedgerows* form a prepositional phrase, used as an adverb, modifying the verb *was divided,* and forming with it the *complete predicate.*

No matter how many other words may be accumulated around it, *the one finite verb* of such a sentence is *the essential predicate.* Thus:

> John Paul Jones,‖with his own hands, *raised* the first American naval flag, under a salute of thirteen guns.

Here *raised*—the one finite verb of the sentence—is the *essential predicate.* It agrees with the subject *John Paul Jones.* All of the words after *Jones* form the *complete* predicate, as analysis will show:

With his own hands and *under a salute,* etc., are prepositional phrases, used as adverbs, modifying the verb *raised,* and showing by what means and to what accompaniment the act was performed. The noun *flag,* modified by the adjectives *first, American,* and *naval,* is the object of the verb *raised.* That is, all the words after *Jones*—sixteen words—form the *complete predicate,* of which the finite verb *raised* forms the *essential predicate.* The sentence is, therefore, correctly constructed.

The length of the sentence makes no difference grammatically. If a sentence, however long or short, contains but one *finite verb,* that sentence is a simple sentence, and *that one finite verb* is the essential predicate.

2. When there is *more than one finite verb in the sentence,* see if each of those verbs agrees with the essential subject (simple or compound). If so, those verbs form a *compound essential predicate* (see pp. 169–170):

John *runs* and *slides.*

Here we have, not two sentences or clauses, but one simple sentence, because both the verbs agree with the same essential subject. The verbs *runs* and *slides* affirm two connected acts of one and the same person, *John.* Those two verbs, therefore, form one compound predicate (see pp. 169–170). The same would be true if the essential subject were compound:

John and James *run* and *slide.*

As the compound essential subject *John and James* consists of two nouns connected by *and,* that compound subject requires a plural verb or verbs (pp. 210–211). Both verbs of this sentence must, therefore, be in the plural, because two persons are performing each action. The essential predicate is, accordingly, *run and slide.* The sentence is correctly formed, and is a simple sentence.

The same treatment is to be given to any number of verbs so joined, as when Tennyson ("Day Dream, Revival," st. 2, l. 6), says of the awakening of life in the enchanted palace:

The palace *banged* and *buzzed* and *clackt.*

The one *palace* did all those acts, and the three connected verbs form one compound predicate in agreement with the one subject, *palace*.

NOTE 1.—If verbs in a sentence *agree with different subjects,* the sentence is *not a simple sentence,* but is a compound or complex sentence. Thus:

> My boat is on the shore,
> And my bark is on the sea.

Here the first *is* agrees with *boat,* and the second *is* agrees with *bark.* We have two subjects, and two predicates, and the sentence is not a simple, but a compound, sentence. (See COMPOUND AND COMPLEX SENTENCES, p. 226–228.)

NOTE 2.—As previously stated, the length of the sentence has nothing to do with the matter. Thus:

> My brother wears a martial plume,
> And serves within a distant land.

There is here one singular noun as subject, *brother,* with which the verbs *wears* and *serves* agree. These two verbs, therefore, form the compound essential predicate, *wears and serves,* of the one simple sentence.

In Synthesis

In framing a sentence (1) determine what the essential subject is to be and (2) choose a verb (or verbs) of the proper person and number to agree with that essential subject, according to the directions already given.

CAUTION.—It is of the utmost importance to remember that appositives (p. 174), possessives (p. 175), and prepositional phrases (p. 175), *have nothing whatever to do with the form of the verb;* the verb reaches past all modifiers and agrees with the essential subject just as if no other words were associated with it. Thus, in the example analysed under the

SUBJECT (p. 196), when we have determined that, out of the seven nouns, the *essential subject* is the singular noun, *plain,* we know that any verb connected with it must be in the singular number, and we must say *was divided,* and not *were divided.*

Or suppose we have in mind a sentence like the following:

> The various kinds of sentence-structure (express, expresses) various relations of thought.

Shall we say *express* or *expresses?* Looking for the essential subject, we see that it is not the nearest noun, *sentence-structure,* because that is the object of the preposition *of,* and can not be the subject of any verb. The essential subject must then be the plural noun *kinds,* requiring the plural verb *express.* Thus our sentence will be:

> The various kinds of sentence-structure *express* various relations of thought.

When we have found the *essential subject* and the *essential predicate,* it is a comparatively easy matter to fit other elements of the sentence about the *essential subject* to form the *complete subject,* and about the *essential predicate* to form the *complete predicate.* It must be noted, however, that the various elements will *not always be found placed in their grammatical order,* which must be learned from the meaning and relations of the words or phrases used. Thus, if I say, "This letter you will deliver at my house," the noun *letter* is the object of the verb *will deliver,* and would regularly follow that verb, but, for the sake of emphasis, is placed at the beginning of the sentence, by what is called *inversion,* as will be more fully explained on pp. 224–226.

EXERCISE A

Find the essential predicate in each of the following sentences and explain its agreement with the essential subject.

(1)   To have read the greatest works of any great poet is a possession added to the best things of life.—SWINBURNE *Essays and Studies,* "Victor Hugo L'Année Terrible."

(2)   According to the state of a man's conscience, so do hope and fear on account of his deeds arise in his mind.—OVID *Fasti,* I, 485.

(3)   An old man in his rudiments is a disgraceful object. It is for youth to acquire, and for age to apply.—SENECA *Epistolæ Ad Lucilium,* xxxvi, 4.

(4)   The confounding of all right and wrong, in wild fury, has averted from us the gracious favor of the gods.—CATULLUS *Carmina,* lxiv, 406.

(5)   The skillful class of flatterers praise the discourse of an ignorant friend and the face of a deformed one.—JUVENAL *Satiræ,* iii, 86.

(6)   O'er Egypt's land of memory floods are level,
              And they are thine, O Nile!
                                        SHELLEY *Sonnet. To the Nile.*

(7)   In lapidary inscriptions a man is not upon oath.
              SAMUEL JOHNSON *Boswell's Life of Johnson.* 1775.

(8)   The glory of ancestors sheds a light around posterity; it allows neither their good nor their bad qualities to remain in obscurity.—SALLUST *Jugurtha,* lxxxv.

(9)   To some men popularity is always suspicious. Enjoying none themselves, they are prone to suspect the validity of those attainments which command it.—GEO. HENRY LEWES *The Spanish Drama,* ch. iii.

(10)   Innocence in genius, and candor in power, are both noble qualities.—MADAME DE STAËL *Germany,* pt. ii, ch. viii.

EXERCISE B

(1)   Vast changes, already in progress, invite the writer.—HAMLIN GARLAND *Crumbling Idols.*

(2)   Perhaps the future poet of these spaces is plowing somewhere like that, because it must be that from the splendor and dramatic contrast of such scenes the poet will rise.—HAMLIN GARLAND *Crumbling Idols.*

(3)   In one place in the *Deerslayer,* and in the restricted space of two-thirds of a page, Cooper has scored 114 offences against literary art out of a possible 115.—MARK TWAIN *Fenimore Cooper's Literary Offences.*

(4)   Cooper's proudest creations in the way of "situations" suffer noticeably from the absence of the observer's protective gift.—MARK TWAIN *Fenimore Cooper's Literary Offences.*

(5)   No one knows so well as I the faults of immaturity and inexperience that characterize this book.—EDWARD EGGLESTON *The Hoosier Schoolmaster* "Preface."

(6)   Wittingly or unwittingly, English fiction and American fiction have recognized this truth, not fully, not in the measure it merits, but in a greater degree than most other fiction. —W. D. HOWELLS *Criticism and Fiction.*

(7)   Doubtful the ideal of those poor islanders will be changed. —W. D. HOWELLS *Criticism and Fiction.*

(8)   Literature should be instructive or amusing. . . . — HENRY JAMES *The Art of Fiction.*

(9)   The cowboy carried Johnny through the drift to the door. —STEPHEN CRANE *The Blue Hotel.*

(10)   His tears plashed upon the livid face beneath his own. —AMBROSE BIERCE *The Coup de Grâce.*

(11)   Is the new presentation of new ways enough?—MARGARET MEAD *Male and Female,* xii.

(12)   This art, the art natural to us, has always been an art of rich detail.—EDITH HAMILTON *The Greek Way to Western Civilization.*

(13)   Another contrast suggests itself, that between the Greek archepelago and the Hebrides.—H. D. F. KITTO *The Greeks.*

(14)   People laugh when a man slips on a banana peel and winds up in an undignified posture with foolish shock on his face.—LOUIS NIZER *My Life in Court,* "Reputation."

(15)   We saw Feeney and Noble go round to the shed and went in ourselves.—FRANK O'CONNOR *Guests of the Nation.*

INDEPENDENT ELEMENTS

Certain words or phrases which may be attached to a sentence and connected with it in thought, but which do not form part of the grammatical structure are called **independent elements.** The independent element contributes to the sense of the sentence without being the subject, object, or the modifier of anything, or without being in any way grammatically connected with the sentence. If a grammatically unconnected element does not make sense, it is either misplaced or incorrect. The *independent elements* to be noted are the following:

1. **The Parenthetical Expression.**—A parenthetical expression is a phrase, clause, or sentence included within a sentence that is complete without it:

> the wind is a Lady with
> bright slender eyes (who
>
> moves) at sunset
>
> E. E. CUMMINGS

Here the parenthetical "who moves" is not essential to the thought of the sentence and can be omitted without injuring it. The two curved marks ( ) used to enclose the injected words are called *parentheses*. Commas or dashes are sometimes used in place of parentheses.

The test of the parenthetical expression is that it may be omitted without injury to the sentence. The parenthetical expression is much less used now than formerly. The current preference is to introduce additional material in a separate clause or sentence.

2. **A Noun or, Rarely, a Pronoun Used in Direct Address** is an independent element: *Charles,* you are wanted at home. Ho, *you!* Where are you going? Similarly a noun or pronoun used in an exclamation is an independent element: The *Niobe* of nations! there she stands.

3. **A Noun or Pronoun Used for Emphasis, Exclamation,** etc. is an independent element:

> The children, *they* above all must be considered.

> In the common people, *in them* only must sovereignty be invested.

The above sentences could be written, "The children above all must be considered" and "In the common people only must sovereignty be invested." But these statements would be less vivid and emphatic.

4. **The Nominative Absolute.**—A participial phrase without grammatical relation to any other word in the sentence is called a *nominative absolute:*

> *The day being warm,* we went to the beach. [Here the phrase does not modify *we,* the subject, or *beach,* the object of the preposition *to;* nor is the phrase itself the subject or verb.]

> *The decision being irrevocable,* they turned their attention to other matters. [The phrase is not the subject or the modifier of the subject *they;* nor does it modify the verb or the nouns *attention* and *matters.*]

The nominative absolute often has the effect of a conditional clause:

> *Because the day was warm,* we went to the beach.

> *Since the decision was irrevocable,* they turned their attention to other matters.

The nominative absolute should not be confused with the construction in which a noun or pronoun is modified by a participial modifier: The sun, *having turned a fiery red,* sank below the horizon. In this sentence *having turned a fiery red* modifies the *sun.*

The nominative absolute is a loose and sometimes awkward construction that is not at home in English. It is therefore not regarded favorably and is not much used. Except for compelling reasons, it should be avoided.

CAUTION.—A participle used as a nominative absolute should, as a general rule, have a definite subject *expressed in the same phrase*. Otherwise the use of the participle may give a false or ridiculous meaning:

> Not *expecting* us, the *horses* had been turned out
> to pasture, and were difficult to catch.

Here *expecting* seems to modify *horses* and thus to make a grotesque statement. The statement should be: "Our *friends* not expecting us, the horses had been turned out," etc.

5. **Many Infinitive Phrases:** *to tell the truth; to speak plainly; to cut the matter short; to be brief;* etc.

6. **Various Adverbs,** used often elliptically: *Away!* (equivalent to *go away*) *Up! Forward!* (Compare INTERJECTIONS, below.)

Yes and *No,* used in answer to questions, are independent elements, each being equivalent to a whole sentence: "Will you go?" "Yes" (equivalent to "I will go").

7. **Many Prepositional Phrases:** *for example; for instance; in fact; in truth; in a word; under the circumstances;* etc. (See also INTERJECTIONS, below.)

8. **Interjections.**—All interjections are considered as *independent elements,* not grammatically connected with the other words of a sentence, though they may deeply affect the meaning of the whole. The exclamation attributed to Wellington at Waterloo, *"Oh,* that Blücher or night would come!" loses most of its force if we omit the introductory interjection "Oh."

Various parts of speech, as nouns, pronouns, adjectives, verbs, or adverbs, when used as exclamations to express surprise or sudden emotion or intense feeling of any kind have the force of interjections: *Well! Hark! Shame! Good! What! Up!*

Forward! Away! An exclamatory prepositional phrase may be used as an *independent element* with interjectional force: Oh, *for rest and peace!*

THE INVERTED CONSTRUCTION

The **inverted construction,** or **inversion,** is the use of words in some other than the regular or usual order, generally for the sake of emphasis or clearness.

Here it will seem to some persons that we are introducing a complication that destroys all simplicity and certainty. On the contrary, *inversion* is one of the most common and familiar things in English speech. Every child understands it. It is used by everyone who asks a question. The direct statement is,

(subject)	(verb)	(pred. nom.)
This *boy*	IS	your *brother*.

As soon as we ask a question, we change the order of the terms, and say,

(verb)	(subject)	(pred. nom.)
IS	this *boy*	your *brother?*

That is *inversion.* It is not mysterious, but is instantly understood by that simple exercise of thought which we call "common sense." Some other forms of *inversion* require more study, but are readily understood or explained by clear and attentive thinking. Some of the chief instances of *inversion* are listed below.

1. **Subject and Verb.**—The verb or auxiliary may by inversion precede the subject:

(*a*) In interrogation: Does he wish to go? (see pp. 118–119).

(*b*) In the imperative sentence where the subject, if expressed, follows the verb or the first auxiliary: *Do* YOU *begin.* This is, however, a highly artificial construction and should be avoided.

(*c*) In exclamatory sentences: What visions *have* I seen!

(*d*) In introducing a quotation: "This is for you," *said* HE.

(*e*) With the subjunctive mood: *Had* I *known* (see p. 84).

(*f*) In relative clauses, for rhetorical effect: He soon reached a neat cottage in which *lived* the WIDOW.

(*g*) In negative statements: Never *was* there a MIND keener and more critical. Not only *does* HE *master* it, but he makes it practical. Neither *was* I *offended*.

(*h*) In sentences expressing a comparison: The longer he toiled, the more hopeless *seemed* the TASK.

(*i*) With adverbs or other designations of place: Here *is* a TELEGRAM. On that hill *is* a fine MANSION.

(*j*) See under ADJECTIVE AND NOUN, below.

2. **Subject and Object.**—(For the regular order of words in English, see THE NOMINATIVE AND OBJECTIVE CASES, p. 18; p. 199; POSITION OF THE DIRECT OBJECT, pp. 203–204.)

(*a*) By inversion the direct object may sometimes precede the subject if no confusion of thought is produced: This land the king gave to his favorite. Here there is no doubt that *king* is the subject of the verb, and *land* the object. It was the *king* who *gave* the land.

(*b*) A relative or interrogative pronoun which is the object of a verb regularly precedes that verb: This is the man *whom* they sent. Here it is evident that *they* is the subject of the verb *sent,* and *whom* the object. Hence we use *whom* just as if the order of words were "they sent *whom*."

3. **Adjective and Noun.**—(See POSITION OF THE ADJECTIVE, pp. 63–65; POSITION OF THE ARTICLE, p. 76.)

The *predicate adjective* may, however, come first in the sentence by inversion: *Certain* it is that this is the field. Such inversion of the predicate adjective often carries with it the inversion of subject and verb: *Wise are* all his WAYS. (Compare SUBJECT AND VERB, pp. 224–225.)

4. **Adverbs and Adverbial Phrases** that really modify some element of the predicate may, by inversion, precede the subject: *There* appears to be your error. *Here* he studied grammar. *Of fuel* they had plenty. *To these peculiarities* Dr. Martoun added another.

Where a number of adverbial elements would overload the concluding portion of the sentence, they may be variously distributed so that the mind follows them without weariness or confusion and gathers their united meaning at the close. The important point to note is that many sentences can not be cut in two at some middle point, with all before that point in the subject and all after it in the predicate. The *meaning and mutual relations of the words* must be the guide to their classification either in the subject or predicate of the sentence.

COMPOUND AND COMPLEX SENTENCES

According to the number and kinds of clauses they contain, sentences are classified as (1) simple, (2) complex, (3) compound, or (4) compound-complex. The simple sentence has already been explained in detail. We will now consider the longer and more complicated sentences that are constructed by combining simple sentences and clauses.

To use only simple sentences, as important as they are, would make our speech or writing choppy and deprive it of logical conditions and qualifications. Thus:

The sun has risen. The birds are singing.

I called. He was not at home.

I overslept. I was late for work.

Instead of these bare and unrelated statements, we often prefer to write:

The sun has risen, *and* the birds are singing.

I called, *but* he was not at home.

Because I overslept, I was late.

These sentences contain the original simple sentences, but each simple sentence is now part of a longer, more complicated sentence.

Clauses

Complex and compound sentences are composed of clauses. A **clause** is a group of words containing a subject and a predicate that is used as part of a sentence.

The following sentence is composed of two clauses, each of which is italicized:

If he is late, he will be discharged.

The essential subject and predicate of the first clause are *he* and *is;* of the second, *he* and *will be discharged.* Both clauses are necessary to express the complete thought. The first clause is logically incomplete and can not stand alone. If he is late—then what? The second clause can stand alone as a simple sentence: He will be discharged. However, this statement is false because the thought to be expressed is that he will be discharged *only if he is late.* Therefore both clauses are necessary to express the complete thought.

The Independent Clause.—An independent clause is a simple sentence used as part of a longer sentence.

Simple Sentence	He was disqualified.
Independent Clause	Because he was too young, *he was disqualified.*

An independent clause is called independent because it may stand alone as a simple sentence; it does not rely on anything else for grammatical completion. Independent clauses are also called main or principal clauses. It will be helpful to remember that an independent clause would be a simple sentence if it stood alone instead of being part of a longer sentence.

The Dependent Clause.—A dependent clause is one that can not stand alone because it does not make a grammatically or logically complete statement. To make sense a dependent clause must be connected with another clause and modify some element of that clause. The following clause is dependent: When the lawyer spoke to the defendants.

Although this group of words has an essential subject (*lawyer*) and predicate (*spoke*), it is logically incomplete because of the subordinating adverb *when*. We are left asking, "What about *when the lawyer spoke to the defendants?*" We are satisfied, however, when the clause is properly related to an independent clause: When the lawyer spoke to the defendants, *he turned around to observe them*. Now the dependent clause acts like an adverb to modify the essential predicate *turned* in the independent clause.

A dependent clause is also called a minor or subordinate clause. A dependent clause is incomplete because it is introduced by a subordinating word that also relates it to another clause, either dependent or independent.

THE COMPLEX SENTENCE

The **complex sentence** contains *one* independent clause and *one or more* dependent clauses. In other words, a complex sentence is a simple sentence to which at least one dependent clause has been attached.

Simple Sentence   He is the vice-president.

Complex Sentence   He is the vice-president *who is in charge of personnel*.

Dependent clauses are joined to other clauses, either dependent or independent, by subordinating conjunctions (pp. 229–

230), relative pronouns (pp. 45–48; pp. 230–231), or by conjunctive adverbs (p. 137).

1. **Subordinate Conjunctions.**—To understand the use of such subordinating connectives, note the two following sentences:

> These flowers are beautiful.
> They are very small.

Each is a principal or independent sentence. Now we may join them with a subordinate conjunction which will indicate that the second sentence is subordinate:

> These flowers are beautiful, *although they are very small.*

The sentence is now a *complex sentence,* showing by its form that the second clause is subordinate to the first. The conjunction *although* makes the second clause *subordinate,* as it is meant to be.

The *subordinate conjunctions* most in use are the following:

although	provided	though
as	save	unless
because	seeing	whereat
except	since	wherever
for	still	whether
however	than	while
if	that	without
lest	then	

Various *conjunctive* or *relative adverbs* are used with the effect of subordinate conjunctions:

how	whenever	wherein
now	where	whither
thence	whereby	why
when	whereon	wherefore
whence	whereupon	

Some of these adverbs have the full effect of conjunctions, and they are often classed as conjunctions. Some other relative adverbs have the conjunctive effect: *after, before, till, until,* etc.

Than as a Subordinate Conjunction.—*Than* (see p. 71; p. 153) when used in comparison connects clauses. The clause following *than* is often incomplete, the verb being understood. A noun or pronoun following *than* may be either in the nominative or objective case according to the verb supplied.

He likes you better than *I* (like you).

He likes you better than (he likes) *me.*

The sentences "He likes you better than *I* and "He likes you better than me" are both correct, but there is a great difference in their meaning. The case to be used after *than* may always be known by mentally supplying a verb to complete the sense, as in the sentences given above.

CAUTION.—An adjective in the positive degree with *as* or *so* should not be used with an adjective in the comparative degree followed by or requiring *than.* Thus:

He is *as* tall or taller *than* I.

He is not *so* old but stronger *than* I.

These sentences are incorrect. They should be written:

He is *as* tall *as* I, or taller.

He is not *so* old *as* I, but (he is) stronger.

2. Relative Pronouns.—A clause connected by a relative pronoun is always a subordinate clause.

A relative pronoun is always a part of the clause which it connects, being either (*a*) the subject, or (*b*) the object of the predicate verb of the subordinate clause, or (*c*) the object of a preposition belonging to the subordinate clause, or (*d*) a possessive modifying some noun or noun-element of the subordinate clause:

(*a*) This is the man *who* sent the message.

(*b*) I found the man *whom* I was seeking.

(*c*) He was the man from *whom* I received the message.

(*d*) The man *whose* message I received met me at the station.

Verbs in Relative Clauses.—The antecedent of the relative pronoun *who* or *which* is usually expressed; the person and number of the relative are known by the person and number of the antecedent. We therefore have the following simple rule:

RULE.—When a relative pronoun is the subject of a verb, the verb takes the person and number of the antecedent of the relative pronoun: John spoke to three *men* who *were* present at the meeting. (Since the antecedent of *who* is plural, *who* is plural and requires the plural verb *were*.)

For the gender, person, and number of a pronoun following a relative in the same clause, see under PRONOUNS AND ANTECEDENTS, p. 61 (2).

Who or Whom.—Care must be exercised in using the nominative *who* and the objective *whom*. Note the two following sentences:

Is this the man *who* was at the door?

Is this the man *whom* you found at the door?

In the first sentence, *who* is the subject of the verb *was;* therefore the nominative is correctly used. In the second sentence, *whom* is the object of the verb *found* and is therefore correctly used: You found *whom* at the door.

RULE.—When the relative is the subject of the predicate verb in its clause, use *who*. When it is the object of that verb, or of a preposition, use *whom:* He is the man *to whom* I spoke.

CAUTION.—A special perplexity arises here, when some parenthetical phrase or clause intervenes between the relative and its verb:

$$\text{I met two men} \left\{ \begin{array}{l} \textit{who} \\ \textit{whom} \end{array} \right\}, \text{I believe, were policemen.}$$

Which is right? That is easily settled by leaving out the parenthetical clause; then the sentence must read:

I met two men *who* —— —— were policemen.

It would be impossible to say "*whom* were policemen."

On the other hand, consider the following sentence:

They were seeking a man *who,* I believe, they found.

Omit *I believe,* and we see at once that we could not say "*who* they found"; we must say "*whom* they found" because *whom* is the object of *found.* Hence the sentence, as given, is incorrect and should be:

They were seeking a man *whom,* I believe, they found.

Try every such sentence by *omitting the parenthetical phrase or clause;* the relative that would be used if that phrase or clause were omitted is the relative that should be used when that phrase or clause is retained.

Who or Whom as Interrogatives.—The rules for the use of *who* or *whom* as *interrogatives* are practically the same as for the corresponding *relatives:*

Subject of verb: *Who* invited you?

Object of verb: *Whom* did you invite?

Object of preposition: By *whom* were you invited?

Similarly in indirect questions:

He asked *who* invited us.

He asked *whom* we invited.

He asked by *whom* we were invited.

(See also CLAUSES WITH WHOEVER, etc., pp. 233–234.)

Dependent Clauses as Elements

A dependent clause of a complex sentence may be used as a *noun,* an *adjective,* or an *adverb*. Dependent clauses are therefore classified as *noun* clauses, *adjective* clauses, and *adverb* clauses.

1. **The Noun Clause.**—A *noun clause* may be:

(*a*) The subject of a sentence: *That you approve the plan* satisfies me.

The entire clause *that you approve the plan* is the only subject that the verb *satisfies* can have. Observe that *you* can not be the subject of *satisfies* because it is of different person and number and is itself the subject of the verb *approve*.

(*b*) The predicate nominative: To be happy is *all that most persons desire*.

(*c*) The object of a verb or preposition: I expect *that the train will arrive on time*. They were eager *for what had been promised them*.

(*d*) An appositive: The proof *that the money was paid* is conclusive. I depend upon your promise *that you will come*.

2. **The Adjective Clause.**—A clause that modifies a noun in the manner of an adjective is called an *adjective clause:* I know the price *that he asks for the property*.

3. **The Adverb Clause.**—A clause that modifies a verb, adjective, or adverb is called an *adverbial clause:* I will come *when I am needed*. Here the clause *when I am needed* modifies the verb *come* just as an adverb might. Adverbial clauses are used to denote place, time, manner, degree, cause, consequence, purpose, concession, etc.

Clauses with Whoever, etc.—The case of the compound relative pronouns *whoever* and *whosoever* is determined by the use of the pronoun in its own clause.

Whoever steps over that line will be shot.

Here *whoever* is the subject of *steps*. The subject of the essential predicate *will be shot* is the entire noun clause *whoever steps over that line*.

Give the job to $\begin{Bmatrix} whoever \\ whomever \end{Bmatrix}$ can do it best.

Here the correct form is *whoever* as subject of the verb *can do*. Note that the required form is not *whomever* as the object of the preposition *to*. The object of *to* is the entire clause *whoever can do it best*.

REMARKS.—In a complex sentence one dependent clause may depend upon another: I met him politely because he brought me the book *which he had promised me*. Here the relative clause *which he had promised me* depends upon the subordinate clause *because he brought me the book*.

However, a speaker or writer should be careful not to make a sentence clumsy or difficult to understand with an accumulation of dependent clauses. A sentence like the following should be avoided: On our way to town we met a wagon which was drawn by a horse which was old and infirm, which was driven by a man who wore a straw hat and a blue shirt which was ill-adapted to the day, which was very cold.

To Parse a Subordinate Clause

1. Treat the whole clause as an element of the complex sentence, telling whether it is a *noun clause,* an *adjective clause,* or an *adverb clause.*

2. Then, treat the clause by itself as a simple sentence, and parse each word it contains as an element of that simple sentence.

EXERCISE

Tell whether each of the following sentences is simple or complex. Identify the independent and dependent clauses in each complex sentence.

1. Beyond a doubt, the officer standing on the corner and talking with the woman in blue is attached to the Sixteenth Precinct.

2. He asked how to go.

3. Here is a glossary of terms for the atomic age.

4. She will can the peaches that I picked yesterday.

5. No one knows how to explain the genius of Mozart.

6. Is he the architect who designed the civic center?

7. Astronauts must be rigorously selected and trained.

8. Much of the computation that was formerly done by men is now done by electronic computers.

9. Many people believe that our hope for peace lies with the United Nations.

10. The boat which docked yesterday is the *Queen Mary*.

11. He believes in advertising as the principal force sustaining our vast commercial-industrial society.

12. Prescott was a great American historian.

13. This book contains scores of Swinburne's letters that have been suppressed for many years.

14. We are now producing glass as hard as most steel.

15. There is no doubt that William Faulkner, who recently died, is one of our greatest writers.

16. I am glad to know that people are still living in the house where I was born.

17. The atom is the smallest unitary constituent of matter.

18. On the test he forgot to say that a proton is a positively charged particle.

19. Intensive research is now being carried on in cardio-vascular diseases.

20. Although England has at least one commercial television company, English television, unlike ours, is not commercially controlled.

THE COMPOUND SENTENCE

When two or more simple sentences are united, the longer sentence formed by their union is a **compound sentence.** When placed in a compound sentence the simple sentences become independent clauses.

Each of the following is a simple sentence: The autumn has come. The apples are ripe. The leaves are falling. We may combine these three simple, independent sentences into one longer sentence which shall include them all:

> The autumn has come, the apples are ripe, and the leaves are falling.

This longer sentence is a *compound sentence.* Each of the simple sentences composing it is now an *independent clause* of the compound sentence, and each of these clauses is a *member* (pp. 227–228) of the compound sentence.

Conjunctions Omitted.—Where several clauses of a compound sentence are connected by the same conjunction, the conjunction may be, and commonly is, omitted, except before the final clause. Since the members of a compound sentence are principal or independent clauses, no one of which is subordinate to any other, they are said to be *coordinate,* or of the same rank.

Coordinate Conjunctions.—The coordinate clauses of a compound sentence are connected by the coordinate conjunctions: *and, but, either, neither, nor, or, for, yet, whereas.*

COMPOUND-COMPLEX SENTENCES

A **compound-complex sentence** contains two or more independent clauses and one or more dependent clauses. That is, the compound-complex sentence contains the essentials of the compound and the complex sentence.

These two abnormalities were the ones that were prepotent in Joan; and they brought her to the stake.—G. B. SHAW *St. Joan,* "Preface."

This sentence contains two independent clauses, thereby satisfying the requirement of the compound sentence: *These two abnormalities were the ones . . . and they brought her to the stake.* The dependent clause necessary to the complex sentence is *that were prepotent in Joan,* an adjective clause modifying the antecedent pronoun *ones.*

In the following sentence each independent clause is modified by a dependent clause. The dependent clauses are italicized.

I know not *how long or short my life may be,* but I do know *that it is my duty to make it good and helpful to others to the utmost of my power.*

TO ANALYZE A SENTENCE

Sentence analysis now becomes a very simple matter.

1. Ascertain whether the sentence is a *simple sentence* with only *one essential subject,* simple or compound, and *one essential predicate,* simple or compound. If so, treat the elements of that simple sentence separately according to the rules and principles stated under THE SIMPLE SENTENCE.

If participial, prepositional, or other phrases are included in the simple sentence, treat each phrase first solidly as an element of the simple sentence, showing its grammatical relation as a phrase. Then take the words of that phrase separately and show their relation to one another as single words.

2. If the sentence is found to have more than one essential subject and more than one essential predicate, separate the clauses and decide whether they constitute a complex, compound, or compound-complex sentence.

3. Show the relation of the clauses to each other as coordinate and independent in the compound and compound-complex sentences (pp. 236–237), or as independent and dependent in the complex sentences (pp. 228–229).

4. Analyze each clause of the compound, complex, and compound-complex sentences according to the rules and principles given for the simple sentence.

EXERCISE

Analyze the following sentences as *complex, compound,* or *compound-complex,* first by *clauses;* then by *words,* treating each *clause* by itself as a *simple sentence.*

(1)   I can look sharp as well as another, and let me alone to keep the cobwebs out of my eyes.—CERVANTES *Don Quixote,* pt. ii, ch. 33.

(2)   The greatest truths are the simplest; and so are the greatest men.—J. C. and A. W. HARE *Guesses at Truth.*

(3)   That is the best government which desires to make the people happy, and knows how to make them happy.—MACAULAY *On Mitford's History of Greece,* 1824.

(4)   He is no wise man that will quit a certainty for an uncertainty.—SAMUEL JOHNSON *The Idler.* No. 57.

(5)   I cannot praise a fugitive and cloistered virtue, unexercised and unbreathed, that never sallies out and sees her adversary, but slinks out of the race, where that immortal garland is to be run for, not without dust and heat.—MILTON *Areopagitica.*

(6)   Oh, don't the days seem lank and long
When all goes right and nothing goes wrong,
And isn't your life extremely flat
With nothing whatever to grumble at.
            W. S. GILBERT *Princess Ida.* act ii.

(7) More helpful than all wisdom is one draught of simple human pity that will not forsake us.—GEORGE ELIOT *The Mill on the Floss,* bk. viii, ch. 1.

(8) Where law ends, there tyranny begins.—WILLIAM PITT (Earl of Chatham) *Case of Wilkes. Speech.* Jan. 9, 1770.

(9) Morality, when vigorously alive, sees farther than intellect, and provides unconsciously for intellectual difficulties. —FROUDE *Short Studies on Great Subjects,* "Divus Cæsar."

(10) In fact, precisely at this transitional point of its nightly roll into darkness the great and particular glory of the Egdon waste region began, and nobody could be said to understand the heath who had not been there at such a time.—THOMAS HARDY *The Return of the Native,* ch. 1.

(11) *Bleak House* begins in the London fog, and the whole book is permeated with fog and rain.—EDMUND WILSON *Dickens: The Two Scrooges.*

(12) I had explored the possibilities of crystallography very carefully during the past months: by the time my apparatus was ready, I was certain of the line I was going to take. —C. P. SNOW *The Search,* ch. 1.

(13) Then hammock, too, ended, and to the south and west lay a broad open expanse that looked at first sight to be a meadow.—MARJORIE KINNAN RAWLINGS *The Yearling,* "Old Slewfoot."

(14) He had had the courage once to steal a necklace but he hadn't carried through his idea.—EDMUND WILSON *Bernard Shaw at Eighty.*

(15) I heard a nervous patter of tiny hoofs, and the animal sneezed from the bushes at my right.—ROY CHAPMAN ANDREWS *This Amazing Planet.*

(16) Farmer Carver had planned to take George to school, but the night before the calf had fallen sick and he could not leave.—SHIRLEY GRAHAM and GEORGE D. LIPSCOMB *Doctor George Washington Carver: Scientist.*

(17) Some of them were musicians, others were Jacks-of-all-trades, but all of them have the imitative instinct.—JOHN J. FLOHERTY *On the Air.*

(18)   He studied physics to try to learn the answer; and he became so fascinated that he began experimenting.—KATHERINE SHIPPEN *The Magic Wheel.*

(19)   As he grew up, he remained a pet and every night he came close to the cabin to sleep.—J. FRANK DOBIE *The Longhorns.*

(20)   He knew that he was committing an enormity by being out of bed in the middle of the night; but he knew too that the look in his father's eyes was not adjusted to his offense. —MARY RENAULT *The Charioteer,* ch. 1.

Part III
PUNCTUATION

PUNCTUATION

There are two kinds of punctuation in English: *significant* and *conventional*. **Significant punctuation** is used as a substitute for the gestures, pauses, and changes of intonation by means of which the speaker clarifies his intentions.

Conventional punctuation is used to present material in a clear, familiar, and convenient form. It satisfies the customs and amenities of writing. For example, meaning does not require a comma or colon after the salutation of a letter; any other mark of punctuation would serve just as well. But convention requires the comma or colon, and the writer must conform.

With the comparatively simple and direct sentences of present-day prose, the trend is to use few marks of punctuation. In order to punctuate effectively one must be able (1) to distinguish between independent and dependent elements in a sentence, (2) to decide how the inclusion or omission of certain punctuation marks will affect the meaning, and (3) to remember the punctuation marks that convention requires in different situations.

THE PERIOD

The period is a terminal mark of punctuation; it is used as follows:

1. To mark the end of a declarative sentence. This is the chief use of the period.

> Rome is the capital of Italy.
> Bread is the staff of life.

2. To mark the end of a deliberately incomplete sentence, an *indirect* question, an unemphatic imperative sentence, or an imperative sentence phrased as a question.

> Children, your attention please.

> He asked why we refused to sign.

> I could hardly believe my ears.

> "May I please go to the circus," he pleaded.

3. After all abbreviations.

> Mr.; Dr.; A.M.; Rev.; Lt.; e.g.

EXCEPTIONS.—The abbreviations of certain names, especially the names of organizations and government agencies, do *not* require periods.

> AAA, CIO, CBS, TVA, NATO, NLRB

In many abbreviations the period is optional.

> MS, MS.; AAUP, A.A.U.P.; CMTC, C.M.T.C.

CAUTION.—The following are not abbreviations and the period is *not* used after them: Roman numerals (I, II, VII); shortened words (*lab, math*); enumerations like *1st, 2nd, 3rd.*

NOTE:—When an abbreviation comes at the end of a sentence, one period is used to mark both the abbreviation and the end of the sentence.

> He is a Ph.D.

However, a question mark or an exclamation point always follows an abbreviation at the end of a sentence.

> Is he a Ph.D.?

Within the sentence an abbreviation is always followed by any mark of punctuation that would be used if there were no abbreviation.

Mr. Jonathan Blair, Jr., who called yesterday, wishes
to talk to you.

The Period with Other Punctuation Marks.—The period is
always placed inside quotation marks. The period is placed
inside parentheses or brackets when they enclose a sentence;
otherwise the period is placed outside.

He said, "History is bunk."

"I have appointed John S. Cassell to the position. (He
is my brother-in-law.")

The entire price is seventeen dollars ($17.00).

The Queen was always uncomfortable with him [Mr.
Gladstone].

Three periods are used to indicate an omission within a
quotation. At the end of a quotation an omission is indicated
by four periods.

Four score and seven years ago our fathers brought
forth . . . a new nation. . . .

THE EXCLAMATION POINT

The exclamation point (!) shows surprise or strong emotion.
It is used to mark the end of an exclamatory sentence.

My goodness, how strong you are!

The exclamation point may also be used after a strong exclamation within a sentence.

He scored ninety-nine per cent—ninety-nine!—on the
mathematics examination.

The exclamation point is placed inside quotation marks or parentheses when it is part of the quoted or parenthetical matter;
otherwise it is placed outside.

She shouted, "Help! Fire!"

You dare call me an "economic royalist"!

THE QUESTION MARK

The question mark (?) is used as follows:

1. To mark the end of any interrogative sentence. This rule applies to questions within a quotation or a declarative sentence as well as to original questions.

> What time shall I come?

> "Who signed the order?" he asked.

> Will the astronaut land safely? was the only question in my mind.

> It is nine o'clock? [A question in the form of a declarative sentence.]

An imperative sentence phrased as a question may be punctuated with either a question mark or a period.

> Will you please submit the report today.

> Will you please submit the report today?

2. To give separate emphasis to interrogative elements in a compound sentence.

> Is the summer cottage on a lake? adequately furnished? shaded?

If separate emphasis is not intended, we should write:

> Is the summer cottage on a lake, adequately furnished, and shaded?

3. Within parentheses to show doubt or uncertainty about the preceding word or fact.

> Chaucer's dates are 1340 (?) – 1400.

> The inventory includes "three sacks (?) for sleeping."

NOTE.—The question mark is placed inside quotation marks or parentheses only when it is part of the quoted or parenthetical matter.

One of his sentimental songs, "Who?", was a sensational hit.

Was the popular song "Who?" written by Irving Berlin?

The ending makes the story ("The Lady or the Tiger?") a minor classic.

CAUTION.—The question mark should not be used as a sign of the writer's humor or irony.

He has submitted several of his poems (?) to the college literary magazine.

EXERCISE

Place the necessary periods, question marks, or exclamation points in each of the following sentences. Indicate any optional punctuation that may be used.

1. "Stop" she screamed are you mad "

2. John L. Lewis, who founded the C I O , was once a coal miner

3. Was my son rejected because of his grades his personality his nationality

4. The president flew back to Washington this morning

5. Will you please type these letters right away

6. Who said, "Give me Liberty, or give me Death"

7. Aha you are a villain indeed

8. Ernest S Stapleton, Jr , has received an appointment to Annapolis

9. Like almost everyone else he practices cleanliness, in my opinion a minor virtue

10. Were you just reading Robert Frost's "Birches "

11. Are the tarpaulins in the cellar, or did we leave them in the car

12. "Don't talk to me you, you rogue " she cried

13. Where did Robert Louis Stevenson die

14. It is time to go

15. Come   keep a civil tongue in your head, Mr   Brown

THE COMMA

The comma is used within the sentence to indicate the least emphatic separation of elements. Since the comma is the most used and abused mark of punctuation, it should be thoroughly mastered. In present-day English the essential and conventional uses of the comma are the following:

1. To separate words, phrases, or clauses in a series.

> apples, peaches, pears, plums
>
> in the house, in the yard, in the meadow
>
> if I take the test, if I pass it, if I am appointed

In a series the comma takes the place of the coordinate conjunctions *and* and *or:* apples *and* peaches *and* pears *and* plums. The final member of the series is usually preceded by the conjunction *and* or *or* to indicate the nature of the series and its termination.

A comma is usually placed before the terminal *and* or *or* to prevent the confusion that might result from the presence of other commas within the members of the series.

> His novel has been rejected by Pierce, Brock and Swift, and Harvest House.
>
> For breakfast the children ate prunes, cereal and milk, bacon, and hot chocolate.
>
> In the summer he likes to hike, play tennis, and fish and swim.

In sentences where no misreading is possible, the comma is optional before the terminal member of a series.

The metals he uses are gold, silver, and platinum.

The metals he uses are gold, silver and platinum.

The singer smiled, bowed, and resolutely left the stage.

The singer smiled, bowed and resolutely left the stage.

I searched for my glasses in the closets, in dresser drawers, and in all my pockets.

I searched for my glasses in the closets, in dresser drawers and in all my pockets.

The snow fell, the wind blew, and we were snow-bound for a week.

The snow fell, the wind blew and we were snow-bound for a week.

If the terminal conjunction *and* or *or* is omitted from a series, the comma is necessary.

He paints portraits, still life, street scenes.

He has played in England, on the continent, in South America.

2. To separate a series of adjectives modifying the same noun or pronoun.

The comma indicates that each adjective in the series separately and individually modifies the noun.

a shallow, muddy, sluggish brook

Note that a comma is not used between the last adjective and the noun.

CAUTION.—Many adjectives modify a noun so closely that they are part of the identification: *flowering shrub, top hat, fine comb, shaving brush.* Another adjective preceding such a phrase modifies the entire phrase and is therefore not separated from it by a comma: *a beautiful flowering shrub; a battered top hat; a soiled fine comb; a soapy shaving brush.*

3. To separate the clauses in a compound sentence joined by the coordinating conjunctions *and, but, for, or, nor, yet.*

> The Wesley brothers were dedicated reformers, and it is generally conceded that they helped to prevent a revolution in England.

> Some members complained that the figure was too high, yet they voted for the appropriation bill.

With clauses short enough to be taken in as a whole, the comma is not required.

I complained and she stopped.

4. To set off a long adverbial clause or phrase preceding the subject.

Since the subject normally comes first in an English sentence, an introductory phrase or clause is concluded with a comma to show that the subject is about to appear. There is no rule that states when a phrase or clause is long enough to require a comma. Phrases and clauses of more than five words frequently require a comma. Some introductory elements this long, or longer, may not require a comma if they are very close in meaning to the independent clause. Most introductory phrases containing an infinitive, a gerund, or a participle are followed by a comma. If there is the danger that the introductory element may be misread, a comma is required. A study of the examples below and of modern writers will give a clearer idea of when a comma is required after an introductory element.

Phrase   On a cold, bleak morning in early December, sixty of us assembled at the induction center.

Clause   When he at last saw the literary idol of his youth, he was bitterly disappointed.

Verbal phrase   Believing that the trapped victims might still
                  be alive, the rescue squad refused to abandon
                  their efforts.

Misreading   This morning as I was bathing, the telephone
                  began to ring.

CAUTION.—Do not use a comma after a short phrase or clause
preceding the subject.

> At breakfast he is always cheerful.

> If you go I will, too.

5. To set off nonrestrictive elements.

A nonrestrictive element is any word, phrase, or clause that
is not essential to the meaning of the sentence. If an element
can be omitted from a sentence without changing or injuring its
meaning, that element is nonrestrictive and is set off by commas.

Words and Phrases

My oldest son, *Robert,* is ill. [Nonrestrictive apposi-
tive]

My son Robert is ill. [Restrictive]

Some books, like *Finnegan's Wake,* are almost impossible to read. [Nonrestrictive phrase]

Books like *Finnegan's Wake* are almost impossible to
read. [Restrictive phrase]

Relative Clauses.—Relative clauses that *describe* an antecedent are nonrestrictive because they do not restrict or limit
the meaning of the antecedent. Since they are parenthetical in
nature, they may be omitted from the sentence. Nonrestrictive
relative clauses must *always* be set off with commas.

Relative clauses that identify or define an antecedent are
restrictive because they identify, limit, or restrict the meaning

of the antecedent. Restrictive relative clauses are *never* set off with commas.

Restrictive	Any act which is retroactive is unconstitutional.
Nonrestrictive	The Field-Melton Act, which was passed yesterday, is unconstitutional.
Restrictive	The people who were on line before six o'clock were able to get seats.
Nonrestrictive	My teacher, who was on line before six o'clock, was able to get a seat.
Restrictive	Advertising which is misleading or injurious should be banned.
Nonrestrictive	Advertising, which is steadily increasing in volume, is vital to our economy.

Adverbial Clauses.—Like relative clauses, adverbial clauses may be restrictive or nonrestrictive. A restrictive adverbial clause may restrict a verb, an adjective, or an adverb.

Nonrestrictive	In the afternoon of December 7, 1941, *while I was reading the Sunday paper,* I heard the announcement of the Japanese attack on Pearl Harbor.
Restrictive	I dislike being disturbed *while I am reading the Sunday paper.*
Nonrestrictive	*No matter where you are,* you must always remember to behave like a gentleman.
Restrictive	The Southern bloc talked for as *long as they could.*

6. To set off nonintegrated sentence elements.

A nonintegrated sentence element is a word or phrase that is not structurally part of the sentence as subject, verb, object, or modifier. The following are the nonintegrated elements that are always set off from the rest of the sentence by commas.

(*a*) Mild interjections: *Ah,* now you've got the idea. *Oh,* that is not the true reason.

An interjection within the sentence is separated by two commas.

> There was, *alas,* no costume that would fit me.

Yes and *no* are frequently used as interjections.

> Yes, we have received the shipment.

Words of direct address (vocatives) are treated as interjections.

> Mr. President, would you like to comment on this matter?

> I reminded you of the recital last week, Margaret.

> Now is the time, Mr. Brown, to purchase more insurance.

(*b*) Sentence modifiers, i.e., words like *therefore, nevertheless, however, moreover, furthermore;* and phrases like *on (to) the contrary, in addition, on the other hand,* etc.

These words and phrases are frequently used to modify the entire sentence. To indicate that they are not intended to modify a single word, they are set off by commas.

> *However,* you may place your application on file.

> I can see no reason, *therefore,* why you should hesitate.

> There is, *on the contrary,* every reason why you should feel confident.

(*c*) To set off absolute phrases (see pp. 222–223).

> We decided, *the roads being crowded,* to picnic in our backyard.

> The principal speaker having already finished his address, we decided not to stay.

7. To separate contrasted sentence elements.

A comma is used to indicate and emphasize the contrast between two coordinate parts of a sentence.

The nominee is Telson, *not Cairns.*

The orchestra is precise, *but spiritless.*

The teacher marks severely, *yet justly.*

8. To set off inserted elements that interrupt the normal word order.

The clerk, *aged and infirm,* should be retired. [The adjectives are transposed from their normal position before the noun.]

Nuclear testing has been temporarily suspended, you will be glad to know. [The noun clause would normally follow the verb.]

The prognosis, *I am happy to report,* is good. [The clause interrupts the flow of the sentence.]

He would, *to save his own neck,* denounce his father and mother.

This work, *it should be unnecessary to remind you,* must be completed within the week.

In the *Odyssey* Queen Areté is loved, *not only by her husband and friends,* but also by the populace. [An emphatic element.]

The burden of the tax, *he protested,* would fall on the poor. [The construction is suspended by the inserted element.]

The inflationary spiral could be halted, *he believed,* by tightening the controls on credit.

EXCEPTION: He has written a novel which he believes will be a popular success. [After a relative pronoun a par-

enthetical *he thought, believed, etc.* is not set off
by commas.]

9. To set off adjectives in abnormal or reversible order.

Normal   She has curly brown hair.

Abnormal   She has brown, curly hair.

Normal   I like a dry white wine.

Abnormal   I like a white, dry wine.

Normal   Proust wrote about a bevy of beautiful young girls.

Abnormal   Proust wrote about a bevy of young, beautiful girls.

Reversible Order

Johnson was an irascible, conservative, eccentric
genius.

Johnson was an eccentric, conservative, irascible
genius.

The company intends to produce a small, light,
inexpensive automobile.

The company intends to produce an inexpensive,
light, small automobile.

10. To satisfy the requirements of convention.

The following uses of the comma have been established by
convention.

(*a*) After the salutation of an informal letter: *Dear Frieda,*

(*b*) After the complimentary close of a letter: *Very truly
yours,*

(*c*) To separate dates and parts of dates: *October 8, 1962.
On August 2, 1916,* he came to this country.

(*d*) To separate parts of an address or of a geographic
expression: *Mr. Richard Bard, 671 Wasson Road, Columbus
19, Ohio.* In *Flagstaff, Arizona,* we met a fascinating tourist.

(*e*) To separate numbered or lettered divisions and subdivisions: *Volume I, chapter 8; I,8; B, e.*

(*f*) To separate names from distinguishing titles: *Elton Sprague Smith, Sr.; Dr. Maldin Mann, A.M., Litt. D., LL.D.*

(*g*) To separate thousands in large figures: *1, 902, 228, 629.*

(*h*) To separate the indication of the speaker from a direct quotation: "We will discuss the matter later," she said. (See QUOTATION MARKS, pp. 274–278.)

(*i*) Before and after introductory words and abbreviations like *viz., e.g., for example:* Let us take, *for example,* his poem "Aftermath."

Misuses of the Comma

Commas should not be inserted where they do not belong. Instead of helping a reader, unnecessary commas confuse and annoy him. The comma should not be used in the following ways:

1. Not between the subject and the verb, or between the verb and direct object or predicate nominative.

Wrong A sound reason for changing the procedure, has not been given.

The foreign ministers of five Latin-American countries, are the group now in conference.

It is well known, that many diseases have a mental or emotional origin.

2. Not after a short essential adverbial modifier that precedes the subject.

Wrong At the meeting, there were two observers from Uganda.

3. Not before the first or last member of a series.

Wrong He wears, small, garrish, ready-made, bow ties. [The
         commas after *wears* and *ready-made* are both
         wrong.]

4. Not before a coordinating conjunction that connects two
dependent clauses.

Wrong While the officials were filing in, and the band was
         playing, everybody cheered. [*While* governs both
         dependent clauses.]

5. Not between the verbs of a compound predicate unless the
verbs are contrasted.

Wrong The doctor weighed, and measured the baby.

6. Not before an indirect quotation or before a restrictive
literary title.

Wrong He replied, that he would be glad to accept the chair-
         manship.

         I greatly enjoyed reading Bellow's novel, *Henderson
         the Rain King*.

But   I have just read a fascinating book, Saul Bellow's
         Henderson the Rain King. [Here the comma is cor-
         rectly used before the title because it is a nonrestric-
         tive appositive.]

7. Not before adjectives that are written in a normally fixed
order.

Wrong He is a handsome, little boy.

8. Not to set off restrictive modifiers or appositives.

Wrong The president, who fought in the Spanish-American
         War, was Theodore Roosevelt.

         Jack, the Giant-killer, is a hero of children's books.

9. Not before correlatives connecting single words or between the elements of compound conjunctions like *as . . . as,
so . . . as, so that,* etc.

Wrong   *Neither* the pleas of the parents, *nor* the threats of the victims stirred the police to action.

When she sits down to practice, she is *so* tired, *that* she can not concentrate.

EXERCISE A

Punctuate each of the following sentences with the necessary commas. Explain the reason for setting off elements by commas or for not doing so.

1. By August 1 1963 the work must be completed.

2. It is a fact unfortunately that Chekhov's play *The Cherry Orchard* rarely receives a satisfactory production in this country.

3. No matter how closely men huddle together they can not alas communicate.

4. In English foreign languages philosophy and the social sciences I always did better than in mathematics and the sciences.

5. When Thomas Mann first came to the United States he was hailed as a representative of the true Germany.

6. After *Buddenbrooks* which Mann completed before he was twenty-five years old he never returned to naturalistic fiction.

7. Malcolm Combs who was last seen at a service station in Las Vegas two weeks ago is wanted for murder.

8. On our European trip armed with cameras and guide books we visited England France Italy Greece and Germany.

9. He wrote you will remember that most men lead lives of quiet desperation.

10. We always travel on the parkways because the expressways are usually hot ugly monotonous and even dangerous.

11. In my little sports car which I purchased last year we went to California this summer.

12. In a letter to his nephew dated July 17 1951 he said, "The best stories in *Dubliners* are in my opinion "Araby" "Eveline" "An Encounter" and "The Dead.""

13. By 1950 the population of our town which is by no means centrally situated had increased to 3926.

14. I have heard this song cycle sung by Berger Lehman Fischer-Dieskau Roland Hayes who was then an old man and of course my wife.

15. Wednesday May 1 1951 was the day on which the general meeting surely the most memorable in the history of our organization voted to open the membership to women.

16. Oh yes the reasons are clearly set forth in the letter we are sending to our patrons.

17. When the time for departure arrived however she began to cry.

18. Marcy you will take charge of the little children those under seven and keep them busy in the library.

19. He is a short stocky swarthy uncouth young man.

20. Lifting his glass he said "I propose a toast to you Margaret and to our only son John."

EXERCISE B

In the following sentences remove all unnecessary commas and give your reasons for doing so.

1. The man, who applied for the position this morning, is unacceptable.

2. When you are in Los Angeles, John, will you please visit my aunt, Helen, and give her my love?

3. Shakespeare's masterpiece is his tragedy, *Hamlet*.

4. At dawn, we rose, and broke camp.

5. This ring is appraised for one hundred dollars ($1,00.00).

6. The ancient Greeks believed, that man is responsible for his own fate.

7. By the end of the month we must submit a statement, explaining, why we should make basic changes in our accounting procedures.

8. Five streets in Earlham, and two avenues in Dornbush will be paved this year.

9. The crowd cheered, as the astronaut rode by in an open limousine.

10. We are expected to finish this task, however, long it takes.

11. The Webster, who compiled the dictionary, is not the famous American statesman.

12. All aliens, who do not report to their local police station, will be deported.

13. A positively charged particle in an atom, is a proton.

14. Medical scientists, who are working on cardio-vascular diseases, are making great progress.

15. By the end of this year all private hospitals, which do not satisfy the minimum standards, will be forced to close.

16. She gasped, and began to cry.

17. We know, that Chatterton died in his early youth.

18. All I want to know about the astronaut's flight is, that he is safely launched, and that he has been safely recovered.

19. The deductions, which you made for professional expenses, have been denied.

20. Multiply the situation by the number of colleges that require a high secondary school average, and you will get a fair picture of the demands, for improving scholastic standing.

EXERCISE C

Explain the use of each comma in the following sentences. If you believe that commas should be added or removed, show where and explain why.

(1)   Of all the great English writers, Charles Dickens has received in his own country the scantiest serious attention from biographers, scholars, or critics.—EDMUND WILSON *Charles Dickens: The Two Scrooges.*

(2)   Fact and fiction are so intermingled in my work that now, looking back on it, I can hardly distinguish one from the other.—W. SOMERSET MAUGHAM *The Summing Up,* ch. 1.

(3)   But I have worked my way through a considerable part of it, slowed down, as all toilers in this rich vineyard must be, by the lack of any suitable indexes.—WILLIAM L. SHIRER *The Rise and Fall of the Third Reich,* "Foreword."

(4)   At six the polls close in urban Alabama, rural Illinois, Indiana, Mississippi, rural Oklahoma, South Carolina, urban Tennessee and Vermont.—THEODORE H. WHITE *The Making of the President 1960,* ch. 1.

(5)   The tests are very plain and simple, and they are perfectly infallible.—W. D. HOWELLS *Criticism and Fiction.*

(6)   So that it comes back very quickly, as I have said, to the liking: in spite of M. Zola, who reasons less powerfully than he represents, and who will not reconcile himself to the absoluteness of taste, thinking that there are certain things that people ought to like, that they can be made to like them. —HENRY JAMES *The Art of Fiction.*

(7)   When, early in December of 1891, William Dean Howells surprised his friends and himself by taking over the editorship of the failing *Cosmopolitan* in New York, he thought it necessary to explain his decision to one of the few friends of

his early years surviving in Cambridge.—ALFRED KAZIN *On Native Grounds,* ch. 1.

(8)   Occasionally, of course, Mencken was not amusing at all, and his loose tongue got in his way, as when he said of Altgeld that "his error consisted in taking the college yells of democracy seriously.—ALFRED KAZIN *On Native Grounds,* ch. 7.

(9)   At the time of the Peace of Ghent, which brought to a close the war of 1812, Gilbert Stuart, the portrait-painter, was an old inhabitant of Boston.—VAN WYCK BROOKS *The Flowering of New England,* ch. 1.

(10)   She turned, she took him by the wrist, a grasp simple, ruthless and firm, drawing him after her.—WILLIAM FAULKNER *The Wild Palms,* ch. 2.

(11)   It was a great night, a historic night in more ways than one.—JACK KEROUAC *The Dharma Bums,* ch. 2.

(12)   She had moved the clothing from his chair to the table, pushing back dishes, bread, milk containers, magazines. —SAUL BELLOW *The Victim,* ch. 1.

(13)   His feet were blistered, he was leaden-tired, but when the ferry moved out of the slip, bucking the little slapping scalloped waves of the river he felt something warm and tingling shoot suddenly through all his veins.—JOHN DOS PASSOS *Manhattan Transfer,* ch. 1.

(14)   Twice round with the little mop, dip, rinse and pile in the rack.—JOHN DOS PASSOS *Manhattan Transfer,* ch. 2.

(15)   Passing on my way aft along the other side of the ship, I observed that the rope side ladder, put over, no doubt, for the master of the tug when he came to fetch away our letters, had not been hauled in as it should have been.—JOSEPH CONRAD *Heart of Darkness,* ch. 1.

THE SEMICOLON

The semicolon is used within the sentence to indicate more of a pause than the comma and less than the period. The semicolon has well-defined uses as follows:

1. To separate independent clauses not joined by the coordinating conjunctions *and, but, for, or, nor,* and *yet.*

This rule governs the use of the semicolon in the following kinds of compound sentences:

(*a*) When no conjunction is used to connect the independent clauses.

The walls are lined with a large number of charts and graphs; they are helpful to the salesmen who wish to know the boundaries of the territories, who covers each, and the volume of sales in each for various periods.

(*b*) When an explanatory expression (instead of a conjunction) is used to connect the two independent clauses.

This syllabus has the advantage of providing the widest possible choice; on the other hand, it makes the scheduling of classes extremely difficult.

(*c*) When a conjunctive adverb (see p. 137) connects the two independent clauses.

The men were under the most rigid surveillance at all times; nevertheless they managed to make off with over a million dollars worth of goods within a year.

2. To separate major word groups from lesser ones.

The semicolon is often used to make the separation between clauses more emphatic. Also it is used to punctuate complex or major elements which themselves contain commas.

I opened my mouth and screamed in terror; but no sound was forthcoming. [Here the semicolon emphasizes the break and the contrast between the two independent clauses.]

To gather data for this educational survey, teams of investigators have visited the elementary and junior high schools in New York City, including the private schools and the various parochial schools; the high schools, both vocational and academic; the independent business schools specializing in shorthand, typing, and clerical skills; and the numerous trade schools. [In this sentence the semicolon marks the major divisions between the various types of schools and thus helps to prevent confusing them with the minor divisions, marked by commas, within the major groupings.]

The following awards have been made: to the boys in High Tor: two gold ribbons for sports, a gold and a silver ribbon for shop, and a bronze ribbon for music; to the boys in Shangri-La: one gold ribbon and two bronze ribbons in sports; to the girls, who this year have not been divided into villages: a gold ribbon in sports, two silver ribbons and one bronze ribbon in shop, and three gold ribbons, three silver ribbons, and one bronze ribbon in music. [Here again the semicolon is used to divide the awards to each group and thus to avoid confusion with the smaller elements which are set off by commas within the groups.]

THE COLON

The colon means "as follows." It is used to anticipate a statement or to introduce a list, frequently in conjunction with the words *following* and *as follows*. The colon is used as follows:

1. To emphasize a word, phrase, or statement that is to follow.

No matter what reasons or excuses are offered, there is only one word for his behavior: cowardice.

There is one problem still to be solved: How can we sustain the task force in the jungle for the required length of time?

2. To introduce a formal list.

The organizations to which we have made substantial contributions are the following: the American Red Cross, the Police Athletic League, the United Hospital Fund, and the Salvation Army.

EXCEPTION.—The colon is not used to introduce a short informal list: He reads novels, biography, and history.

3. To indicate the structural balance between two independent clauses not joined by a conjunction.

I sighed as a lover: I obeyed as a son.

4. After the salutation of a business letter: Dear Sir:; To Whom it May Concern:

5. To divide subdivisions from major divisions in recording time (3:45) or in Biblical references (Exodus 3:6).

EXERCISE

Wherever necessary in the following sentences, change the commas to semicolons or colons. Be prepared to explain each change you make.

1. The order was received this morning, the goods were immediately shipped.

2. The qualifications for the position have been increased, consequently we are receiving fewer applications.

3. The new employees have been assigned as follows, Mae Thompson, stenographic pool John Risto, boiler room, Ann Sparrow, complaint desk, and Mable Riston, inspector's division.

4. Dear Sir, We have arranged to have our representative call on you within a week.

5. Remove the skillet, it's burning.

6. The four generations in Mann's *Buddenbrooks* are represented by Old Johann, the founder of the business, Consul Johann, his son, Thomas, under whom the business is most profitable, and Hanno, who dies in childhood.

7. Over the gates of Hell were inscribed these words, "Abandon all hope ye who enter here."

8. The bill is too loosely drawn to be administered, furthermore it is so severe that it will never be invoked.

9. The fateful words sounded through the room, the Japanese have attacked Pearl Harbor.

10. Fallon made a fortune in a decade, his son squandered it in a year.

11. Every man has but one prayer, make me a healthy animal.

12. The sky has grown dark, the wind is howling around the house, the frightened children are huddled in the living room.

13. For two days we drove continuously at an average speed of forty-five miles an hour, thus we were able to report at the air base on time.

14. Our next issue will contain the following features, two short stories, three poems, all in free verse, a profile of Samuel Allman, the newest Texas oil millionaire, and an article on the common market by Arthur Aufhalt, the economist who teaches, I think, at Yale.

15. Go to the next traffic light, turn right into Fairfax Drive, proceed for about a mile to the blinker, and bear left into Oakside Street where you will immediately see the monument.

16. The problem is this, Where can we house the computer?

17. To the rector of our church, to the vestrymen, to the ladies of the auxiliary, to all parishioners, Greetings.

18. We have every requirement for success, a new and essential product, a large capital, an astute director, a first-rate market analyst, and an experienced sales force.

19. Man proposes, God disposes.

20. Beat, drums, beat, blow, bugles, blow, march, men, march, forward to victory!

THE APOSTROPHE

The apostrophe indicates the possessive form or the plural number. It is used as follows:

1. The apostrophe is used with *s* to form the possessive of singular and plural nouns not ending in *s:*

Singular   boy's, week's, John's

Plural   oxen's, women's, mice's

To form the possessive of plural nouns ending in *s* the apostrophe is used alone: *cats', companions', husbands'*

The possessive of singular nouns ending in *s* varies according to usage. We may write either:

> E. E. Cummings' *or* E. E. Cummings's
>
> Paul Barnes' *or* Paul Barnes's
>
> Henry Edwards' *or* Henry Edwards's

However, the apostrophe without *s* is generally used to avoid three sibilant sounds: *Jesus'; Odysseus'; Rameses';* the *masses'*

The apostrophe with or without *s* is added to the last member of a group that is regarded as a unit: *Abraham and Straus's policy; Barnes and Noble's catalogue; Simon and Schuster's list.*

If the members of a group are to be taken separately, however, each member forms its own possessive by adding the apostrophe with or without *s: Faulkner's and Steinbeck's novels; the boy's and girl's swimming pools; Hobbes' and Locke's essays.*

In names of institutions, organizations, and places, the apostrophe is frequently omitted.

the Teachers Union   the Bankers Trust

Queens Village   Jones Beach

But the apostrophe is used in *Martha's Vineyard; St. George's Channel; St. John's, Newfoundland.* When in doubt about the use of the apostrophe in names, consult a standard dictionary.

The apostrophe with *s* is also used to form the possessive of phrases and of indefinite pronouns.

Phrases   the other man's hat
my father-in-law's business

Indefinite pronouns   somebody's, nobody's, one's
everybody's, another's

CAUTION.—The personal pronouns do not form the possessive with the apostrophe: *his, hers, yours, ours, theirs, whose.*

2. The apostrophe is used to indicate missing figures and letters in contractions: *What's wrong?* We *aren't* ready. It happened in *'48.*

3. The apostrophe is used to form the plurals of words, figures, or letters referred to as such.

Are there two *s's* in *misspelled?*

Let's have no more *if's, and's,* and *but's.*

How many *9's* and *5's* are there in this column?

The apostrophe is also used to indicate the plural of signs for which there is no acceptable plural: Use **'s* and *†'s* sparingly.

EXERCISE

Use the apostrophe correctly in the following sentences.

1. Hows the argument to be resolved?

2. The little boy said, "I took Uncle Joe for a walk to the woods, but we couldnt find the woods."

3.   This word has two *s*s and two *p*s.

4.   The girls gymnasium is being refloored.

5.   Its never too late to mend.

6.   He is everybodys friend but nobodys love.

7.   Frost and Hammers prices are the lowest in town.

8.   This evening he discussed two of Salingers short stories and one of Cummings poems.

9.   Charles friends are always welcome.

10.   Show me Lands End on the map.

Form the possessive of each of the following.

1.   Peter the Great

2.   Kennedy and Johnson campaign

3.   Nicodemus

4.   New York, New Haven and Hartford request

5.   sister-in-law

6.   geese

7.   Frances

8.   women

9.   The *Post-Dispatch* editorial

10.   Tennyson and Browning poems

11.   Rodgers and Hammerstein musical comedies

12.   Archimedes

13.   Brown and Wheelock department store

14.   Tristan and Isolde love

15.   Dickens

16.   Henry the Eighth

17. The CIO

18. Oxford University

19. my mistress eyes

20. the shepherd crook

THE HYPHEN

The hyphen is used to join two or more words in a compound that is intended to be read as a single unit.

a holier-than-thou expression

The Franco-Prussian Alliance

a sure-fire method

the Army-Navy Game

The hyphen is used to prevent misreading and ambiguity which occasionally results when a prefix is added to a word: *re-cover; ex-wife; non-co-operative; re-establish.*

When a word is broken at the end of a line, a hyphen is used to indicate that the remainder of the word is to follow. Words may be broken only between syllables. In case of doubt about how a word is divided, consult a standard dictionary.

> For the position of typists all applications must be filed with the Supervisor of Personnel by May 1, 1963.

THE DASH

The dash is used to indicate a sudden break or shift in the expected flow of sentence structure or thought. It is an informal mark of punctuation which should be used sparingly in formal writing. In typing, the dash is represented by two hyphens.

I have a surprise—but I won't tell you now.

He fully expected—can you believe it?—that I would entrust my money to him.

1. The dash is sometimes used to separate parenthetical ideas or ideas introduced as an afterthought.

Many of Picasso's pictures—I am referring especially to the *Guernica* period—are full of violence and horror. [A break in sentence structure]

His mood is so black that he will undoubtedly commit some act of violence—possibly against himself. [An afterthought]

It is my pleasure, now, to introduce the most gracious lady of our day—Mrs. Eleanor Roosevelt. [A parenthetical appositive]

Occasionally the dash is used with an apparent afterthought to achieve emphasis and suspense.

You may think that I have no means of persuading you, but I have a way, a most powerful one that you have probably not thought of—a pistol!

2. The dash is also used to introduce a summary of a preceding thought.

A childhood without love, a broken home, drunken parents, grinding poverty and deprivation—these are the conditions that have made this youth and this crime.

3. In dialogue the dash is used to indicate hesitating or faltering speech.

"He told me—that man—the man at the desk, I mean —he said I should ask for—for Mr. Jones—or was it Mr. James?

Note that when a sentence ends with a dash the period is omitted. After a dash an exclamation point or a question mark is used if the sentence requires it.

You know that we have long hoped—

He is a rather charming man, but his wife—!

A belief in nihilism—you know what nihilism is, don't you?—pervades everything he wrote.

PARENTHESES AND BRACKETS

Parentheses and brackets are used to enclose interpolated or supplementary material which would otherwise be an annoying interruption of sentence structure.

Parentheses

Parentheses are used to enclose material which is loosely connected with the main thought.

> He said that the boldness of his proposal (his proposals are always bold!) would ensure its adoption.

> This syllabus was drawn up by the principal (acting principal to be exact) of Buena-Vista Academy.

NOTE.—No punctuation is used before the first parenthesis mark in a sentence, but the second mark is followed by any punctuation that would be used if the sentence contained no parentheses. Capitals and periods are not used with parentheses within a sentence, but question marks and exclamation points may be used: He apologized and promised (*as usual!*) not to act without authorization. A parenthetical sentence standing by itself is punctuated like any other sentence.

Parentheses are also used to enclose numbers, letters, and dates that are used to assure numerical accuracy or to indicate divisions and subdivisions.

> The storm windows cost twelve dollars ($12.00) apiece installed.

> The year of my father's death (1922) I entered college.

The ladies proposed to raise the necessary funds (1) by taxing each member $5.00, (2) by seeking contributions from friends, and (3) by holding a dance.

The directory classifies children's camps as (*a*) private, sectarian; (*b*) private, nonsectarian; (*c*) organizational camps, nonsectarian; (*d*) organizational camps, sectarian; and (*e*) training camps for arts and sciences.

Brackets

Brackets are used to enclose any kind of material that an editor inserts in any kind of quoted matter.

"It is difficult for me to understand how he [William Carlos Williams] could produce so much poetry while being a busy practicing physician."

EXERCISE

Punctuate the following sentences with the required dashes, brackets, or parentheses. Be prepared to justify each mark of punctuation that you use.

1. He has married, passed his qualifying examinations, established an office, and become the secretary of the local medical board all within a year.

2. In syllabication, digraphs, two letters representing one sound must not be split.

3. Odysseus's tasks were these 1 to get home safely, 2 to drive the suitors out of his home, 3 to put his house and kingdom in order, and 4 to placate Poseidon.

4. "We take our ideas of Hell from three of the greatest fools who ever lived an Italian Dante, an Englishman Milton, and a German Goethe."

5. "Give me that whistle at once, or I'll   "

6. To go to college, to own a sports car, to make a fortune, to travel around the world these were his goals.

7. "After questioning his wife about her former lover Michael Fury Gabriel is ashamed of himself."

8. Dante sees and talks to Paolo and Francesca among the carnal sinners in the third ? canto of the "Inferno."

9. You told me don't deny it that you would refund my money if the merchandise were unsatisfactory.

10. I knew that if there were children in the audience and there were dozens of them the performance would be spoiled.

QUOTATION MARKS

Quotation marks are used as follows:

1. To indicate the title or name of short works or parts of a work such as essays, articles in magazines, short stories, short poems, one-act plays, chapters of books, short motion pictures, paintings, sculpture, etc.

"Ulysses" [a short poem]

"The Dead" [a short story]

"Young Faustus" [Book II of Thomas Wolfe's *Of Time and the River*]

Picasso's "Guernica" [a painting]

"Queen Mary" [a ship]

2. To set off words or to define or translate words.

Words which the writer wishes to call special attention to are enclosed in quotation marks. Words so punctuated include the following:

(*a*) Technical words in nontechnical writing.

The ills of the heart and the blood vessels are called "cardio-vascular" diseases.

(*b*) Colloquial words in formal discourse.

Perhaps the lonely Queen Victoria began to think of Disraeli as a "pal."

(*c*) Nicknames.

Our new secretary is "Porky" Smith.

(*d*) Slang.

My son informs me that my former student Joseph Salip has become a "beatnik" and lives in a "pad" on Thurston street near the docks.

(*e*) Coined and humorous words.

To my Irish Republican grandfather a rich man was a "plutorat."

3. To enclose direct quotations.

Quoted material, either oral or written, is enclosed in quotation marks. The quotation marks are used to enclose only the exact words of the writer or speaker. Paraphrases, indirect quotations, and summaries of what was said or written are not enclosed in quotation marks.

Direct	The president said, "I will not consent to a reduction in taxes at this time."
Indirect	The president said that he would not consent to a reduction in taxes at this time.
Direct	He said, "I have several reports to finish this afternoon."
Indirect	He said that he has several reports to finish this afternoon.
Direct	The first sentence of Shirer's *Rise and Fall of the Third Reich* states: "On the very eve of the birth of the Third Reich feverish tension gripped Berlin."

Indirect   The first sentence of Shirer's *Rise and Fall of the Third Reich* says that Berlin was extremely tense before the Third Reich was established.

Combined   He declared that he was "monumentally displeased" with our behavior.

Note that in direct quotations *he said, she said,* and other indications of the speaker are separated from the quotation by a comma. Sometimes a colon is used for this purpose: These were the words he spoke: "Let the little ones come unto me."

If the indication of the speaker occurs within the sentence, it is marked off by two commas: "Now at last," he said, "we can get down to business."

When the indication of the speaker follows a quotation ending with a question mark or an exclamation point, the comma is omitted.

"Will the press be ready in time?" he asked.

"God help me!" he exclaimed.

In a quotation consisting of more than one sentence, only one sentence is joined to the indication of the speaker:

"The next step is simple," he said. "We merely cover the surface with a coat of shellac."

In quotations like the above, note that *he said* is not enclosed by the quotation marks. The quotation must be closed before the indication of the speaker and opened again after it.

In quotations of anything written or said by someone else, the punctuation and the capitalization must be reproduced exactly as it stands in the original.

Reader! we, as well as Pliny, had an uncle, an East Indian uncle; doubtless you have such an uncle; everybody has an Indian uncle.

In quotations longer than one paragraph, all paragraphs are prefaced by quotation marks, but only the last paragraph is concluded by end quotation marks. According to current usage, long quotations (ten or more lines) from writings are not enclosed in quotation marks. Instead they are separated from the context in which they appear by space and indentation. Single spacing is used for typewritten material, and small type face is customary for printing.

Quotations Within Quotations.—A quotation within a quotation is indicated by *single* quotation marks.

> In her last letter she wrote, "Nothing else I have seen is as thrilling as Michelangelo's 'David.' "

Double and single quotations are regularly alternated for the indication of quotations within quotations within other quotations. Whenever possible such a complex should be avoided.

> "I would like to remind you," my sister said, "that Father's very words were, 'I will disown any child of mine who says "I can't" or "I won't" or who dares to say "Frank's father let him read 'Lovers by Appointment to her Majesty the Queen.' " ' "

Quotation Marks with Other Punctuation.—For the sake of uniformity and the physical appearance of the page, printers have established standard procedures for the placement of quotation marks in relation to other marks of punctuation. These procedures are now generally followed:

Commas and periods are always placed inside quotation marks.

> "Tomorrow," he said, "will be soon enough."

Semicolons and colons are always placed outside end quotation marks.

> Find the word "Penobscot"; now count off ten words more.

Schubert wrote "Die Forelle": Mme. Ostrawsky ruined it.

Question marks and exclamation points are placed where they logically belong: inside the quotation marks if they punctuate the quotation; outside the quotation marks if they punctuate the sentence containing the quotation.

Why should I believe that "Honesty is the best policy"?

"Who said 'A thing of beauty is a joy forever'?" he asked.

Shun "the primrose path"!

The Punctuation of Dialogue.—In the punctuation of dialogue, standard practice requires a new paragraph for every change of speaker. Any descriptive or explanatory material related to the speaker is included in the paragraph that contains the quotation. The correct method of writing dialogue is illustrated by the following passage from Joseph Conrad's *The Secret Sharer.*

"Yes," I said, replacing the lamp in the binnacle. The warm, heavy tropical night closed upon his head again.

"There's a ship over there," he murmured.

"Yes, I know. The *Sephora*. Did you know of us?"

"Hadn't the slightest idea. I am the mate of her—" He paused and corrected himself. "I should say I *was*."

"Aha! Something wrong?"

"Yes. Very wrong indeed. I've killed a man."

"What do you mean? Just now?"

"No, on the passage. Weeks ago. Thirty-nine south. When I say a man—"

"Fit of temper," I suggested confidently.

EXERCISE

The following extract from *A Christmas Carol* by Charles Dickens has been printed without quotation marks or capitals, except at the beginning of each sentence. Place quotation marks where they are required and capitalize every proper noun and adjective. (See CAPITALS, pp. 284–288.)

What's today! cried scrooge, calling downward to a boy in sunday clothes, who perhaps had loitered in to look about him.

Eh? returned the boy, with all his might and wonder.

What's today, my fine fellow? said scrooge.

Today! replied the boy. Why, christmas day.

It's christmas day! said scrooge to himself. I haven't missed it. The spirits have done it all in one night. They can do anything they like. Of course they can. Hallo, my fine fellow.

Hallo! returned the boy.

Do you know the poulterer's, in the next street but one, at the corner?

I should hope i did, replied the lad.

An intelligent boy! said scrooge. A remarkable boy! Do you know whether they've sold the prize turkey that was hanging there? Not the little prize turkey; the big one?

What, the one as big as me? returned the boy.

What a delightful boy! said scrooge. It's a pleasure to talk to him. Yes, my buck!

It's hanging there now, replied the boy.

Is it? said scrooge. Go and buy it.

Walk-ER! exclaimed the boy.

No, no, said scrooge. I am in earnest. Go and buy it, and tell 'em to bring it here, that i may give them the direction where to take it. Come back with the man, and i'll give you a shilling. Come back with him in less than five minutes, and i'll give you half a crown.

The boy was off like a shot. He must have had a steady hand at a trigger who could have got a shot off half so fast.

I'll send it to bob cratchit's! whispered scrooge, rubbing his hands, and splitting with a laugh. He shan't know who sends it. It's twice the size of tiny tim. No one ever made such a joke as sending it to bob's will be.

The hand in which he wrote the address was not a steady one, but write it he did, somehow, and went downstairs to open the street door, ready for the coming of the poulterer's man. As he stood there, waiting his arrival, the knocker caught his eye.

Part IV
MECHANICS

MECHANICS

The conventions of English writing and printing that pertain to capital letters, abbreviations, numbers, italic type, and the division of words into syllables are called **mechanics**. The conventions of mechanics are dictated by custom and are subject to change. In these matters, however, a reasonable degree of consistency is demanded, and the failure to maintain it is likely to attract unfavorable attention.

ITALICS

The term *italics* designates a special font of printer's type that is distinct from regular or roman type. The letters in italic type slant upward to the right as in the word *italic*. Underlining is used to indicate italics in written or type material. Italics are used as follows:

1. To indicate foreign words and expressions (or abbreviations thereof) used in English, but still regarded as foreign and still marked off by convention.

Examples of foreign words still italicized: *Geist, Weltschmerz, hacienda, Lied, passé, bistro*.

Examples of foreign words no longer italicized: rodeo, café, debutante, aria, legato, opera, libretto, mesquite.

Examples of abbreviations requiring italics: *loc. cit., ibid., op. cit., viz., q.v.*

Since the status of borrowed words is constantly changing in English, one should consult a standard dictionary to see if a borrowed word is still regarded as foreign and therefore italicized; or if it is Anglicized and does not, therefore, require italics.

Examples of abbreviations that do not require italics: A.M., P.M., B.C., A.D., e.g., i.e.

2. To indicate the titles of full-length works.

The titles of books, plays, long poems, full-length motion pictures, etc. are indicated by italics: *The Grapes of Wrath, Way Down East, Paradise Lost, Hamlet.*

Italics are also used to indicate the names of magazines and other periodicals: *The Atlantic Monthly, Variety, Women's Wear.*

EXCEPTION. The Bible and the books of the Bible are not italicized or placed in quotation marks: Ruth, Exodus.

Although the place of publication of newspapers is normally regarded as part of the title, it is frequently not italicized. The writer should follow the practice of the publication itself: The New York *Daily News,* The St. Louis *Post-Dispatch.*

3. To indicate words or letters as such.

Words or letters used as terms independent of their meaning are italicized.

The word *companion* is of French origin.

The letter *c* has no distinct sound of its own.

4. To emphasize a word or group of words.

A word or group of words is occasionally italicized for emphasis. This usage is rare and should be avoided unless there is no other way of securing emphasis, as in writing a play or reporting dialogue: "I didn't call you; I called your *brother.*"

CAPITALS

Capital letters are used chiefly to mark the beginning of every sentence and to distinguish nouns and adjectives (and occasionally other words) as proper and not common.

Capitalization of the First Word of a Sentence.—The first letter of the first word in every sentence is always capitalized. In addition to normal sentences this rule also applies to the following:

1. Fragmentary sentences: Not now. Perhaps tomorrow. So long. Be seeing you.

2. A quoted sentence within a sentence: Waving a small flag and shouting *"We demand to see the president himself,"* he started to run down the aisle toward the dais.

EXCEPTION.—A parenthetical sentence inserted in another sentence does not begin with a capital: He took the bar examination in June—*this was his first attempt*—but failed it.

CAUTION.—An indirect quotation within a sentence does not begin with a capital: Without the slightest hesitation he uttered the lie *that he saw a small boy run off with the purse.*

3. A sentence that is used as the subject or complement of a verb: *"How shall we accomplish our objective?"* is the question to be asked. He chalked on the wall *"It is later than you think"* and walked nonchalantly off.

4. The first word of every line of conventional poetry:

> She dwelt among untrodden ways
>   Beside the Springs of Dove,
> A maiden whom there was none to praise
>   And very few to love.

WORDSWORTH *Lucy.*

Capitalization of Proper Nouns and Adjectives.—All proper nouns and adjectives and all words derived from them are capitalized. A proper noun is the individual title of a person, place, or thing. A proper noun is always singular and definite and is never modified by a limiting adjective such as the article *a* or *an* or by words like *many, few, largest,* etc. Some examples of proper nouns are: *Samuel Johnson, France, Judge Manning, Brown University.*

A proper noun which is occasionally used to refer to a group of objects becomes a common noun. Although it is written with a capital letter, it takes a plural form and limiting modifiers.

EXAMPLES: Vermont is the *Switzerland* of America.

The lad is talented, but he is no *Mozart.*

If a proper noun is frequently used in this way to represent a class of objects, it is generally regarded as a common noun and is not capitalized. Some common nouns of this kind are *ohm, watt, volt, boycott, guillotine, sandwich,* and *billingsgate.*

To show respect and courtesy, some common nouns are capitalized: *New Testament, the Pope, the Bible, the Saviour.*

Many proper names are phrases: *the Rocky Mountains, the Golden Gate Bridge, the Cape of Good Hope, the Mississippi River, the Methodist Church,* etc.

Like proper nouns, proper adjectives are capitalized. A proper adjective is a derivative of a proper noun: *Canadian, German, Methodist, American, Jewish.*

A proper noun used as an adjective or part of an adjective phrase is also classified as a proper adjective: *the Washington Monument, the Labor Party, the University of Pennsylvania.* When two or more proper adjectives modify a plural noun, the noun is not capitalized: the George Washington and the Bronx-Whitestone *bridges;* the East, Harlem, and Hudson *rivers;* Columbia and Brown *universities.*

The following are the most important classes of proper nouns:

1. Names of individuals: *John Doe, Theodore Roosevelt, William Wordsworth.*

2. Names of institutions, organizations, and agencies: *Reed College, Merchants Trust, Department of State, Simon and Schuster.*

3. Names of individual artifacts: *Leonardo Da Vinci's "Mona Lisa," the Wilbur Cross Highway, Gainsborough's "Blue Boy," Lever House*.

4. Geographical names: *Cape Cod, Spain, Lake Huron, Westchester County, Green Mountains*.

5. Titles of works of art: the *New World Symphony, The Return of the Native, Long Day's Journey into Night, "Pietà," "The Lost Chord."*

6. Names of epochs and historical events: *the Victorian Age, the Russo-Japanese War, the Middle Ages*.

Capitalization of Titles of Office and Honor.—Titles of office and of honor that precede a name are always capitalized: *Dr.* Smithson Jones, the *Reverend Mr.* Dinwoodie, *President* Truman, *Mayor* Finch. A title that stands alone is capitalized only if it is one of the highest respect and clearly refers to a particular person: the *Pope* (meaning Pope John); the *President* (meaning President Kennedy). But: The *president* has the power of veto. How many *cardinals* are there now?

All degrees which follow a name are capitalized: *Jasper Bruhns, Ph.D.; Sylvester Sims, Ph.D., Litt.D.*

The titles of relatives are capitalized when (1) they are used in direct address: *"Father,* are you listening to me?" "I'll get it for you, *Grandmother";* (2) they are used without any limiting modifiers: We were all a little afraid of *Father*. We always waited for *Mother* to kiss us goodnight. When these words are used with limiting modifiers like *my, your*, etc., they are not capitalized: His *aunt* and my *father* and *mother* saw the accident.

Capitalization of Titles of Works of Art.—In the titles of all works of art, the first and last words and every other important word are always capitalized. This rule applies to an individual's own work and to the titles of books, poems, plays, stories, essays, articles, paintings, sculpture, magazines, lectures, motion pictures, songs, symphonies, ballets, etc. In titles the articles, prepositions, and conjunctions are not capitalized except when they occur first or last: *The Return of the Native, Of Mice and Men, If Winter Comes.*

However, in the titles of magazines and newspapers, an initial *the* need not be capitalized:

> the *Christian Science Monitor*
> the *Saturday Review*
> the *Nation*
> *The Mill on the Floss*
> "The Rime of the Ancient Mariner"
> "The Pit and the Pendulum"

EXERCISE

In each of the following sentences, supply capital letters and italics wherever they are required.

1. after years of rivalry the cio and afl finally united.

2. everyone knows the myth of george washington's throwing a silver dollar across the potomac.

3. on the town is a musical comedy with music by leonard bernstein and book by betty comden and adolph green.

4. the green, white, catskill, and adirondack mountains are all in the east.

5. my mother was always in awe of dr. sweet much to father's amusement and exasperation.

6. in recent years the baptists, presbyterians, and methodists have been meeting in the old river road church.

7. negroes, indians, and mexicans have suffered from discrimination.

8. in the summer american teachers travel abroad.

9   next summer we will go to the northwest and the canadian rockies.

10. in the book of job satan is a tempter who tests man and reports to god in heaven.

11. debut is not a verb, and one can not travel something, not even smoke.

12. parking is not permitted on fairlawn avenue or western boulevard from 11 a.m. to 2 p.m. daily, except sundays.

13. we adore the virgin mary and pray to her as our intercessor in heaven.

14. in the fourth grade we memorized longfellow's poem "the children's hour"; in high school we read evangeline.

15. this volume contains milton's paradise lost and a selection of poems by the cavalier poets.

SYLLABICATION

In any kind of manuscript, words should not be broken at the end of a line unless absolutely necessary. When it is necessary to break a word, it must not be broken arbitrarily, but by syllables according to the established rules of syllabication. The most frequently used and most helpful of these rules are given below. Anyone who is in doubt about how a word is divided should consult a standard dictionary.

1. The mark of division between parts of a word is the hyphen. The hyphen must always be placed at the end of the first line and never at the beginning of the second.

2. A word must be divided between syllables, and the part on each line must be pronounceable by itself: *con-sult, de-ac-ti-vate, gen-er-al, me-te-or-o-log-i-cal.*

3. A word must not be divided so that a single letter stands alone as a syllable. Two letters are seldom written as a syllable,

except for prefixes and suffixes: *over* (not o-ver); *again* (not a-gain); *into* (not in-to).

4. Monosyllables are never divided. The guide should be the pronunciation of the word, not the spelling. For examples, *walked, talked,* and *passed* look like two-syllable words, but they are pronounced as monosyllables: *walkt, talkt, past.*

5. Two consonants and double consonants are normally divided, except for words in which the base ends in a double letter and for words with digraphs, i.e., two letters that represent a single sound. The combinations *th, ch, sh, ph* are examples of digraphs.

EXAMPLES: *ter-ror, din-ner, sum-mit, traf-fic.* BUT *moth-er, mach-in-a-tion, crush-able.*

6. Three or more consonants are divided so that those pronounced together are in the same syllable: *en-snare, in-strument, pros-trate.*

7. Compound words are broken into their components: *baseball, type-writer, air-plane.*

8. Prefixes and suffixes are treated as separate syllables. The exception to this rule is *ed* which stands alone only when it is pronounced as a syllable: *trans-action, pro-vide, intro-duction.*

EXERCISE

Divide the following words into syllables.

1. basement	9. fallacious
2. incontrovertible	10. geometric
3. postmortem	11. piscatorial
4. picturesque	12. preternatural
5. euphonious	13. morphology
6. abstention	14. neologism
7. conspicuous	15. retrogression
8. disproportionate	

NUMBERS

The writing of figures and the spelling of numbers should be consistent. The formal practice in written discourse is to write out all numbers of one or two words and to use figures for all others: *ten little Indians; twenty-five applications; 732 parishioners; one million dollars; $1,672,003;* a population of over *seventy million people.*

Note that this rule applies to sums of money as well as to numbers of objects. For sums less than a dollar, the dollar sign is not normally used.

Numbers are not spelled out when used with the following:

1. Dates: *May 2, 1902*

2. Addresses: *210 Maple Street, Ashton, Pa.*

3. Pages and sections of books: *p. 3; pp. 34–39; Book II, chapter 1.*

4. Hours when used with A.M. and P.M.: *3* P.M. *2* A.M.

5. Cardinal numerals preceded by an indication of enumeration or division: *Locker G326 in Room 3.*

The following conventions in the use of numbers should also be observed:

1. A number at the beginning of a sentence is always written out: *Thirty* days hath September. . . .

2. A number should not be repeated with parenthetical figures (unless extreme accuracy is desired): She is *sixteen* today. But it is understood that the cost will not exceed *twenty-five dollars ($25.00).*

3. Use commas to set off large figures in groups of three: *3,826; 8,901,273.*

EXCEPTIONS.—In the following uses figures are not set off in groups of three:

Dates: A.D. *1066*

Pages: *page 1136*

Addresses: *1671–26 Argyle Road*

4. In compound numbers less than a hundred, hyphens are used: *twenty-nine, seventy-four*.

5. After numbers the abbreviations *th, st, nd, rd* should not be used. They are unnecessary and usually omitted:

April 2 (not April *2nd*)
January 9 (not January *9th*)

EXERCISE

Write the following numbers and phrases correctly as they should appear in written discourse.

1. seventy eight
2. two million five hundred and three thousand and three
3. seven hundred and twelve forty seventh boulevard.
4. may fourteenth, nineteen hundred and forty-three
5. thirteenth at the table
6. in ten hundred and sixty six A.D.
7. page twelve hundred and three
8. invoice six hundred and seventy three L dash fourteen A
9. three thirty P.M.
10. one hundred and fifty nine

THE FORM OF THE MANUSCRIPT

All papers should conform to the following rules of manuscript form. The form of a research paper is too specialized and technical to be dealt with here. Anyone interested in learning about the form of research papers should consult manuals of style like those produced by the University of Chicago and the Modern Language Association, or the various style sheets and pamphlets prepared for the particular professions and disciplines.

Neatness and Legibility.—A paper should be typewritten if possible; if not, it should be neatly and legibly written by pen in blue or blue-black ink. Erasures and corrections should be avoided; there should be no more than three to a page, and they should be neatly made and present no difficulty in reading and no possibility of misreading.

The Writing Paper.—All manuscript should be written on paper approximately 8½ x 11 inches, the standard size of typewriter paper. Typed manuscript should be written on unlined paper and should be double-spaced. If the manuscript is handwritten, lined paper should be used, the lines wide enough apart to separate each line of writing from the lines above and below it. Only one side of the paper should be written on for both handwritten and typewritten manuscript.

Spacing.—A generous margin should be left on all sides of the paper to avoid a cramped, unpleasant appearance. The writing should not be crowded to the bottom of the page. A part of a line should not be left blank except at the end of a paragraph or preceding a quotation that is indented below the introductory words. One space is left between words, two spaces between sentences. A typewritten paper should be double-spaced except for footnotes and indented quotations.

Indention.—Each paragraph should be uniformly indented, five spaces for typewritten material and the equivalent space (about an inch) in handwritten material. Quotations and verse should be centered inside the margins of the manuscript.

The Title.—The title should be centered near the top of the page. The first and the last words of the title and any other important words should be capitalized. In many papers the author's name is placed immediately below the title.

The Last and the Least

by
Stephen R. Cross

However, formal reports are normally concluded by the complimentary close "Respectfully submitted," followed by the author's signature. A student in a writing class should, of course, follow his teacher's instructions.

Between the heading and the first line of text, additional space should be left, three or more spaces for typewritten material and a line or two for handwritten material.

The title is not followed by a period, but may be followed by an exclamation point or a question mark. The title is not italicized or enclosed in quotation marks unless it is a quoted title. The title is not considered to be a part of the paper; the first line of the text must be intelligible without reference to the title.

Paging.—The pages of a manuscript should be numbered and arranged in proper numerical order. The first page is not numbered; each succeeding page should be numbered with an Arabic numeral placed in the upper right-hand corner or centered at the top or bottom. The paper should never be numbered on the top left. The upper right-hand corner is preferred because it makes reference to any page quick and easy.

INDEX

sions of, 26; expressed or omitted, 29–30; gender in, 27–29; number in, 31–33; person in, 29–30; and relative clauses, 61; special uses of, 31–33; used with or without nouns, 29. *See also* Pronouns

Personification, in nouns, 8–9; in pronouns, 28–29

Phrases, defined, 167

Plurals, foreign, 13; double, 14; irregular, 13; of nouns, 11–15; nouns unchanged in plural, 14–15; plural noun treated as singular, 15; regular, 11

Position of the adjective, 63–65. *See also* Adjectives

Position of article, 76; of direct object, 203–4; of preposition, 145

Positive degree, of adjectives, 66

Possessive after *of,* 38

Possessive case, of a compound word, 21; defined, 17; double possessive, 22–23; equivalent for, 22; of groups of words, 21; of inanimate objects, 22; of irregular plurals, 21; in nouns, 19, 21–22; of plural nouns ending in *s* or *es,* 21; of singular noun, 21. *See also* Complete predicate; Complete subject

Possessive pronouns, used with nouns, 37; used without nouns, 37; with *else,* 51

Predicate adjective, 65

Predicate adverb, 213

Predicate nominative, 19

Predicate, complete, 170; defined, 161–62; essential, 169, 197, 215–20; parts of speech in complete, 198–220; simple and compound,

197

Prepositional phrases, 149–50, 189; used as noun, adjective, or adverb, 149. *See also* Special uses, suggestions, and cautions

Prepositions, 144–51; antecedent of, 144; connectives, 143; combined, 149; defined, 144; listed and discriminated, 146; object of, 144; participial, 148; position of, 145–46; used as adverbs, 149; used in complete predicate, 214; used in complete subject, 189–91

Present tense, 88, 95–96, 97 98. *See also* Conjugation of verbs

Principal parts of a verb, 95

Principal and auxiliary verbs, 81. *See also* Verbs

Progressive conjugation, 117–18

Pronominal adjective, 53

Pronoun, classes of, 26–53; defined, 25; personification in, 28; properties of, same as nouns, 25. *See also* Complete subject

Pronouns, and antecedents, 55–61; agreeing with antecedents, 56–60; used as adjectives, 63; without antecedents, 56–60

Pronoun, in complete predicate, 201

Pronoun, in complete subject, 178–81

Proper noun. *See* Nouns, classes of

Properties of adjectives, 65; of nouns, 5; of pronouns, 25; of verbs, 82–94

Punctuation, 243–80; conventional, 243; in dialogue, 278; double, 21; significant, 243. *See also* Comma; Dash; Hyphen, etc.